COMIC BOOKS
AND THE COLD WAR,
1946–1962

Comic Books and the Cold War, 1946–1962

Essays on Graphic Treatment of Communism, the Code and Social Concerns

Edited by CHRIS YORK *and* RAFIEL YORK

McFarland & Company, Inc., Publishers
Jefferson, North Carolina, and London

LIBRARY OF CONGRESS CATALOGUING-IN-PUBLICATION DATA

Comic books and the cold war, 1946–1962 : essays on graphic
  treatment of communism, the code and social concerns / edited
  by Chris York and Rafiel York.
        p.   cm.
  Includes bibliographical references and index.

  ISBN 978-0-7864-4981-1
  softcover : acid free paper ∞

    1. Comic books, strips, etc.— Social aspects — United States.
  2. Comic books, strips, etc.— Political aspects — United States.
  3. Cold War — Caricatures and cartoons.   4. Cold War in popular
  culture.   I. York, Chris, 1969–   II. York, Rafiel.
  PN6725.C633 2012
  741.5′30973 — dc23   2012001984

  BRITISH LIBRARY CATALOGUING DATA ARE AVAILABLE

© 2012 Chris York and Rafiel York. All rights reserved

*No part of this book may be reproduced or transmitted in any form
or by any means, electronic or mechanical, including photocopying
or recording, or by any information storage and retrieval system,
without permission in writing from the publisher.*

On the front: Cover art from *T-Man*, No. 23, March 1955
(Quality Comics).

Manufactured in the United States of America

*McFarland & Company, Inc., Publishers
  Box 611, Jefferson, North Carolina 28640
    www.mcfarlandpub.com*

To Robyn and Dwight York:
Thanks for the comics

Table of Contents

Preface	1
Introduction: Frederic Wertham, Containment, and Comic Books CHRIS YORK and RAFIEL YORK	5

PART I : CONTAINING COMMUNISM, CONTROLLING THE ATOM

1. Lights, Camera, Action 101: A Brief Lesson on How to See an Atomic Bomb
   NATHAN ATKINSON 19
2. Decrypting Espionage Comic Books in 1950s America
   PETER LEE 30
3. "He Was a Living Breathing Human Being": Harvey Kurtzman's War Comics and the "Yellow Peril" in 1950s Containment Culture
   CHRISTOPHER B. FIELD 45
4. "I Can Pass Right Through Solid Matter!": How the Flash Upheld American Values While Breaking the Speed Limit
   FREDERICK A. WRIGHT 55
5. Jack Kirby's *Challengers of the Unknown*: Establishing Order in an Age of Anxiety
   PHILLIP PAYNE and PAUL J. SPAETH 68
6. Red Menace on the Moon: Containment in Space as Depicted in Comics of the 1950s
   JOHN DONOVAN 79

PART II: CONTAINING SEXUALITY IN THE COLD WAR

7. Girls Who Sinned in Secret and Paid in Public: Romance Comics, 1949–1954
   JEANNE GARDNER 92

8. Rebellion in Riverdale
    RAFIEL YORK   103
9. The Amazon Mystique: Subverting Cold War Domesticity in *Wonder Woman* Comics, 1948–1965
    RUTH MCCLELLAND-NUGENT   115
10. The Girls in White: Nurse Images in Early Cold War Era Romance and War Comics
    CHRISTOPHER J. HAYTON and SHEILA HAYTON   129
11. Horror Camp: Homoerotic Subtext in EC Comics
    DIANA GREEN   146

PART III: THE PROBLEM OF CONSENSUS

12. "Dedicated to the Youth of America": Deviant Narration in *Crime Does Not Pay*
    CHRIS YORK   156
13. *MAD*'s Guest Writers
    LAWRENCE RODMAN   169
14. Beyond the Frontier: *Turok, Son of Stone* and the Native American in Cold War America
    CHRIS YORK   179
15. East Europeans in the Cold War Comic *This Godless Communism*
    ALEXANDER MAXWELL   190
16. *The Fantastic Four*: A Mirror of Cold War America
    RAFIEL YORK   204

About the Contributors   217
Index   219

Preface

Like many other people who have chosen comics as the focus of their scholarly work, we started reading comics when we were kids. Our mother tells the story of when she attended Chris's kindergarten parent-teacher conference. When the teacher asked if Chris read outside of school, mom responded, "just comics." Mom expected the teacher to insist that Chris focus on "real books." Surprisingly, the teacher gave her approval to comics, and we ran with it. Our parents were soon buying comics before every family road trip, paying us allowances to feed our hobby, buying Mego superhero dolls for birthdays (and one summer, Dad bought them every week, just because they were cool, but Mom still doesn't know about that). There was an expectation that when we bought comics, Dad got to read them too (he liked *Thor* the best), and each time he borrowed a comic it would sit on the table next to his recliner for weeks before we'd get it back and have the chance to read it for the first time. In retrospect, it seems inevitable that we would turn to comics when we entered the world of academia.

When we attended the 2009 national conference of the Popular Culture Association (PCA) in New Orleans we came prepared to approach publishers with a book proposal. However, as we were getting ready to go to the first day's sessions we talked about how to pitch the book, all of a sudden it hit us, separately but simultaneously — we didn't want to write the book we were getting ready to pitch. We spent the time between sessions that day talking about the gaps that existed in this relatively young field of comics scholarship, and our most promising idea was a book that examined comics as artifacts of containment-era America. We would focus on analyzing comics in much the same way as Frederic Wertham, examining both images and stories and how these elements combined to reveal the influence of world events on the stories and characters, and, conversely, how the stories and characters influenced the world. We also decided that rather than writing the entire book ourselves, it would be best to edit a collection of essays from several contributors, as the years following World War II saw many genres of comics emerge and gain popularity. We figured that the more people we had writing the book, the less chance there would be we'd leave something out, or overdo something.

We do not claim that *Comic Books and the Cold War, 1946–1962* addresses every issue faced by post-war America, nor does it include every genre of comic being published during those years. It does, however, cover a range of genres. The big names of the era, like EC, Superman, and romance comics are revisited, but other comics that haven't received much scholarly attention also find their way into these pages as well. It is important to note that this book is not intended to present a comprehensive history of comics in America after World War II. The analysis of comics as artifacts of an era cannot occur without the inclusion of some history, but our interest was in performing close readings of specific titles or characters, rather than tracing the history of the industry. There are many excellent books that examine various aspects comics history during this era, David Hajdu's *The Ten Cent Plague*, Amy Kiste Nyberg's *Seal of Approval*, and Bradford Wright's *Comic Book Nation* among others, and many have been instrumental in the production of this book.

As we prepared, we faced another conundrum. Comics being relatively new in the world of academia, many style manuals do not include a format for documenting them. We found two possible documentation styles for comics, one from the Modern Language Association (MLA) and one by Allen Ellis and recommended by the Comics and Comic Art area of the Popular Culture Association. Most sources in this volume are documented using MLA format, but we found the MLA guidelines for documenting comics to be lacking, so we opted for PCA's more complete documentation. The MLA documentation of comics places emphasis on the writer, with any other contributors relegated to secondary status, with their names listed after the title of the work. The creation of a comic is often a collaborative effort between a writer and an artist, or several artists, and the PCA takes this into account. In the PCA's format, the writer and artist(s)'s names are listed before the title of the story, giving them equal status as creators of the comic.

Authorship of comics, particularly from the 1940s and 1950s, was often uncredited. Yet, given the large fan base and the collectability of the work of certain authors and artists, authorial information will often emerge long after publication. When information not found in the comic itself appears in a citation, it appears within brackets.

A book like this could not be produced without the assistance of many people and entities. We would first like to acknowledge the contributions the various comic book publishers have made to sustain the study of comics. Through "archive editions" and reprints, the comics of the post-war years are readily available to scholars and collectors. This preserves the history and the artifacts of the medium, and promotes scholarship, which is important to the continued existence of comics as the subject of scholarly inquiry.

Another source of comics for analysis that deserves mention is the online comics museum sites. Websites like the Digital Comics Museum and Golden Age Comics contain digital versions of many comics that have fallen into public domain, and therefore have little chance to be reprinted. Many of these comics would be difficult to find through comic dealers, and even if one were able to find the comics, buying them could prove to be cost prohibitive.

For the comics that are not available through either of these outlets (reprints or online), writers turned to the many libraries that maintain comic collections. The libraries at Michigan State University and Bowling Green State University, as well as the Library of Congress, were utilized. There are many other libraries across the country, public and academic, that hold comics, and as the field of comics studies continues to grow more libraries are sure to follow suit.

A couple of final acknowledgments. Trish York, Chris's wife, was instrumental in the production of this book. Not only has she always supported Chris's interest in comics (she even went so far as to attend the Chicago Comic Con with us one year), but she offered her opinion when we asked her for help; she proofread our essays; and she allowed Chris to put his duties as a father on hold while we worked (Rafiel was allowed to temporarily shirk his responsibilities as an uncle as well). Chris's sons, Finn and Otto, also sacrificed some of their time with their father and uncle, and while they may not realize it right now (being a toddler and an infant), this was much appreciated.

At one point Rafiel found himself needing help conducting research for the chapter "Rebellion in Riverdale." One of his students, Leslie Handzus, came forward and offered to help out of the goodness of her heart. We greatly appreciate the assistance she gave, even though she has no interest in comics whatsoever.

Introduction: Frederic Wertham, Containment, and Comic Books

Chris York and Rafiel York

Any discussion of comic books in the era between World War II and the cultural revolutions of the 1960s almost inevitably finds its way to Frederic Wertham. The much maligned psychologist and social reformer turned his attention to comic books in the late 1940s with the culmination of his work coming in 1954, the year that his book *Seduction of the Innocent* was published. The attention he gave comics was singular. Not only was he the most prominent critic of comic books, he also saw them as important cultural texts. As Bart Beaty notes, "From a historical vantage point, [*Seduction*] is the only sustained work from the postwar period that took comics seriously or treated them as if they were important in any way" (198). That same year, Wertham also testified before the Senate Subcommittee Hearing on Juvenile Delinquency, which would lead to the Comics Magazine Association of America (CMAA) publishing its Comics Code, a list of directives governing the content of comic books that essentially eliminated the sex, violence, and graphic content that had made the industry so controversial from 1946 to 1954.

Wertham found his way into the anti-comics campaign of the postwar period through his work at the Lafargue Clinic in Harlem, a psychiatric clinic for underprivileged clients that he opened in 1944. By 1948 he had become one of the leading figures in the anti-comics campaign, participating in the Association for the Advancement of Psychotherapy's "The Psychopathology of Comic Books" and publishing his article "The Comics...Very Funny!" in the *Saturday Review of Literature*.

Wertham believed that social conditions influenced psychological health and stability, and one pattern that he saw in his young clients at the clinic was an enthusiasm for comic books. Such a connection was not surprising considering the sheer numbers of children reading comics at the time. Wertham himself was aware of this, stating that they were "the greatest mass influence on children" ("The Comics"). The more he investigated the connection, however, the more convinced he was that a causal relationship existed. Wertham's concern was, in part, that, unlike other popular forms of children's entertainment, like radio and movies, comics had no regulations governing their content. He never claimed that comics were the only factor that caused juvenile delinquency, but saw them instead as a contributing factor; they led to what he called a "moral disarmament" that deteriorated a child's values and beliefs (*Seduction* 91).[1]

Though comic book publishers and readers balked at his conclusions, Wertham's reading of comics was insightful and, in some cases, ahead of his time. No place is this more evident than on the subject of race. In jungle comics, for instance, Wertham identified the enduring racist stereotypes that both reflected and perpetuated an America divided along color lines. In the 1940s and early 1950s there was a surfeit of jungle stories featuring white protagonists, both male and female. Almost invariably they lived in the jungle and, through their wisdom and physical might, ruled with benevolent authority over misguided and superstitious native tribes. Wertham noted the superior traits of the white protagonists compared to the black natives, and also observed how that superiority was communicated through visual representations: "While white people in jungle books are blonde and athletic and shapely, the idea conveyed about natives is that they are fleeting transitions between apes and humans" (*Seduction* 31–32). A look at nearly any jungle comic from the era bears out his analysis. *Jungle Comics* #86, a representative example of the portrayal of Africans in jungle comics, illustrates the savagery of the black tribesmen generally portrayed in jungle-themed comics of the era. The juxtaposition of the hunched and heavily pierced tribesmen to the bound white woman in an evening dress not only illustrates the animalistic characterization of Africans, but implicitly hints at miscegenation as well.

Wertham argued that such representations not only reflected a nation still plagued by racism, but also projected those beliefs toward the readers of the comics. The consequences were substantial. The foreign policy narrative of containment set the world as a struggle between two spheres of influence: one democratic and free, the other totalitarian and oppressed. It was the duty of the United States, as the leader of the free world, to increase the free and democratic sphere, while preventing the expansion of the oppressive communist sphere. The race issue, however, threatened to undermine the freedoms

Narratively and visually, jungle comics generally portrayed Africans as savage and uncivilized. From Mack, "Tabu," *Jungle Comics* #86 (February 1947). Glen-Kel [Fiction House]. Print.

the United States championed overseas (Field 88). In an era when the civil rights movement was in its early stages, and the United States was committed to convincing the world that racism was not part of the American social fabric, Wertham noted that, "At the same time, millions of American comic books ... give the impression that the United States is instilling race hatred in its young children" (100). And certainly one didn't have to look too far in the postwar era (no further than the hostile reaction to Jackie Robinson, Rosa Parks, or the Arkansas Nine, to name but a few) to see the validity of Wertham's assessment.

Even after the implementation of the Comics Code, Wertham was unsatisfied and saw few changes in the industry. This belief was substantiated by the representation of minorities after 1954. The Comics Code stated explicitly that "[r]idicule or attack on any religious or racial group is never permissible," yet the few representations of minorities that did exist in mainstream comic books continued to be damagingly stereotypical. Though jungle comics almost completely disappeared after the code was instituted (a suggestion that the Comics Code did result in substantial changes), the jungle narratives that remained were built on the same basic pre-code narrative formula. Black characters were slightly less hunched and primal, but they were still superstitious, childlike, and subjugated to the wills of white men and women. One of the few jungle heroes to survive the code, for instance, was the Phantom. Though he appeared infrequently, he did show up in the pages of *Harvey Hits* during the 1950s and early 1960s. A look at the composition from a panel in a 1956 issue depicts a clear hierarchy — the white (though masked) Phantom stands authoritatively at the prow of the boat while the black tribesmen row him to his destination. For a man whose scholarship has been questioned for over a half-century, Wertham certainly seems to have gotten some important things right.

Though he condemned comics as poorly written and poorly drawn, Wertham understood through conversations with his young clients that comics were capable of doing complex cultural work. His once infamous proclamation that Batman and Robin's world was "like a wish dream of two homosexuals living together" now seems to have been nearly a half century ahead of its time (*Seduction* 190). In retrospect, it is not surprising that such a reading of Batman and Robin was possible. In fact, most recent scholarship supports the validity of Wertham's reading.[2] Rather, it seems shocking that a social reformer and enlightened thinker on such a volatile issue as race could react so conservatively toward homosexuality and the homoerotic potential of a text.

Wertham's alternative reading of Batman represents another important element in his examination of comics. As Bart Beaty observes, Wertham's work "forcefully brings out the idea that reading [comics] is an active process and that texts are polysemic" (204). Certainly Wertham noted that meaning

The Code did little for the representation of other cultures in Jungle Comics. They were either ignorant in their resistance or subservient in their alliance with the white lords of the jungle. From "Hoodoo of the Pirate Ship," *Harvey Hits* #44 (May 1961). Harvey Hits. Print.

is made in the space between the text and the reader of the text. He writes that one cannot study the effects of comics without studying the comics themselves, but "to read them like an adult is not enough. One must read them in the light of how children read them" (*Seduction* 20). In other words, not all components of a comic are weighed equally by the reader. Based on the testimony of his patients, he deduced that the title and cover of the comic book were centrally important to the reader's perception, as was the opening splash page of the story. Furthermore, printed text was not as important as images. "A picture," he explained, "stands out in the mind of a child quite independent of the story" (103) and often children will look at the pictures with little or no recourse to the written components. He called this the "picture gazing method" (120, 122). Text only components in comic books — short narratives, letters from the editor, educational content — were, according to Wertham, often ignored by young readers: "The educational page skipped by many children, pointed to with pride by publishers and approved (but not sufficiently scrutinized) by parents and teachers, could conceivably contain a counter-stimulant to the violence of the stories, but often it just gives some historical rationalization of it" (Wertham 22).

But if Wertham's work implied the polysemic potential of the comic form, as Beaty suggests, he chose to emphasize a reading of comics that supported his pre-established agenda rather than celebrate the potential of comics as an art form. His famous confrontation with William Gaines over the anti-racism story "The Whipping" during the Senate subcommittee hearings illustrates this well. Wertham noted to the subcommittee the derogatory language in the story as an example of the race hatred one can find in comics, but failed to note, as Gaines pointed out, that the story very explicitly condemned bigotry and hate crimes (Hajdu 267; Nyberg 64; Wright 167). Here Wertham not only ignored the polysemic potential of the narrative, but went against his own "picture gazing" theory, choosing text over image. Despite these inconsistencies, at a time when few comic book writers and artists were thinking theoretically about comic books as an art form, Wertham was giving them serious attention.

Wertham's influence is felt throughout this book. Nearly all of the authors position their subjects in relation to either the anti-comics crusade, *Seduction of the Innocent*, or to the Code itself. Perhaps his presence is felt most fundamentally, however, because of the scrutiny he gave comics and because he saw that comic books as a medium were capable of sustaining complex narratives.

Like Wertham, *Comic Books and the Cold War, 1946–1962* returns to the comic books of the post-war era because they are important cultural documents. Far from the widely held misconception that the comic books of the postwar era (with a few exceptions) were poorly drawn, poorly written publications notable only for the furor they raised, the authors in this volume find that many of the comics from the era, both before and after the implementation of the code, are texts that create a dialogue between mainstream values and containment ideologies on the one hand, and alternative beliefs that question or complicate the grand narratives of the era on the other.

This book is divided into three parts. In the first part, "Containing

Communism, Controlling the Atom," the authors explore the primary sources of Cold War anxieties and the motivating factors behind containment ideology: the threat of communism and the threat of nuclear annihilation. Nathan Atkinson demonstrates how quickly attempts to address the anxieties over atomic bombs found their way into popular culture. The 1946 Superman story "Crime Paradise" superficially reads as an endorsement of the atomic bomb tests over the Bikini Islands and their stated purpose of demystifying atomic power. Upon closer inspection, however, Atkinson sees the comic and the actual tests as "a testament to the deep ambivalence about the bomb."

Comic books also addressed the communist threat. Peter Lee looks at espionage comics of the era and notes that, to a large extent, they were vehicles for endorsing containment ideologies. Spies fought to increase the American sphere of influence abroad against sinister communist agents and blatantly totalitarian regimes. He also observes, however, that there are times when containment ideologies collided. This was particularly true of female characters whose involvement in international intrigue often demanded some kind of rationalization to justify deviating from the feminine domestic ideals of the era.

If espionage comics generally painted the communist enemy with broad, malignant brush strokes, Christopher B. Field demonstrates that Harvey Kurtzman's war comics undermine such oversimplified characterizations in an attempt to create a more "truthful" representation of war. Kurtzman was interested in humanizing both sides of the Korean War — Americans were not as morally righteous as we wanted to believe and the North Koreans were not the inhuman savages portrayed in the "yellow peril" convention.

The 1956 reintroduction of the Flash in the wake of the Comics Code ushered in the Silver Age of comics, an age when superheroes, often emerging from the haphazard application of science and technology, would again return to prominence. The Flash, Frederick A. Wright observes, is the ultimate purveyor of containment, preventing the spread of any potential threat to Central City. At the same time, his powers make him a metaphor for unlimited possibility, allowing for a symbolic liberation from the forces of constraint and anxiety that acted on Americans.

Jack Kirby's *Challengers of the Unknown*, which, like the Flash, first appeared in DC's *Showcase Comics*, pits a team that is what Phillip Payne and Paul J. Spaeth refer to as "a throw-back to the masculine combat teams of World War II comic books" against decidedly modern technologies (at times conflated with sorcery or mysticism) that promised destruction of atomic proportions. This formula, the authors state, offered World War II era certainty in the ambivalence of the Cold War and at the same time was a harbinger of the Marvel comics of the 1960s.

John Donovan, in "Red Menace on the Moon," shows how the battle for the new frontier of space was imagined in comic books, and how that imagining differed from Truman era rhetoric of "Space for Peace." This battle for space initially pitted Earth against other planets, but, with the success of Sputnik, science fiction comics took on more explicitly Cold War themes that, at times, saw Soviets and Americans working together to further the cause of humanity. Often, though, comic books would sidestep Truman-era rhetoric, and suggest that space would be where the Cold War would ultimately turn hot.

The second section, "Containing Sexuality in the Cold War," turns to the home front, where, after nearly a half century of expanding opportunities and personal liberties for women, gender roles became more restrictive. In an anxious climate in which there was the perception that the woman who challenged conventional gender roles "placed the security of the nation at risk," women were asked to find meaning in the home (May 99). Jeanne Gardner looks at romance comics that illustrate the complex, constricting nature of gender expectations for young women when it came to courtship. Dating had become an elaborate ritual with consequences for the young woman's reputation but also her perceived class affiliation. Gardner sees the best instances of these comics as sympathetic to the young women who were trying and, at times, failing to stay within the boundaries of the moral order. Rafiel York explores the difficulty of operating within moral expectations, as well. Focusing on behaviors that challenge the moral, sexual, and gender codes of the era, he notes that the gang from Riverdale often found themselves transgressing social norms and expectations.

Ruth McClelland-Nugent looks at the peculiar case of Wonder Woman. A character originally developed by William Moulton Marston for the expressed purpose of subverting 1940s gender roles, McClelland-Nugent argues that even Wonder Woman felt the pressure to conform in the postwar era. Though she would never fully succumb to those pressures, by the 1950s the oppositional characteristics of Wonder Woman are gradually replaced by qualities more synchronized with conventional feminine expectations.

One profession women were still encouraged to pursue (at least until they got married) was nursing. Christopher J. Hayton and Sheila Hayton analyze the way nursing stereotypes manifest themselves in comic books of the era. They argue that, while comic representations of nurses generally conform to several types that are both consistent with the portrayal of nursing in other media but also with the conventions of the containment era, these representations did provide a degree of agency for young women.

In addition to the pressure for women and men to conform to narrowly defined social roles, the 1950s were virulently homophobic. Diana Green turns to the publisher most celebrated for their attack on mainstream conventions, EC Publications, and sees within their comics a thread of transgendered motifs that, while inconsistent, at times attack the rigid roles of the 1950s and suggest a less constricting vision of gender.

The essays in the final section of this volume all address the notion of consensus, a term often used to describe the 1950s. Though the consensus portrayed through the mass media was illusory, each of these chapters explore the dynamic between consensus and alternatives to perceived norms. As Douglas Field notes, the postwar period was "characterized by an anxiety over boundaries," and not exclusively the boundary between us (the United States) and them (the USSR) (6). For comic books, the boundaries of decency were always being contested. The comic book *Crime Does Not Pay* for instance, subverted the illusion of a moral and enlightened America by showing the discord in our own society through "true crime" narratives. Chris York demonstrates, however, that as criticism of comics escalates, *Crime Does Not Pay* subtly changes the tone of its feature narrative in an attempt to walk a fine line between appeasing critics without losing readers. Similarly, Lawrence Rodman shows how *MAD*, which had adopted the magazine format in order to survive the Comics Code, sacrificed some of its satirical edge when Al Feldstein took over editorial duties. Feldstein wanted to grow the fan base by hiring "big name" contributors from TV and radio. The result, Rodman argues, was a much milder form of satire.

The boundary between the minority experience in America and the white mainstream is largely unexplored in the comic books of the era. This is not to say that minorities didn't appear at all. Rather, they appeared from distinctly stereotypical points of view. Wertham's critique of the portrayal of Africans in jungle comics is one example, and Christopher B. Field, as noted earlier, explores the portrayal of Asian characters in war comics. Native Americans, for the most part, were left to fill the role of the savage, noble or otherwise, in Western comics. Chris York explores *Turok, Son of Stone* and finds that removing Native Americans from the context of the Western liberates them, if only partially and problematically, from the stereotyping inherent in the genre.

Alexander Maxwell also addresses stereotyping, arguing that the lay Catholic comic *This Godless Communism*, while clearly a didactic anti-communist narrative, actually seeks to broaden young readers' understanding about the Soviet Union, teaching them not to conflate communism with the diverse Russian people, most of whom suffered greatly under their government.

The volume ends with "The Fantastic Four: A Mirror of Cold War America," which, though set within part three, provides an appropriate coda to the book as a whole. It takes many of the themes throughout — the family, gender roles, atomic anxieties, science and technology, and communism — and brings them into the '60s. Rafiel York suggests that Stan Lee and Jack Kirby created superheroes that were more human than the Silver Age superheroes DC had resurrected. As a result of creating more human, more three dimensional, characters, *Fantastic Four* comics were also more liable to show the cracks that were beginning to form in the foundations of containment ideologies and expose the illusion of cultural consensus.

In the end, what this book demonstrates is that the popular culture of the postwar era was far from monolithic in its representation of American values and beliefs. Certainly this was true prior to 1954, but even after the Comics Code is instituted it is clear that the narratives contained in comics of the era are multi-faceted. Texts that seem, superficially, to endorse the status quo are capable of harboring subversive elements, while controversial comic books are still created within and therefore influenced by the culture they critique. This book only begins to dig under the surface of comic books in this fascinating period, but our hope is that this book becomes part of an enduring discussion of comic books in the early Cold War era.

Notes

1. There have been several excellent books that give substantially more detailed accounts of both Wertham and the anti-comics campaign of the 1940s and 1950s. Please see Amy Kiste Nyberg's *Seal of Approval*, Bradford Wright's *Comic Book Nation*, David Hajdu's *The Ten-Cent Plague*, Bart Beaty's *Frederic Wertham and the Critique of Mass Culture*, and John Lent's *Pulp Demons*.

2. Will Booker, Andy Medhurst, and Chris York, for instance, have all supported the validity of Wertham's homoerotic reading of Batman and Robin.

Works Cited

Beaty, Bart. *Frederic Wertham and the Critique of Mass Culture*. Jackson: University of Mississippi Press, 2005. Print.
Brooker, Will. *Batman Unmasked: Analyzing a Cultural Icon*. London: Continuum, 2000. Print.
Field, Douglas. Introduction. *American Cold War Culture*. Ed. Douglas Field. Edinburgh: Edinburgh University Press, 2005. Print. 1–13.
_____. "Passing as a Cold War Novel: Anxiety and Assimilation on James Bladwin's *Giovanni's Room*." *American Cold War Culture*. Ed. Douglas Field. Edinburgh: Edinburgh University Press, 2005. 88–113. Print.
Hajdu, David. *The Ten-Cent Plague: The Great Comic Book Scare and How It Changed America*. New York: Farra, Straus, and Giroux, 2008. Print
"Hoodoo of the Pirate Ship." *Harvey Hits* #44. (May 1961) Harvey Hits. Print.
Lent, John. *Pulp Demons: International Dimensions of the Postwar Anti-Comics Campaign*. Madison, NJ: Fairleigh Dickinson University Press, 1999.
Nyberg, Amy Kiste. *Seal of Approval: The History of the Comics Code*. Jackson: University Press of Mississippi, 1998. Print.

Mack. "Tabu." *Jungle Comics* #86. (Feb. 1947) Glen-Kel [Fiction House]. Print.
May, Elaine Tyler. *Homeward Bound: American Families in the Cold War Era.* New York: Basic, 1988. Print.
Medhurst, Andy. "Batman, Deviance, and Camp." *The Many Lives of Batman* Eds. Roberta Pearson and Robert Uricchio. New York: Routledge, 1991. Print.
Wertham, Frederic. "The Comics...Very Funny!" *Saturday Review of Literature* 29 May 1948. Web. 10 May 2011. Web.
_____. *Seduction of the Innocent.* Laurel, NY: Main Road, 2004. Print.
Wright, Bradford. *Comic Book Nation: The Transformation of Youth Culture in America.* Baltimore: Johns Hopkins University Press, 2001. Print.
York, Chris. "All in the Family: Homophobia and Batman Comics in the 1950s." *International Journal of Comic Art* 2.2 (Fall 2000), 100–110. Print.

Part I
Containing Communism, Controlling the Atom

Context

Purpose of the comic?
Cultural contexts?
Purpose/role of images

Craft

- Explication of visual elements
- Paraphasing
- Incorporation

1

Lights, Camera, Action 101: A Brief Lesson on How to See an Atomic Bomb

Nathan Atkinson

On July 1, 1946, a joint United States military task force called Joint Task Force One (JTF-1) detonated the first of two atomic bombs over a fleet of decommissioned and captured Naval vessels moored off the Bikini Atoll in a series of tests called Operation Crossroads. Operation Crossroads was by most accounts the story of the year, having become the focus of a larger, public controversy over the future of nuclear weapons and nuclear policy. The tests were announced and implemented at a time when the Truman Administration was still publicly committed to pursuing a plan for the international control of nuclear technology, and as Congress debated what role, if any, the military should have in the development of said technology. Critics of the military, most prominently some outspoken atomic scientists making a case against the nuclear weapons, seized on the timing of Crossroads, arguing that the tests would do nothing to further nuclear science, but would jeopardize efforts to establish a lasting peace (Weisgall 159). This peace, they warned, was crucial given the terrible consequences of nuclear war — consequences these scientists were not afraid to highlight in what was by all accounts an anti-weapons rhetoric that exploited fear to maximum effect (Boyer 49–64, Weart 114–118).

In response to this controversy, JTF-1 mounted a massive public relations campaign. The commander in charge of JTF-1, Admiral William H. P. Blandy, worked with the Navy's Office of Public Relations to promote Operation Crossroads as something more than an extravagant military exercise. The tests would, according to JTF-1, serve as a counterweight to the frightening "myths" and "stories" circulating about the bomb, and facilitate reasoned deliberation on nuclear policy (JTF-1 PC#2). In speeches, press releases, and public statements, Blandy and other task force members argued that by making the effects of the bomb visible, largely by means of film and photography, the tests would provide the public with a "ringside seat" at the tests, and a factual basis for deliberation of the bomb's future (JTF-1 PR #25, "Operation Camera"). This association between the tests as an experiment designed gain knowledge into the bomb, and the public as rational witness to this experiment via film and photography, proved a recurring feature of JTF-1's response to the controversy over Crossroads, and a common topic for newspaper and magazine coverage of the tests. Even the newsreels covering the tests got in on the act, showcasing the massive photographic effort underway, and touting their role in keeping the public abreast of events at Bikini.[1]

"The Old Type Atom Bomb"

As newspapers, magazines and newsreels covered Operation Crossroads, so too did *Action Comics* #101. The comic announces its contents on the cover: "In This Issue! Superman Covers Atom Bomb Test!" Yes, that Superman; more powerful than a locomotive, faster than a speeding bullet, able to leap tall buildings in a single bound, and now able to film the bomb. And the bomb really is the star here. The featured explosion appears in bright primary colors, yellows and reds erupting from the ocean's blue. These are, of course, the same colors worn by the title's featured character, Superman. As for Superman himself, he is dramatically front-lit by the blast, reduced to a camera-wielding silhouette. That bomb test is clearly the star here speaks to the bomb's hold on the popular imagination at the time. The comic does more, however, than simply exploit the novelty of the bomb and the notoriety of the tests. Rather, in the story "Crime Paradise" the comic weighs in on the ongoing, public debate about the purpose and significance of the tests, suggesting that the tests and the technologies for making them public will make possible the clear-eyed deliberation necessary for charting the future of nuclear policy. Specifically, it invites the reader to see the tests as a mediated, public event designed to manage fear and anxiety about the bomb. In so doing, the comic draws heavily on period discourses about the function of film and photography as information mediums. As such, it provides insights into the potentials and pitfalls of the nuclear test film as a means to contain threats, both international and domestic.

The comic opens with Superman lazily blowing bubbles in a park. A jewel heist is in progress across the street. A bank window explodes onto the street next door to the heist. And a concerned onlooker asks Superman why he's just sitting idle, as Metropolis descends into chaos. "Because I'd rather blow bubbles, that's why!" responds the Man of Steel, exclamatory even in his indolence (Siegel 1). The third person narration in the text box asks if the reader can "imagine the Man of Tomorrow refusing to lift a finger to stop the evil, destructive forces of the underworld ... or willfully bringing confusion and disaster into the lives of thousands of citizens" (Siegel 1). This question is, of course, rhetorical. The comic goes on to unfold this scenario in loving detail, leaving little to the imagination. Over the course of several pages Superman runs amok. He flies upside-down and backward, and ignores a drowning swimmer in order to pick up a glittering seashell from the ocean floor. As the lifeguards step in, he flies away. Next he disassembles a stalled car, then dismantles a building and reassembles it upside down. The citizens of Metropolis are understandably confused, angry, and above all frightened. At the end of this third page a caption asks: "What's this all about? Has Superman gone berserk?" (Siegel 3) The answer appears in a flashback depicted in the pages to follow.

It turns out that one Specs Dour, the "brains" of a small "mob" of crooks, created an insanity-inducing elixir from a recipe discovered in an "ancient book of drugs" (Siegel 4). Specs Dour and his mob "dose" unsuspecting "rich men" and "make their families pay high for the antidote" (Siegel 4). Everything goes according to plan until Lois Lane discovers their operation, and the gang in turn discovers her. Dour wastes little time in forcing her to ingest the drug. Fortunately for Lois, though as we will see less fortunate for Metropolis, Superman is already fast behind. Having used his "photographic memory" and "telescopic, x-ray vision" to unravel Dour's plot and track him to his hideout, Superman crashes onto the scene (Siegel 9). At first glance it appears the game is over for Specs Dour and his gang, but the myopic mobster threatens to withhold the antidote from Lois unless Superman takes the drug himself. Superman agrees, and "berserk" with the elixir he flies backward through the wall, "says hello and leaves" (Siegel 10).

The page following Superman's drug crazed egress brings the reader to the narrative present.[2] The first panel depicts Superman as he flies "helpless, his mind twisted by the drug ... far out over the pacific ... to a lonely atoll, scene of a Navy Atom bomb test." His pose reflects his mental state — he soars upside down and backward, eyes to the sky, high above a fleet of ships anchored at a dubiously rendered atoll, which looks less like a ring of islands than circular sand jetty (Siegel 11). The naval officer in the second panel is less dubiously rendered; he bears more than a passing resemblance to Admiral Blandy. The officer watches over the test scene, binoculars in hand, and announces that the "old-type atom bomb will explode first" (Siegel 11). Meanwhile, a photographer laments his inability to get closer to the blast. The photographer's newsboy style hat marks him as a civilian journalist, and the camera is clearly designed for motion pictures. He is a newsreel cameraman, and he is there to record the detonation on the public's behalf.

Throughout its public relations campaign, JTF-1 stressed newsreels as a key element in the larger effort to make Operation Crossroads public. In press releases and public statements task force members consistently downplayed censorship, and focused instead on the military's efforts to provide comprehensive coverage of what it insisted was not a show of force, but a scientific experiment. For example, in an early press release JTF-1 details a plan to establish special air transports for getting photographic materials to the United States in good time, and promises to station "still and newsreel crews" aboard ships and planes to better capture the "test" on behalf of the public (JTF-1 PR #12). This press release, like the ringside seat press release quoted earlier, positioned the viewing public as witness to a test or experiment. This language of scientific experiment and observation reinforced JTF-1's promise that the tests were being conducted as part of an effort to help the public understand the bomb and its policy implications, and not simply to determine (or worse still flaunt) its military applications. Also, by promoting newsreels as transparent windows onto a laboratory experiment designed not "to prove or disprove anything," JTF-1 sought to contain the potential for differing interpretations of the tests themselves (Shurcliff 36). They are not in this account part of a "spectacle ... intended to show the world what a powerful weapon the atom is," but a test designed to gather information (Lindley 21). The problem for JTF-1 was, of course, that a test of an atomic bomb on decommissioned ships was (presuming success) bound to produce a spectacle, and a violent spectacle at that. "Crime Paradise" reflected this tension between the explicit purpose of the tests, as promoted by JTF-1, and the implicit purpose of the tests that was suggested by the publicity.

Returning now to our story, the bomb explodes in the third panel, just after Superman's arrival at the scene of the "test," whereupon he "is engulfed in a man-made holocaust" (Siegel 11). Superman reappears in the fourth panel plummeting alongside pieces of ship. The caption explains: "Instead of being destroyed by the fearful blast, heat and radiations [sic], Superman's mind is cleared by it" (11). At first strike, this turn of events seems a ham-fisted narrative contrivance — an effort to lend an air of topicality to what is basically a *deus ex machina* resolution to an otherwise by-the-numbers Superman story. And to an extent it is. That said, in so doing it takes part in a popular discourse about the significance of the tests. Yes, this is a man-made holocaust, but it is a holocaust in service of clarity. The test fixes Superman, after all. It makes him sane. In this respect "Crime Paradise" echoed JTF-1's insistence that Operation Crossroads was designed not as spectacle, but as a response to myths and stories circulating about the bomb — myths and stories that received considerable press coverage following the announcement of the tests. Not only was the public still hearing the dire warnings of atomic scientists who regularly used fear tactics in their effort to ban nuclear weapons, it was also hearing the speculations about the tests made by less circumspect sources. These speculations included the notion that the tests could create "tidal disasters" or perhaps even blow up the world (Weisgall 64). That the military had itself trumpeted the power of the bomb in the wake of Hiroshima and Nagasaki, and even sensationalized its effects in some of the early, pre-test publicity for Crossroads, added to the perception that reasonable discussion of nuclear policy had been infected by a widespread and irrational fear of the bomb.

The tests and films of the tests would, according to the narratives forwarded by both "Crime Paradise" and JTF-1's public information team, put an end to this fear of the unknown. As one task force official put it in his opening remarks at a press conference, the tests would remove the bomb "from the myth class," from the realm of the magical and mysterious, and make it available for reasoned, science based deliberations (JTF-1 PC#2). No longer would the public be subject to the doom-sayings of atomic scientists, or to hastily composed propaganda written in the fraught, final days of World War II. Testing the bomb was, in this account, necessary to contain the threat to reason and rational action posed by unchecked, baseless fear. The *Action Comics* #101 sequence neatly reflects this narrative; they clear Superman's mind,

Superman cured by a holocaust. From Jerry Siegel and Win Mortimer, "Crime Paradise," *Action Comics* #101 (October 1946). New York: DC Comics. Print.

and in so doing enable him to restore order to a world thrown into chaos by his confusions.

If we understand the test as an antidote to the fear created by the bomb's opponents, the apparently random series of events leading up to Superman's appearance at Bikini makes an imperfect, but nevertheless, plausible sort of sense. Specs Dour is a character named for pessimism and an inability to see clearly. He is, moreover, an ascetic, bow-tied, button down brain. His mien is more professorial than criminal. What's more, his power derives from a fear of the unknown; he wields his knowledge like a weapon, using it to control the actions of those around him. As such, it is not too much of a stretch to read Dour as a proxy for the atomic scientists and public intellectuals opposed to the tests. This portrayal has unsettling implications. After all, Dour reduces Superman, a symbol of truth, justice, and the American way to blithering ineffectuality. He is portrayed, above all, as a threat to the social order. What's more, Superman's photographic memory, X-ray vision, and super-hearing aid in the undoing of Dour's scheme. All told, this depiction of threats from within and the good that comes from surveillance reads as an advance justification for the sort of domestic surveillance and ferreting out of ill-defined threats that would become so common later in the Cold War. Matters of surveillance aside, it is Operation Crossroads that ultimately leads to the downfall of Specs Dour. However, before the newly well Superman returns to Metropolis to deal with Dour he volunteers to help film the second detonation.[3]

"A New Type of Bomb"

The Naval officer announces the second detonation of "a new type atom bomb" in the fifth panel, and the newsreel cameraman laments his inability to get closer to the blast (Siegel 11).[4] This is, to invoke the language of *Action Comics*, a job for Superman. In panel six he takes the camera from its astonished operator and announces: "I've only got five seconds to spare, but I'll handle the camera for you! These photos will be a warning to men who talk against peace" (Siegel 11). Superman's characterization of the film's purpose is revealing. Phrased as it is, the film will do the warning — not the United States, not the newsreel producers, not the photographer, but the film. Superman thus shifts the burden of warning from the test, and by implication the actors conducting the test, onto the nuclear test film itself. The film speaks, so to speak, for itself. This shifting of agency continues onto the next page of the story. In the first panel Superman flies high above the mushroom cloud in an image that recalls the cover. He gets the camera into position to shoot a "film that no other mortal could take" So positioned, Superman lets the

1. Lights, Camera, Action 101 (Atkinson) 25

Superman doing "anything for a scoop" from Jerry Siegel and Win Mortimer, "Crime Paradise," *Action Comics* #101 (October 1946). New York: DC Comics. Print.

camera tell the story: "Filmed — the most colossal film of all time" (12). Note the absence of grammatical subject. The "film is filmed," and authorship is elided in a single linguistic bound. Upon completing the task he returns the camera and quips, "anything for a scoop" (12). This sequence offers insight into then prevalent assumptions about film and photography, and the synergistic overlap between an emerging Cold War visual rhetoric, and emerging professional discourses about photojournalism.

Specifically, Superman's phrasing suggests the extent to which JTF-1's promotion of the test films as transparent windows onto the events at Bikini piggybacked on what Dona Schwartz calls the "dual rhetoric of photojournalism" (Schwartz 160). The dual rhetoric of photojournalism locates the art of photography in the cameraperson's ability to erase him or herself from the scene of production, and to let the subject matter author the image. In other words, the art of photography is successful only when it is artless. This dual rhetoric was particularly popular with professionals in the newsreel industry hoping to establish the informational value of their product vis-à-vis print journalism. For example, an editor from Fox Movietone argued that his studio's policy to "let the camera tell the story" gave the newsreel an edge over written reports with regard to objectivity (Doherty 359). If such a claim seems a little overblown, that is because it is. We know today, as many knew then, that the newsreels were themselves constructed, their perspectives skewed, and their depictions of events managed for rhetorical effect. Yet despite some lingering reservations about them, the newsreels were enjoying a final flush of respectability following World War II, during which they served as important sources of information for audiences at home about events overseas. So extensive was wartime coverage that even former critics of the newsreels argued for their potential to facilitate understanding of distant events and to bring them to life such that the public could more fully appreciate their implications (Fielding 292–94). Given the newsreel's growing respectability, it is not surprising that JTF-1 consistently cited their presence at Bikini as evidence that the tests would provide the public with a basis for understanding the bomb and its implications.[5]

Once again, by framing Superman's act as journalistic (anything for a scoop!), "Crime Paradise" perpetuates JTF-1's preferred interpretation of the films and their purpose. That the films happen to serve as a warning to men who talk against peace — here meaning the USSR, or any country seeking to develop their own bomb — is a consequence of the enormity of its content, and not of authorial intent. However, by acknowledging this consequence, "Crime Paradise" suggests the capacity of the nuclear test film to contain the threat posed by the bomb. And while somewhat at odds with JTF-1's official narrative, this suggestion points to an alternate use for the nuclear test film, one that would prevail in the years to follow.

The idea of containment had, of course, only recently been articulated at the time of Operation Crossroads and the publication of "Crime Paradise," and the policies it inspired had not yet been put into motion. However, many of the assumptions underpinning this policy are very much in evidence in the comic, just as they were in the culture itself. By the time it was published, U.N. negotiations between the United States and USSR on a treaty banning nuclear weapons had collapsed, and suspicions about the Soviets and their nuclear aspirations were on the rise. To paraphrase a Crossroads newsreel, by the autumn of 1946 the question was no longer one of "can man control the atom," but rather, "can man control himself" (*Underwater Blast*)? Can we avoid an arms race? Can we avoid nuclear war? The answer implicit in "Crime Paradise" is a qualified yes. Man is capable of self-control, but requires incentives. Fear is a time-honored incentive. And what better to create fear than a film depicting controlled nuclear detonation? The film, unlike the detonation itself, is mobile, re-viewable, and as such an ongoing reminder of high stakes of nuclear war. In short, it seems an excellent resource for managing fear.

While Superman's offhand remark suggests the potential of images to manage fear in service of foreign policy, it also portends the use of the nuclear test film as a resource for managing fear in the domestic realm. Film's capacity to manage domestic anxieties about the bomb was not, of course, lost on JTF-1. Blandy cited it in a speech given after a showing of one test film when he expressed his hope that the tests might substitute "a healthy fear of the known for an unhealthy fear of the unknown" (Blandy 1946). Inculcating a healthy fear of the known in the American public became increasingly important as the Truman, and later the Eisenhower administrations adopted and implemented a policy of deterrence — a policy largely motivated by the goal of containing the Soviets. Deterrence policy held that the best way to prevent nuclear war is to prepare for it, and to demonstrate to the enemy a nation's willingness to commit to a full scale nuclear exchange if attacked. Because nuclear exchange assumed the destruction of American cities, a.k.a. metropolises, a policy of deterrence implied existential risks to a citizenry. With this risk came anxiety and fear, and with anxiety and fear the potential for resistance and/or resignation.

To contain this anxiety and fear the Federal Civil Defense Administration (FCDA) produced a series of civil defense films designed to sell the public on the survivability of atomic attack. These films portray the nuclear bomb as at once necessary to containing the threat posed by the Soviet Union, while at the same time promising that the threat posed by a policy of deterrence is containable. That is, the FCDA films suggest that the risks inherent in a policy of deterrence can be mitigated through thoughtful preparation and a refusal to panic. They mix terrifying images of nuclear war with facile guides to self-preservation—just duck and cover. Their chief purpose was, in the language of the day, to contain feelings of helplessness and panic among their audiences. The Superman of "Crime Paradise" is thus a sort of proto–Bert the Turtle, the stalwart cartoon mascot of civil defense and friend to so many children of the nuclear age. The tests, and films of the tests, are characterized as a means to containing a threat. The bomb is survivable, the atom a friend of civil society. At the same time, however, the comic's description of the test as a "man made holocaust" serves as a reminder of the dangers posed by the bomb, a danger that according to the logic of deterrence requires more weapons, and more tests. These tests and weapons will in turn require more films, and so on.

This escalating logic of deterrence highlights the problem with managing fear to achieve a goal. Namely, that once loosed both fear and images are notoriously difficult to contain. The atomic scientists found this out the hard way, when the fear they inculcated in their effort to gain public support for a ban on nuclear weapons had the opposite effect, creating "a fertile psychological soil for an ideology of nuclear superiority" that was exploited to justify an arms race (Boyer 106). And not only was the success of efforts by the FCDA to "inoculate citizens" by "exposing them to selected images of nuclear war" debatable at best, the frightening images in those films were eventually used in late Cold War documentaries challenging nuclear policy (Weart 130, Atkinson forthcoming). It is fitting, then, that Specs Dour also fails in his efforts. His plan meets its end when Superman dunks him in a vat of juice spiked with the drug. As Superman (disguised now as Clark Kent) puts it in the story's final panel, "he fell prey to the fate he tried to force on others! That's justice" (12). This last line of the story suggests a level of ambivalence with regard to the prospects of fear management as a strategy of containment. Fear can turn on you.

Inasmuch as we can read "Crime Paradise" as an artifact of a larger debate about the bomb and its filmic representations, we can discover insights into a culture still coming to grips with the implications of nuclear weapons. Paul Boyer characterizes the mood at the time as "shaped by two intertwined cultural moods: intense fear and a somewhat unfocussed conviction that an urgent and decisive public response was essential" (Boyer 32). Operation Crossroads was, in many respects, a response to this uncertainty — an attempt to maintain a space for the bomb in national and international politics by aligning it not with war, but with its prevention. This was, as would become all too clear after the Soviets conducted their first nuclear test, a dicey proposition that depended on the assumption that fear could be managed through psychological (perhaps even pictorial) warfare. That a comic produced so early in the discussion points to the limits of this assumption suggests that what at first reads as a bald apology for the actions of JTF-1 is also a testament to the deep ambivalence about the bomb, and the tests at Bikini. This ambivalence is reflected in the story's title, "Crime Paradise," which refers explicitly to the story, (Metropolis becomes a crime paradise in Superman's absence), but also alludes to the location of the tests at Bikini (a crime in paradise). This dual valence suggests there remained some question about exactly what happened at Bikini. All told, the title, the last line, and the fear and paranoia driving the plot collude to reflect an abiding unease about the bomb that would ultimately prove impossible to contain.

Notes

1. For example, the Universal Newsreel "Operation Crossroads Underway" depicts the preparations for filming as the narrator boasts: "More cameras were trained on Bikini than at any other single event in world history."

2. If my summary seems a bit ropey, it's because the story itself unfolds in a decidedly weird way, and it's often difficult to figure out when certain events occur relative to others in the story. For example, on first read Superman's appearance at the scene of the test seems to follow immediately after his exit from Dour's hideout, but on second read, it is clear that there is an unspecified amount of time — punctuated by acts of mayhem — between that exit and his arrival at Bikini. Ferenc M. Szasz remarks that early comics featuring the bomb, including AC#101, often "made for some awkward storytelling" (Szasz 15). Szasz suggests that this awkwardness owes to the bomb's powers matching the heroes. Broadly speaking, there's probably something to this. In this particular example, however, I think the awkwardness might have just as much to do with the ambivalent public response to the bomb, a response I will discuss at the end of the chapter.

3. The creators behind this story are taking some poetic license as the two detonations were actually held almost a month apart. A planned third detonation never took place.

4. The "new type" bomb is another bit of poetic license. The bombs tested at Bikini were of the same sort dropped on Nagasaki. Concerns about getting close to the blast were, however,

real enough. Films of the first test were famously anticlimactic, as observers were stationed too far away. Films of the second test did not disappoint. Not only were the cameras closer, but the detonation itself occurred underwater, which produced the massive dome of water that remains to this day an iconic image of nuclear testing.

5. For a full account of how JTF-1 used newsreels to promote the tests, see Atkinson, "Newsreels as Domestic Propaganda."

Works Cited

Atkinson, Nathan. "Newsreels as Domestic Propaganda: Visual Rhetoric at the Dawn of the Cold War," *Rhetoric and Public Affairs* 14(1): 69–100. Print.
Blandy, William H.P. "Atomic Power for Peace." New York Herald Tribune Forum. New York, 29 Oct. 1946. Speech.
Boyer, Paul. *By the Bomb's Early Light: American Thought and Culture at the Dawn of the Atomic Age*. Chapel Hill: University of North Carolina Press, 1994. Print.
Doherty, Dan. "The Newsreel: Its Production and Significance." *Journal of the Society of Motion Picture Engineers* 47 (1946): 357–360. Print.
Fielding, Raymond. *The American Newsreel: 1911–1967*. Norman: University of Oklahoma Press, 1972.
Joint Task Force One (JTF-1)*Minutes of Press Conference*. 23 April 1946. NARA. Records to the Department of the Navy. RG 428, Box 99.
_____. *Press Release #12: Complete News, Radio, and Pictorial Coverage Planned for Atomic Bomb Tests*. 3 March 1946. National Archives. Records Administration (NARA). RG 428, Box 99.
_____. *Press Release #25: Radio and Press Coverage of Bomb Drop*. 23 March 1946. NARA. Records to the Department of the Navy. RG 428, Box 100.
Lindley, Ernest. "Significance: The Good That May Come From the Tests at Bikini." *Newsweek* 1 July 1946: 21–22. Print.
"Operation Camera," *New York Times Sunday Magazine*, 23 June 1946: 49. Print.
Shurcliff, William A. *Bombs at Bikini: The Official Report of Operation Crossroads*. New York: William H. Wise, 1947. Print.
[Siegel, Jerry (w) Win Mortimer (a)]. "Crime Paradise." *Action Comics* #101 (Oct. 1946). New York: DC Comics. Print.
Szaz, Ferenc M. "Atomic Comics: The Comic Book Industry Confronts the Nuclear Age." *Atomic Culture: Howe We Learned to Stop Worrying and Love the Bomb*.
Weart, Spencer. *Nuclear Fear: A History of Images*. Cambridge, MA: Harvard University Press, 1989. Print.
Weisgall, Jonathan. *Operation Crossroads: The Atomic Tests at Bikini Atoll*. Annapolis, MD: Naval Institute Press, 1994. Print.
Zeman Scott C., and Michael A. Amundson, ed. Boulder: University Press of Colorado, 2004. Print.

2

Decrypting Espionage Comic Books in 1950s America

Peter Lee

The hyper-patriotism prevalent in American comic books during World War II continued with the onset of the Cold War, and with good reason: the Red Menace. The FBI considered communism a major concern during the Second World War. However, only after 1945 did comic book commies loom large, as the nation, according to one historian, became "sweat-drenched in fear" (Caute 11). Indeed, Communist Party USA courier Elizabeth Bentley's 1948 Congressional testimony concerning dozens of alleged Soviet spies in America had "convinced millions of Americans" that Soviet espionage was not just "a few isolated bad apples, but of a systematic and substantial assault on the integrity of the government" (Haynes and Klehr 73). Something was rotten in the state of the union.

Subversive activity was opaque, but the objective was obvious. Comic heroes such as U.S. Treasury Agent Pete Trask in *T-Man* comics agreed with White House counsel George Elsey's 1946 Clifford Report that the "ultimate aim of Soviet policy is world domination" (qtd. in Sibley 180). However, publishers added little to the definition of communism: references allude to an impending revolution for "the common people," but offered little ideological substance. The superhero Marvel Boy sums up the industry's comic book communism as he investigates the corrupt "financial minister of Upper Stalinia." "This I could never understand," the boy hero muses,

> Commies — champions of the *common* people, heroes of the *"downtrodden masses,"* degraders of individualism, incentive, and wealth, scorning all manner of worldly riches — yet wearing the finest clothing, riding in the sleekest limousines, eating

the grandest food, living in the most expensive hotels, and *amassing great sums of United States currency by fair means or foul*! What *hypocrisy*! I don't get it! [Everett, "Phantom"][1]

What Marvel Boy did understand was that whatever communism represented, it imperiled American freedom and democracy.

With such fundamental American values at stake, publishers conveyed real-life anxieties in their work. With the Hollywood blacklist, Alger Hiss's trials for espionage and perjury, and public concerns about subversive threats from the 1940s onward, creators catered to those fears as they crafted espionage tales to simulate real-life suspense and thrills. In the uncredited story "A Word Here.... A Word There" one inspired agent describes the explosive uses of playing cards and brass bearings, while another comic inaugurates a "School for Spies" with lessons on invisible ink and truth serums. "The Attractive Smuggler" from *Top Secret* #1 reveals ways in which women tried to hide contraband from customs agents. The *Spy-Hunters* story "Assault in Armenia!" even discussed the hydrogen bomb: "220 pounds of heavy hydrogen — or deutonoium — when set off by a powerful electric discharge through a thin wire, will provide 24.916 kilograms of neutrons — and an explosive force equal to *1,700,000 tons of TNT!*"

Creators especially utilized "classified information" in storylines. In one issue, a "top secret" file is rendered as squiggly lines and "censored" is stamped on the illegible text, with an editor's note that "for security reasons, actual plans have been censored," thus generating an illusion of authenticity that the reader was witnessing an actual case based upon fact ("Operation"). Another story, the "Robart Report," was "authorized" to be "released to the press" by "John Sloan, U.S. Secret Service" ("Smashing"). An additional disclaimer noted that "all the names of places and people have been changed except for the American agent, Pete Trask," adding realism to a fanciful story about a fictional spy uncovering an improbable hydrogen bomb in an outdoor planter ("Two Days"). While the medium of comic books may have been socially regarded as lowbrow literature, other children's texts confirmed the dangers of foreign spies. The schoolbook *Exploring American History* warned pupils that "the FBI urges Americans to report directly to its offices any suspicions they may have about communist activity on the part of their fellow Americans" (qtd. in Whitfield 102).

Primers and comics underscored the lurking threat communists posed to Americans and introduced their young audience to the anxieties and paranoia of the era. Since communism had no restrictions on demographics, "parlor pinks" could be anyone, and Cold War comic books vividly presented American traitors and sympathizers. As one Red boasted, "Our agents are everywhere, working for the glorious revolution!" ("Homicide"). Indeed, on assignment in Iraq, U.S. Treasury agent Pete Trask observes Soviet-hired assassins that included English, French, Italians, and Americans. So baffled was Trask in "Assassins of Baghdad!" that he implored, "For heaven's sake — *tell me! What side are you on?*" Similarly, agent Brad Kendall, also from *T-Man* comics, deduces in one story that his peers have turned traitors and were murdering fellow agents ("Ring").

T-Man was not the only comic to find communist sympathizers in seemingly benign places. In a *Spy Cases* story, "The Traitor," FBI agent Van Langley is stunned that the bureau was leaking secrets. Langley's superior is dismissive: "What's so strange? The enemy places it's [sic] agents in *every* position of responsibility ... right down the line!" Langley discovers that the line led to his boss. In "Beautiful but Deadly," one shapely FBI employee sunbathes on the building's roof to project semaphores, which "with some imagination, could look exactly like the map of *Europe*!" In *Date with Danger*, agent Bruce Kimball spots fifth columnists in Tokyo — an injured vet and a commissioned army nurse — spreading distrust among soldiers "when they were down, filling their wondering minds with doubt!" ("Captain Coward") In *Spy Thrillers*, agent Rick Davis uncovers a ploy to poison American crops, targeting "the countries we ship to, and half the world will be wiped out!" Heading the scheme was an American whom Davis tags as "a solid citizen, no trace of red connections!" ("The Unseen") Similarly, in the *Spy Cases* story "The Fjords of Fear!" agent Doug Grant calls one ally a "four-square, entirely trustworthy volunteer," but he proves otherwise. In Korea, G2 informs four army radio operators that one of them is a traitor. After pointing fingers, they realize that the culprit is the G2 agent who was sowing suspicion among them ("One is a Traitor!"). In every instance the message was clear: foreign spies were everywhere, they could be anyone, and no one could be trusted.

Compounding the dangers were those who ignored the Reds. In one case, Pete Trask enrolls in the "Kremlin Sabotage School" where co-ed Zorita demonstrates tactics to destroy Western landmarks. Alarmed, Trask hurries to England, but the English do not believe that the Russians could cross the Channel. While being hounded by an untrusting Scotland Yard, Trask barely saves Parliament ("Shocking").[2] In *Kent Blake and the Secret Service*, an American guerrilla fighter in the Soviet Union broadcasts worldwide: "We're not going to sit by and enjoy life while the rest of the world suffers and dies a slow death! [...] If we don't stop them here, they're coming over there and do the same thing!" ("The Voice").

One issue of *Astonishing* summarized the dangers of American complacency. When a friendly witness, Sherry Davis, is subpoenaed by a Senate Committee, she fears lurking fellow travelers. Davis informs Marvel Boy about the hidden enemy and the teenager gasps, "Even in the *FBI*??? Oh, no, Sherry!

Marvel Boy takes a moment to preach to the readers about the dangers of Complacency. From Bill Everett, "Time-Bomb Terror!" *Astonishing* #3 (April 1951). 20th Century Comic [Marvel Comics].

That's impossible!" Davis confirms that the Reds placed a bomb in the heart of American intelligence, with plans to "*blow the entire bureau to Kingdom Come!*"

Marvel Boy hurries to inform the police and federal agents, but the authorities laugh at the pleading youngster. The hero shares his observations about the achievements of fifth columnists through the fourth wall. Marvel Boy speaks while looking at his audience; his furrowed brow implicates the readers as among those contributing to the nation's unprepared state. Marvel Boy finally apprehends the spy, but the FBI building goes up in dynamite. Marvel Boy concludes with a biting summation, again to the reader:

> We weren't quite in time, thanks to the pig-headed complacency of certain 'loyal Americans' — but no one was hurt and [the army] had sense enough to remove all the F.B.I. records of communist agents and activities before the explosion! It's all over now but the shouting — among the members of the Senate Investigating Committee! [Everett, "Time Bomb Terror!"].

The Uranian Marvel Boy usually displayed admiration for American authority, but his wisecrack suggests that politics as usual could be dangerous.

Uniting the Free World

While Marvel Boy observed human behavior at home, others, especially *Spy-Hunters'* Jonathan Kent and *T-Man*'s Pete Trask were "world-wide Trouble

Shooters," scouring the globe to implement the Truman Doctrine; their international intervention built solidarity for the United States as the sole superpower after 1945.[3] In doing so, Trask supported American values abroad, particularly in the hotly contested Middle East and Southeast Asia; the latter, as President Eisenhower publicly explained in 1954, was predicted as the first domino to fall to communist aggression. In 1952, Trask saves the Iranian oil pipelines in *T-Man* #3, inspiring the Iranians to turn the industry over to the British and Americans. However, after Iran nationalized the then British controlled oil pipelines, the political atmosphere became turbulent. Quality Comics revised the story a year later. In *T-Man* #9, Trask marvels at an American-built pipeline in an undisclosed location ("Censorship stops me from telling where my new assignment was, but you'll get the idea if you know it was in one of the six Moslem kingdoms!") and stops the Reds from demolishing it ("Pipeline to Peril"). In this issue, Trask defends the joint efforts of the Americans and the "Moslem kingdom" from Soviet aggression. Although both *T-Man* stories support the United States position in Iran, the latter, with its setting classified and its omission of the British, masks the escalating tensions in Iran, in which Mossadegh's anti–Western regime would be overthrown by MI6 and the CIA later that year.[4]

In another issue, Trask journeys to Southeast Asia and alludes to the country's mixed population as a mirror of the United States, describing "Country X" as "a melting pot of Eastern peoples — Hindus, Arabs, Malays, Chinese, white rubber planters." In applying a label used to describe the United States of America, Trask establishes a parallel between east and west. While in Country X, Trask deduces that Mr. Karabi, a "loyal man respected by everyone" who "has contributed hundreds of thousands of dollars to fighting communism," was "obviously of the Malayan race. As for his wife, she was a winner in any race!" ("Red Ticket"). Trask certainly appreciates Mrs. Karabi's physical attributes, which also transcend international and racial borders. Unfortunately, Trask misreads the situation; Mrs. Karabi is a Communist agent who guns down her husband. Nine issues later, Trask extends the "melting pot of the Orient" metaphor to Singapore and misjudges another woman who kills her pro-American spouse ("Operation Blowup!"). Trask rarely operated on the home front, yet in wading through various foreign melting pots looking for impure elements, *T-Man* suggested that America's own cosmopolitan society had subversive dangers as well.

Despite communist sympathizers lurking about, comics made clear the unity between western powers and their allies. When operative Ernest Barnes stops a Communist from duping the locals in Madagascar into wanting independence, the populace flocks back to Western-led brotherhood: "We go! Back to the mines — to our French friends!" (Whitney). Similarly, when

Jonathan Kent eliminates North Korean operatives in the United States, a grateful South Korean official declares, "With the assistance of Americans like yourself, we can smash *any* Communist plot! We have waited years for democracy — and we will never give it up!" ("Adventures").

In India, Trask assesses that the Maharaja's "despotism has fallen on evil days since India became self-governing"—a jab at Prime Minister Jawaharlal Nehru's non-alignment policy and maintaining relations with China despite the Chinese invasion of Tibet in 1950 ("Tigers"). Indeed, Trask suspects that a Pakistani communist, Ali Mustapha, was spearheading an invasion of India through the Himalayas. This time, Trask was fortunately mistaken; Ali is a double agent for the United States. In Rumania, Trask meets Terente, a vigilante who robs foreign powers for his countrymen. Trask expands Terente's horizons beyond Rumanian borders with a "wake up" call, and by the end of the narrative brings him within the American sphere of influence.

In his assignments abroad, Trask stressed respect for cultural differences, relaying that violations of local customs could land one "in the middle of a full scale riot!" Even when he compromises that respect, however, his allies understand where the true threat lies. To give an example, Trask narrates that, while in India, he dutifully removes his shoes before entering a mosque. Unfortunately, later in the story, Trask learns of subversive activities taking place in the Islamic house of worship, and is forced to demolish an "altar" housing a "black rock from the holy Kaaba in Mecca" ("Elephant"). Before Trask's offense escalates into an international incident, all is forgiven when the agent reveals that the Soviets had hidden a printing press to spread anti–American literature. Unlike the respectful Trask, the communists had usurped the mosque for their

Pete Trask doing the physical and rhetorical work of the Cold War. From "The Red Robbers!" *T-Man* #29 (November 1955). Comic Magazines [Quality Comics].

own agenda and their lack of esteem for other people's values led to their defeat.

As Trask had found out, anti-communism was an international endeavor and comic books showcased ethnic groups uniting to thwart various Red schemes. In *Men's Adventures*, while battling communist aggression, Captain America encounters an Egyptian, Adu Bey. Adu praises, "America is great! She is wonderful! I like her people and I want them to like me!" He adds, "I hate wars and violence! But the Reds ... ugh! They threaten us all!" Captain America suspects that Adu might be a spy, but Adu proves himself by collapsing his ancestral tomb on a raven-haired Red. Like Trask's demolition of the mosque, the ancestral tomb is acceptable collateral damage. Captain America apologizes, but Adu is "honored to have it serve as a *tomb* for the *betrayers* of my country!" (Romita). His ancestral past, it seems, is not as valuable as containing the communist threat in the present.

Chinese American agents were also involved in spying against their recently-turned mother country. Undersecretary of State Dean Acheson issued a government White Paper in 1949 stating that "the unfortunate but inescapable fact is that [the Communist takeover in China] was beyond the control of the United States" (qtd. in Patterson 171). Times were dire: *Yellow Claw* depicted the "Chinese Communist High Command" contemplating invading Taiwan, even with U.S. Navy's Seventh Fleet "protecting the battered remains of the Nationalist army!" (Feldstein, "Coming").

However, even as Chang Kai-shek's chances of retaking the Middle Kingdom faded, comics showcased Chinese Americans fighting for the free world. Shoring the defense against Yellow Claw was agent Jimmy Woo, one of the few non-white protagonists in comics. Another pro-American Asian was Hong Kong detective Charley Loo, who casually uses American slang ("dollars to doughnuts!") and enjoys a British "spot of tea" with Trask ("Girl with Doom"). Other Chinese American spies weren't as fortunate: in "Incident!" American agent Lee Chan sneaks into China to investigate a series of "international incidents," but in doing so, Chan strands himself in the mainland. If Chan fails to escape, the story concludes, "Lee Chan will be ... another 'incident!'"[5] Similarly, when agent Mike Chang is killed, Trask eulogizes that Chang was "as American as baseball and hotdogs!" ("Operation Blowup"). Agent Lee Tsui helps operative Kent Blake destroy North Korea's germ warfare program, but she catches the virus and commits suicide ("Unseen Death"). Crossing ethnic lines, two Russian defectors steal a vial containing "the most deadly plague of germs known to science" and flee from the Iron Curtain (Ditko). Unfortunately, both are killed and the plague is released.

The use of science as a communist means for mass destruction echoed the escalating arms race, joined by concerns about radioactive fallout. By the end of the 1950s, strontium-90 was detected in everyday items such as milk, and, as one historian notes, even pet owners were warned about possible contamination in dog food (Winkler 103). Mounting fears of radioactive poisoning, coupled with heightened awareness of Soviet espionage, including Senator Joseph McCarthy's red-baiting hearings, the trials and executions of Julius and Ethel Rosenberg in 1953, and the discrediting of the esteemed scientist J. Robert Oppenheimer six months later, infused a sense of pessimism in pre-code comics. Winning the Cold War, these unhappy endings suggested, would have a high cost, and agents, regardless of ethnicity or gender, paid the price with their lives.

Dames, Domesticity, and Danger

Young Jane Warren intuitively knew that her "marriage was a mistake," even before her husband Harry slapped her on their honeymoon. Indeed, Harry was a Communist gun-runner. Warren provides a first-person narrative in the spirit of a romance comic's confessional. However, Warren isn't a teenager confiding to her diary, but a civilian caught up in international intrigue as she testifies before a military tribunal concerning her troubles with Harry. Happily, the tale ends with Warren finding "peace and fulfillment" in the arms of agent John Hawks, with whom she will make a more idyllic marriage ("Incident in Shanghai"). Such marriages were vital to American Cold War culture; as one historian posits, the household was a shield to "protect the nation by containing the frightening potentials of postwar [atomic] life (May 90).

Jane Warren's feminine intuition recognized that her sweetheart had dangerous loyalties. Disaster struck Eliana, a lovelorn secretary to diplomatic courier Sam Lacey. Eliana pines away for her boss, while avoiding Taragov, her ex-spy partner and ex-boyfriend. In switching sides, Eliana spurns her old loyalties for her new boss, and when she is wounded while on duty, Lacey awards her with a kiss. In a mix of passion and patriotism, Eilana survives her date with danger ("Betrayal").

Like their civilian counterparts, female American espionage agents also managed to balance patriotism with patriarchy. Fortunately, the 1950s ideals of western womanhood — home, hearth, and husband — meshed well with comic book espionage. Czech chemist Kurt Riner defects to the United States to pursue his work. His assistant, Betty, is a CIA agent, and when Riner is kidnapped, she guns down the enemy, devises a rescue plan, locates Riner, and singlehandedly bluffs them to surrender. With Riner safe, Betty coos, "It's not Operative X you're holding now, Kurt, just the woman who loves you!" ("Man Hunt"). In *Top Secret*, Soviet "master spy" Jorge Lootens tries to snare American agent "Twenty-One" by kidnapping his wife, homemaker Cora Rogers. The ploy fails because Lootens didn't consider that Twenty-One was Rogers herself, who strings the Communists along in an effective blend of domesticity with counter intelligence ("Agent Twenty-One").

However, like it did religion and race, anti-communism could also supersede romance. In Belgrade, Luba Slanic's partner is killed and the American Doug Grant forgets himself as he asks her to team-up with him. Her reply: "My job is here! I must stay as long as I am able ... and then ... my lips will be yours forever, darling!" Grant realizes, "She's right! We must win the peace ... or nothing ... not even love is worthwhile!" ("Smashing"). A happier ending occurred in "Jeopardy in the Jungle!" American plantation owner Greg suspects that Slavonian guerrilla fighter Tania was a Philippine Communist Party dupe. After defeating the Huks, Greg tells her, "I kept thinking of you so much [...] that I couldn't work on my accounts!" Tania cracks, "Maybe you'll find it easier — Greg — now that I'm not on the *red* side of the ledger!" Safely in the black, Greg embraces Tania, a double victory.

Although American women learned to suppress their innate womanhood while on duty, they made up for lost time after they accomplish their missions. In contrast, their communist counterparts squashed all sentiment for domesticity underneath the party line. In "The Death House at Bergenstrasse 13" Trask instructs that one "basic law of the department" was "never turn your back on the female of the species," and with good reason. Agent Doug Grant learns this the hard way in *Spy Cases* #7, when a valued scientist is murdered by the scientist's stepdaughter Greta. Greta coolly shrugs, "I begged him to sell out to the Reds! When he refused, I killed him! What does it matter? The cause is everything!" Having no qualms about eliminating her family for the good of the state, Greta meets a fitting end when she throws herself from a plane rather than be captured. Grant quips, "If she likes Red territory better than Western, good riddance [...]! Heaven knows she'll be in buried deep enough in the soil she murdered for!" (Hartley). The last panel shows Greta face down in the dirt, her comrades ignoring her crushed body as they watch Grant escape. Her death didn't matter; the cause was everything.

The same occurred for Captain America's foe "The Executioner," who masterminded a network of spies in the United States. The Executioner assigns Lupa Ludoff to seduce an American safeguarding an "atomic cannon." Ludoff describes her superior as having "no mercy ... no heart! He'd kill anyone standing in his way of Communist victory!" (Romita, "Top Secret"). The Executioner shoots Ludoff's husband when he fails. The next panel reveals that Ludoff herself is the Executioner — a cog in the communist machinery. Having removed all possibility of marital bliss after killing her husband, Ludoff turns the gun on herself. Despite the rhetoric of the cause, this ending suggests that for some communist women, the cause was not necessarily all they lived for.

Fortunately, opportunities for redemption abounded. Women who rediscovered their capacity for love and romance inevitably found their way to the Western powers. In Egypt, Pete Trask encounters Margot La Rocherlie, the "curved serpent of the Nile," who murders for her Soviet masters. However, her comrade wonders, "A girl may be beautiful, unscrupulous, greedy, dedicated to our cause ... But what if she falls in love? What then? [...] I have known women who were excellent agents until their heads were turned! Love

America's secret weapon versus communism: love. "Assault in Armenia!" *Spy-Hunters* #15 (December 1951–January 1952). Best Syndicated Features [American Comics Group].

makes traitors!" Indeed, after Trask captures La Rocherlie's heart, she dies content: "For the first time ... The only time ... *gasp* I knew what it meant to ... love!" ("T-Man").

The fundamental characteristics of female spies found agreement across geography and ideology. When agent Charles Lockwood travels to Mount Ararat, he finds his wife, Tanya, heading a spy ring. Tanya plays the cold warrior, but Lockwood's devotion overwhelms her. Tanya announces that "it was love that made me see the light." Lockwood's chief concurs, having pegged womanhood down to a science: "we knew that only *love* would make you come to this country and tell us all you knew!" ("Assault").

Perhaps the most effective female agent was Pete Trask's sometime partner, Terry Gordon. Gordon is perky, patriotic, and completely platonic in regards to Trask. In "Red Murder Incorporated!," Trask lauds, "Our job's done, Terry! And who's responsible? *You!*" Gordon smirks, "All in a day's work of a *T-Woman*! Or wouldn't you know — just being a *T-Man*?" Uninterested in domesticity and her boss, Gordon's presence was awkward for Trask; her appearances restrained Trask from asserting his American manhood abroad. As a result, Gordon made few appearances; by *T-Man*'s end, her role was greatly diminished — a casualty of Cold War gender roles.

One story that highlights many themes of American containment was the lead story in *Spy and Counterspy* #1, published in 1949. Spy Jonathan Kent introduces himself because readers "ought to learn what we're doing." Kent's family emigrated from an unnamed totalitarian state to America and Kent has "done his best to fight for liberty and democracy — and today, the world needs them more than ever," as Kent casts his services "on the side of *freedom*!"

Kent soon learns that "vital plans for the detonator of the atom bomb" had been stolen. The agent deduces that the culprit "spells only *one power*": the Soviet Union. While investigating, operatives Gregg and Toby are killed. Since Kent's family hailed from the same anonymous nation, he is able to travel behind the Iron Curtain to avenge his friends. There, Kent finds Greg, or, rather, Greginovsky, who gloats, "See how easy it is to fool you stupid Yankees? Me, a foreign operative — and I duped you enough to get into your spy training school to learn your methods!" Kent kills Greginvosky, sneaks into an atomic research lab, and meets Vera Blanoff, who possessed "a yum-yum figure!" Blanoff, a.k.a. Soviet Operative 617, captures Kent, despite his protesting, "You *can't* betray me! We serve different masters, but I love you — and you've told me you love me!"

Kent's plea works. Blanoff confesses, "I thought I was doing my duty, that my country meant everything to me — but I've found out that I'm *more* than Operative *617*! I'm a *woman*, too — and *I love you*!" Blanoff helps Kent while re-discovering romance and religion: "I know what it is, God help me!

There is nothing I can say — but I wish I were dead for what I've released you to do!" With Kent safe, Blanoff "can die happy now" and promptly does so. Kent concludes that "I try not to think about Vera — to remember only that she really died for the right to love and live — for the same values we're trying to protect! And we'll protect those and all democratic rights —*just as along as American countrymen are on the job!*" ("Jonathon Kent"). In his first issue, Kent loses friends, a love interest, and learns the threat his ancestral fatherland poses to the United States. But he willingly sacrifices all in the service of his country.

Post-Code Epilogue

The implementation of the Comics Code in 1954 tempered comic book illustrations of spice and vice, and though critics did not delve too deeply into anti-communist espionage titles, publishers played it safe nevertheless. Toward the end of *T-Man*, Quality reprinted their earlier stories, but sanitized these "top-secret" exposés. In one issue, violent visuals — a dead policeman or Trask being gunwhipped — disappeared. Objectionable insults ("Cochran! Pig!") were muted. Even the villain vanished from his death scene, leaving a blank spot on the page ("Parisian"). Readers took heart that Americans, whether cowardly or criminal, would never turn traitor, and the casualty rates of American agents dropped to near zero. Pete Trask continued to troubleshoot until Quality exited the industry. "I haven't had a real vacation in four years," Trask comments in 1955, as his career winds down ("Death House"). The public outcry against comics achieved what the Comintern could not: censorship of the comics.

The number of espionage titles diminished, but the themes of subversive activities threatening the American way of life and the infiltration of American society continued in various genres. EC Comics publisher Bill Gaines had revulsion for his early espionage pieces, calling one tale "the most dreadful, horrible, stupid story" (Cochran 42). However, EC routinely depicted aliens overtaking key positions in American politics and military — greater coups than the Soviets ever achieved. Over at DC Comics, news of frog-faced shape-shifters in Metropolis start a panic: "He — he might be of us ... right here in the crowd! He can change shape, they say!" Superman realizes that "the mob hysteria is spreading" but manages to prevent disaster (Finger). The Man of Steel safeguards the "American Way," and his heritage reflected those same values: Superman's parents were even portrayed as Krypton Bureau of Investigations agents who apprehended subversive elements in Kryptonian society (Binder, Swan, and Kaye). Likewise, Supergirl journeys to a parallel Earth where strangers without identification papers are automatically "arrested under suspicion of being a spy from another planet" (Binder and Mooney). Espionage was an interstellar concern.

While aliens meddled with America's military industrial complex, communism remained a continual threat. The "Silver Age's" revival of superhero titles reinforced the danger of Red agents. Soviet espionage contributed heavily to early Marvel Comics heroes, including the Hulk and Iron Man, while World War II vet Nick Fury would lead a globetrotting, troubleshooting taskforce, S.H.I.E.L.D. As one reader wrote, she and her husband "feel that sometimes using Communists as villains gives a story impact and promotes an interest in world affairs" (Morse). This would change as the postwar consensus broke down, and comic books would later challenge Cold War policies in later decades, thawing the Cold War culture that Fury's predecessors had sought to contain.

Notes

1. In another story, "For Services Rendered," the Reds tell one of their own he "joined the Communist party when you thought it would do you good ... just as you once joined the Nazis for the same reason! And now you've joined the enemy, eh? It will be wise for you to switch back to us, comrade!" The opportunist returns to his old loyalties, but when foiled by the FBI, fellow travelers gave him a lead-lined payoff. On the cinematic front, *I Was a Communist for the F.B.I.* (1951) mirrored Marvel Boy's sentiments, showing Soviets living the high life in America while espousing sympathy for the common people. The film earned an Academy Award nomination for Best Documentary.

2. In "The Man in Black" from *Menace* #2, a more rigorous course of study is depicted for budding Soviet agents. Students are required to kill their own parents ("You didn't even flinch when your father collapsed on the floor [...] After all, it was over in just a few seconds!"). Instructors maintained a torture chamber under the campus, where they branded underperformers with hot-iron hammers and sickles.

3. *T-Man* bore little resemblance to the 1948 film *T-Men*, which focused on counterfeiting. The television show *Treasury Men in Action* (1951–1954), based on cases from the Secret Service, had a domestic setting. *T-Man* was more in line with *The Man Called X* (1955–1957), a television show which centered on international espionage, although the program premiered after Trask's book had ended. For synopses of television Cold War spy programs, see Michael Kackman's, *Citizen Spy: Television, Espionage, and Cold War Culture*.

4. The historian Bradford Wright posits that *T-Man* #3 was influenced by the overthrow of the Mossadegh government in Iran. However, that issue has a cover date of January 1952, a year before the coup. See Bradford W. Wright, *Comic Book Nation: The Transformation of Youth Culture in America*, 126.

5. The comic may have played off then-recent headlines: the United States lost aircraft over the Siberian coast in 1954, which the press dubbed as "incidents." See "U.S. Bids U.N. Act on Soviet Attack on Patrol Bomber," *The New York Times*, September 7, 1954: 1.

Works Cited

"Adventures of a Spy." *Spy-Hunters* #3 (April 1951), 20th Century Comic [Marvel Comics].
"Agent Twenty-One." *Top Secret* #1 (Jan. 1952), Hillman Periodicals.

"Assassins of Baghdad!" *T-Man* #9 (Jan. 1953), Comic Magazines [Quality Comics].
"Assault in Armenia!" *Spy-Hunters* #15 (Dec. 1951-Jan. 1952), Best Syndicated Features [American Comics Group].
"The Attractive Smuggler." *Top Secret* #1 (Jan. 1952), Hillman Periodicals.
"Beautiful but Deadly!" *Spy Cases* #26 (Sept. 1950), Hercules Publishing [Marvel Comics].
"The Betrayal!" *Date with Danger* #5 (Dec. 1952), Standard Magazines.
Binder, Otto (w), Curt Swan (p), and Stan Kaye (i). "The Three Magic Wishes." *Superman* #123 (Aug. 1958), National Comics [DC Comics].
Binder, Otto (w), and Jim Mooney (a). "The Supergirl of Two Worlds!" *Action Comics* #273 (Feb. 1961), National Comics [DC Comics].
"Captain Coward." *Date with Danger* #5 (Dec. 1952), Standard Magazines.
Caute, David. *The Great Fear: The Anti-Communist Purge Under Truman and Eisenhower.* New York: Simon and Schuster, 1978. Print.
Cochran, Russ. "The Birth of Two-Fisted Tales." *Two-Fisted Tales Archives,* vol. 1. York, PA: Gemstone, 2007. Print.
"The Death House at Bergenstrasse 13." *T-Man* #29 (Nov. 1955), Comic Magazines [Quality Comics].
[Ditko, Steve] (a). "The Pay Off." *Strange Suspense: The Steve Ditko Archives,* vol. 1. Ed. Blake Bell. Seattle: Fantagraphics, 2009: 217–223. Print.
"The Elephant Who Loved Flowers!" *T-Man* #30 (Dec. 1955), Comic Magazines [Quality Comics].
Everett, Bill (a). "The Phantom Pen!" *Astonishing* #6 (Oct. 1951), 20th Century Comic [Marvel Comics].
_____. "Time-Bomb Terror!" *Astonishing* #3 (April 1951), 20th Century Comic [Marvel Comics].
Feldstein, Al (w), and Joe Maneely (a). "The Coming of the Yellow Claw!" *The Yellow Claw* #1 (Oct. 1956), Marjean Magazine [Marvel Comics].
_____, and Werner Roth (a). "For Services Rendered!" *The Yellow Claw* #1 (Oct. 1956), Marjean Magazine [Marvel Comics].
Finger, Bill (w), Curt Swan (p), and Stan Kaye (i). "The Contest of Heroes." *World's Finest Comics* #74. (Jan.-Feb.1955), National Comics [DC Comics].
"The Fjords of Fear!" *Spy Cases* #7 (Oct. 1951), Hercules Publishing [Marvel Comics].
"The Girl with Doom in Her Hands!" *T-Man* #30 (Dec. 1955), Comic Magazines [Quality Comics].
Hartley, Al (a). "Nightmare at Noon!" *Spy Cases* #7 (Oct. 1951), Hercules Publishing [Marvel Comics].
Haynes, John Earl, and Harvey Klehr. *Early Cold War Spies: The Espionage Trials That Shaped American Politics.* Cambridge: Cambridge University Press, 2006. Print.
"Homicide Holocaust!" *T-Man* #11 (May 1953), Comic Magazines [Quality Comics].
"Incident!" *Spy-Thrillers* #2 (Jan. 1955), Prime Publications [Marvel Comics].
"Incident in Shanghai." *Spy-Hunters* #15 (Dec. 1951- Jan. 1952), Best Syndicated Features [American Comics Group].
"Jeopardy in the Jungle!" *Spy-Hunters* #3 (Dec. 1949-Jan. 1950), Syndicated Features [American Comics Group].
"Jonathan Kent, Counterspy." *Spy and Counterspy* #1 (Aug.-Sept. 1949), Best Syndicated Features [American Comics Group].
Kackman, Michael. *Citizen Spy: Television, Espionage, and Cold War Culture.* Minneapolis: University of Minnesota Press, 2005. Print.
Lee, Stan (w), George Tuska (a). "The Man in Black." *Menace* #2 (April 1953), Hercules Publishing [Marvel Comics].
Man Hunt from the East!" *Spy and Counterspy* #1 (Aug.-Sept. 1949), Best Syndicated Features [American Comics Group].
"May, Elaine Tyler. *Homeward Bound: American Families in the Cold War Era.* New York: Basic, 1988.

Morse, Mrs. Danny Lee. Letter. *The Amazing Spider-Man* #16 (Sept. 1964), Non-Pareil Publishing [Marvel Comics].
"One Is a Traitor!" *Kent Blake of the Secret Service* #8 (July 1952), 20th Century Comic [Marvel Comics].
"Operation Blow Up!" *T-Man* #17 (Aug. 1954), Comic Magazines [Quality Comics].
Patterson, James. *Grand Expectations: The United States, 1945-1974*. New York: Oxford University Press, 1996. Print.
"Pipeline to Peril." *T-Man* #9 (Jan. 1953), Comic Magazines [Quality Comics].
"Red Murder Incorporated!" *T-Man* #13 (Nov. 1953), Comic Magazines [Quality Comics].
"The Red Robbers!" *T-Man* #29 (Nov. 1955), Comic Magazines [Quality Comics].
"A Red Ticket to Hell," *T-Man* #8 (Nov. 1952), Comic Magazines [Quality Comics].
"The Ring of Doom," *T-Man* #13 (Nov. 1953), Comic Magazines [Quality Comics].
Romita, John (a). "The Girl Who Was Afraid!" *Men's Adventures* #27 (May 1954), Comic Combine [Marvel Comics].
_____. "Top Secret!" *Young Men* #25 (Feb. 1954), Comic Combine [Marvel Comics].
"School for Spies." *Spy-Hunters* #3 (Dec. 1949-Jan. 1950), Syndicated Features [American Comics Group].
"Shocking Red Sabotage." *T-Man* #24 (April 1955), Comic Magazines [Quality Comics].
Sibley, Katherine S. *Red Spies in America: Stolen Secrets and the Dawn of the Cold War*. Lawrence: University of Kansas Press, 2004. Print.
"Smashing the Iron Curtain." *Spy Cases* #26 (Sept.1950). Hercules Publishing [Marvel Comics].
"T-Man." *T-Man* #8 (Nov. 1952), Comic Magazines [Quality Comics].
"The Tigers of Balipur!" *T-Man* #8 (Nov. 1953), Comic Magazines [Quality Comics].
"The Traitor!" *Spy Cases* #26. (Sept. 1950). Hercules Publishing [Marvel Comics].
"Two Days to Doom." *T-Man* #15 (April 1954), Comic Magazines [Quality Comics].
"The Unseen Death!" *Kent Blake of the Secret Service* #8 (July 1952), 20th Century Comic [Marvel Comics].
"The Unseen Killers!" *Spy Thrillers* #2 (Jan. 1955), Prime Publications [Marvel Comics].
"The Voice!" *Kent Blake of the Secret Service* #13 (May 1953), 20th Century Comic [Marvel Comics].
Whitfield, Stephen. *The Culture of the Cold War*. Baltimore: Johns Hopkins University Press, 1991. Print.
Whitney, Ogden (a). "Menace in Madagascar!" *Spy-Hunters* #6 (June-July 1950), Best Syndicated Features [American Comics Group].
Winkler, Allan. *Life Under a Cloud: American Anxiety About the Atom*. New York: Oxford University Press, 1999. Print.
"A Word Here ... A Word There..." *Top Secret* #1 (Jan. 1952), Hillman Periodicals.
Wright, Bradford. *Comic Book Nation: The Transformation of Youth Culture in America*. Baltimore: Johns Hopkins University Press, 2001. Print.

3

"He Was a Living Breathing Human Being": Harvey Kurtzman's War Comics and the "Yellow Peril" in 1950s Containment Culture[1]

Christopher B. Field

In a 1981 interview conducted by Kim Thompson, Gary Groth, and Mike Carton with celebrated comics creator Harvey Kurtzman, Groth asks Kurtzman about his groundbreaking war comics for William Gaines's Entertaining Comics (EC Comics), *Two-Fisted Tales* and *Frontline Combat*. Kurtzman responds,

> what I was trying to tell my reader was what I perceived as being true. I didn't want to be a preacher, but I did want to tell the truth about things.
>
> For instance, I was absolutely appalled by the lies in the war books that publishers were putting out. What they did when they produced a war book is they focused on what they thought the reader would like to read, which was "Americans are good guys and anybody against us is the bad guys. We're human. And God is always on our side." This trash had nothing to do with the reality of life [104].

Kurtzman's contention that he was only trying to "tell the truth about things" is especially important for examining the development of *Frontline Combat* and *Two-Fisted Tales*, because his attempts to produce truthful war comics occur at a time when truth was not exactly encouraged in popular mediums.[2] In American culture, truth was frequently subverted in an attempt to formulate a consistent narrative about the dangers of communist influence. The solution to dealing with American anxieties regarding the spread of communism was the policy of containment which, as Alan Nadel contends, was a pervasive element of American culture to the point that it influenced discourse in numerous settings (3). As Nadel illustrates, containment became a way of life for many Americans where even the most relatively mundane activity, like reading a comic book, for instance, related back to the idea that communists were trying to infiltrate and subvert, or to simply destroy American culture. Therefore, in this highly combustible cultural landscape, every cultural artifact, including comic books like Kurtzman's, were potential vehicles for infiltration.

The development of the first of Harvey Kurtzman's war comics, *Two-Fisted Tales*, started with Kurtzman approaching Gaines with the idea of doing an adventure book, but the concept quickly turned to war with the onset of the Korean War.[3] Kurtzman was able to persuade Gaines to try out the concept, and the first issue of *Two-Fisted Tales* debuted in late 1950, with one story by Kurtzman.[4] The story that Kurtzman wrote and illustrated for the first issue, "Conquest," is a tale of Spanish conquistadors who attempt to conquer the "heathen savages" of Campeche in order to steal their gold. The Spanish are at first successful, overwhelming the Mayans with their advanced military tactics (i.e., guns and cavalry), and the subsequent mistreatment of the injured and captive natives at the hands of the Spanish. However, the Mayans do not give up, and they begin to stage counter-attacks at night when they are protected by the darkness. The final panels of the story show the natives defeating the Spanish and subjecting them to the same type of treatment that they were subjected to. This story, while not explicitly addressing American involvement in the Korean War, does establish some themes that Kurtzman would revisit and further develop in his later stories dealing with the Korean War, such as the invasion of a technologically superior army, the identification of the indigenous population with "savagery" by the invading force, and the resulting irony of the invaders subjecting the natives to inhumane treatment. While the subtext of "Conquest" might be easy to miss when it is hidden beneath a story of Spanish invaders and Mayan natives, when the same subtext is included in a story that deals with the Korean War it becomes abundantly clear that Kurtzman is voicing some powerfully stated objections to American involvement in the Korean War. Therefore, when Kurtzman's work is compared to the more culturally conservative works of his contemporaries in comics, for instance, the stories included in *War Comics*[5] published by Atlas Comics (later Marvel) it is possible to see how Kurtzman's war comics are skillfully constructed critiques of the American policy of containment through their sympathetic portrayal of enemy combatants, specifically in regards to the depictions of Asian characters.[6]

Yellow Peril and the Korean War

The most common portrayal of Asian characters in the works of Harvey Kurtzman's contemporaries is in the tradition of the "Yellow Peril." William F. Wu defines

3. "He Was a Living Breathing Human Being" (Field) 47

the "Yellow Peril" as the threat to the United States that some white American authors believed was posed by the people of East Asia. As a literary theme, the fear of this threat focused on specific issues, including possible military invasion from Asia, perceived competition to the white labor force from Asian workers, the alleged moral degeneracy of Asian people, and the potential genetic mixing of Anglo-Saxons with Asians, who were considered a biologically inferior race [qtd. in Ma 7–8].

In the first chapter of his book *The Deathly Embrace: Orientalism and Asian American Identity*, Sheng-mei Ma traces the use of the "Yellow Peril" in classic adventure comic strips from the 1930s, such as Alex Gillespie Raymond's *Flash Gordon* and Milton Caniff's *Terry and the Pirates*, to mark Asian characters as racial "others" and create an aura of exoticism by positioning these characters as either threats to Caucasian American values, or as comedic relief for their inability to fully assimilate in to American society. Ma describes a typical portrayal of the "evil Chinaman" exhibiting characteristics of "Yellow Peril" caricatures as being "garbed in a long robe often decorated with dragons, his head shaved or sporting a cap with a dragon, long and thin goatees, eyes half-closed or slantingly drawn, and, at times, long fingernails and pointed ears" (9–10). The last two characteristics that Ma describes, the "long fingernails and pointed ears," are meant to accentuate the character's animalistic qualities so that the reader can clearly identify the character as bestial and subhuman. Each of these characteristics is utilized in portrayals of Asian characters in the more conservative war comics, with some slight variations in order to update the stereotypes. Because of the popularity of these strips, many of the comics writers and artists during Kurtzman's time were familiar with these strips, and in works like those found in *War Comics* there is an undeniable influence from the earlier strips, where the American everyman, the superhuman protector of American values, must confront and defeat the feral, subhuman threat.

The portrayals of American troops in the stories in *War Comics* are unabashedly positive, and they immediately call to mind Kurtzman's assessment of his contemporaries. They show "Americans are good guys and anybody against us is the bad guys. We're human. And God is always on our side" (Thompson, Groth, and Carton 104). For example, issue #26 features the story "Midway," in which a sailor aboard the Yorktown finally gets his wish for more action as the Japanese attack Midway during World War II. The sailor, Mulrooney, fights valiantly against the Japanese onslaught, and he is shown keeping a cool head as the attack causes the ship to list, and he and another crew member, Tim, have to abandon ship. The first two panels on the last page of the story show Mulrooney and Tim's rescue by a lifeboat, which is followed by Tim praising Mulrooney for being "cool as a cucumber" in the next two panels. The fifth panel shows Mulrooney finally losing his cool and passing out now that he is out of the battle and safely aboard the boat. This story is only one example of numerous stories in *War Comics* that feature American soldiers that are able to suppress their emotions and excel under the pressure of combat. The story's frame starts with an overview of Japan's original attack on Midway and the subsequent decision to focus on larger targets. When the Japanese decide to shift their focus back to Midway, the story then shifts to focus on Mulrooney throughout the course of the battle. By using Mulrooney as a focal point for the action of the battle, the writers make Mulrooney a representative for the entire American side during the battle. The implication is that the American military is filled with men like Mulrooney, men that can suppress their humanity in battle, fighting valiantly and showing no weakness in front of the enemy, who can only show weakness around other American soldiers, whom they see as equals.

The pattern of the American soldier exhibiting superhuman traits during the course of a battle is a common one in *War Comics*, and a variation of this pattern occurs when American soldiers display a spiritual superiority in comparison to the enemy. An example of this variation occurs in the story "The Prayer," in issue #18. The story starts with four marines, Brown, Connolly, Kaplin, and Big Jim Johnson, being volunteered to stay behind and stop the advance of a North Korean unit to give their own unit a chance to get away and meet up with reinforcements. The four marines come up with a plan to use the snow banks on the cliffs around them to start an avalanche and bury the North Korean troops. The plan works, but as the marines flee the surviving North Koreans to meet up with their unit, they find that there is a reservoir blocking their unit from advancing. Seemingly trapped with the enemy closing in behind them, several of the men resort to prayer while Big Jim refuses to take part. Big Jim defiantly shouts at the praying men that their prayers are not going to bring a bridge to help them cross the reservoir, when suddenly sections of a bridge are airdropped from the heavens to assist the men. After the troops have successfully assembled the bridge and crossed to the other side of the reservoir where the army unit is waiting for them, Big Jim drops to his knees in prayer, declaring, "Nobody calls Big Jim an ingrate!" (30). This story underscores the strong theme of moral superiority that persists in *War Comics*. At one point in the story the troops are shown discussing God, with Big Jim claiming that their prayers are useless because they cannot even agree on which god is the correct God. One of the troops replies that it does not matter what God is called, because all gods are the same God. The point here is that it does not matter which god a person believes in, because God believes in America. God's favor of the American cause is illustrated in the bridge being delivered just in time to aid the Americans. The story leads the reader to believe that God's interest in the American cause is an active interest, hence the intervention to aid the cause, rather than a passive interest. This leads to the question, with an army of Mulrooneys and God's protection, how could America possibly lose? The answer, of course, is meant to be in the negative; that America cannot possibly lose.

The conflation of the American fighting spirit with God's favor of capitalism and American values gives the reader a clear picture of the views of the conservative comics, like *War Comics*, but there is still one thing that could possibly defeat the American cause, and it is inextricably bound up in the depictions of the enemy. Many of the depictions of Asian characters in *War Comics* are similar to the characteristics that Ma describes as prevalent in the "Yellow Peril" tradition. The story "Tooth and Nail," in issue #13 starts, "Suddenly you're face to face with the enemy! You stare at each other in silence and know that one of you has to die!" (1). In setting the stage for the conflict, the narration tells the reader that the fight will be a "hand to hand, tooth and nail, beast-like encounter!" (1). The story then shifts to providing a background for the conflict, where "you" are accidentally left behind by the unit and forced to catch up on foot. As "you" walk toward the next point, "you" stumble upon a North Korean soldier. A scuffle ensues in which "you" disarm the North Korean soldier, but he has the advantage in hand-to-hand combat. That is, until he insults capitalism. This insult gives "you" the strength to fight off the North Korean soldier. He claws "your" face, and "you" respond by sinking "your" teeth in to his forearm. He kicks "you" in the stomach, and "you" pick up a rock and pummel the man until "you" know that he is dead. When "you" finally arrive in camp after the encounter, a fellow soldier tells "you" that it looks like "you" have been in a fight with "some wild beast" (5). The final panel of the story is a close-up shot of "your" beaten and scratched face, with "your" response that "you" have. This story includes several jarring effects for the reader that help to emphasize the major theme of the story. The first is the use of second-person perspective ("you") to place the reader in the story. This has the effect of emphasizing the reader's complicity with the American soldier's actions in the story. The next is that the splash panel on the first page of the story shows the American soldier and the North Korean soldier facing-off across the page from each other. The men have their teeth clinched in a grimace that makes it appear as if they are growling at each other. This effect is further enhanced by the sixth panel on page four, which depicts a close-up shot of the North Korean soldier raking his nails down the American soldier's face like a "claw." The eighth panel shows a close-up shot of the American digging his teeth in to the North Korean's forearm, like a dog chewing on a bone. The purpose of portraying the fight in this manner is to show that the American soldier has been forced to match the ferocity of the North Korean by becoming just as animalistic as he is. Both of these

An American soldier becoming an "animal." From "Tooth and Nail," *War Comics* #13. U.S.A. Comic Magazine. 4. Print.

effects, the second-person perspective and portraying the American as animalistic in response to the North Korean's attack, combine to underscore the story's theme of shifting identity. The story starts by assigning the reader with an identity, that of the American soldier, but this identity is later replaced by an animalistic one, which then reverts back to that of a soldier. The shift in identity is fluid, and it acts as a parable for containment culture at this time, as the soldier must be able to shift his identity to defend himself against the attack from the North Korean soldier, but at the same time he must retain his ability to shift back to a soldier after the conflict has ended. This shift in identity stands in stark contrast to the identity of the North Korean soldier, who is portrayed as an animal in his attack on the American, and who is still left with this identity at the end of the story when the American soldier categorizes him as a wild beast. The story stands as a reminder to the reader that it is necessary to match the ferocity of the opposing force to win the fight against communism, and that after the fight is over, it will be necessary to shift back to a more human identity, an identity that is still withheld from the soldiers that fight to uphold the values of communism.

Kurtzman's Korea and the "Truth about Things"

In direct opposition to the view on containment culture that the stories in *War Comics* offer, stands the view of Harvey Kurtzman's war comics. In *Two-Fisted Tales* and *Frontline Combat*, Kurtzman portrays both sides of the Korean War, the Americans and the North Koreans, as human beings. This approach may seem simplistic but, in reality, it actually helps to make more complicated narratives. For example, the story "Enemy Assault!" in the first issue of *Frontline Combat* depicts an American soldier who rounds a corner in a trench and finds an enemy soldier with his gun drawn. The two stare each other down, guns trained on each other. The tension builds as the reader

3. "He Was a Living Breathing Human Being" (Field) 51

wonders which soldier will be the first to fire, the American or the Korean. Each soldier issues a threat to take the other captive, and it is at this point that the American soldier realizes that the Korean soldier speaks English. This realization sparks a conversation, and within a few panels the two soldiers have gone from enemy combatants to proud fathers sharing pictures of their families. This scenario is indicative of an important departure in Kurtzman's war comics from the depictions of Asian characters in the comics of Kurtzman's contemporaries, like those in *War Comics*. In "Enemy Assault!" the Korean soldier is not drawn with the exaggerated, animalistic features indicative of "Yellow Peril" characters, like those found in "Tooth and Nail." In Kurtzman's hands a Korean soldier loses the racist features a contemporary audience was used to seeing, or as the American soldier puts it, "He was a living breathing *human being* with a *wife* and *children* and *hopes* and *plans just like me!*" [emphasis in the original] (24). However, the burgeoning friendship is cut short when soldiers from each side advance on the trench, and when an American soldier shoots a North Korean soldier that has taken aim at the American in the trench, it frightens the North Korean and he shoots the American soldier that shot the North Korean. The American in the trench is then forced to react, and as he levels his gun at the North Korean soldier he thinks, "I had to choose sides! I had to! You can't fight in a war by comparing baby snapshots!" (25). The next panel shows the American soldier in the trench firing at the North Korean soldier, and the subsequent panel depicts the dead North Korean soldier with the photos of his family laying on top of him. While the ending of "Enemy Assault!" may match the end of "Tooth and Nail," with the American soldier killing the North Korean soldier, the tone at the end of this piece is vastly different. The soldier's repetition of the phrase "I had to" indicates that he is trying to convince someone, possibly himself, that he made the right decision in killing the North Korean.

His realization that the North Korean was a "human being" and not an "automatan" is reinforced here by the photos on the dead

Reminders of humanity. From [Harvey Kurtzman (w), Jack Davis (p), and Marie Severin (i)], "Enemy Assault!" *Frontline Combat* vol. 1. York, PA: Gemstone, 2008, 25. Print.

man's chest, which forces the American to accept that he has killed a human. With this knowledge he then turns his attention to advancing figures far off in the distance, and he prepares himself for the next assault. The shift in focus at the end of the story, from the dead man to the figures in the distance, is a reversal of the soldier's earlier shift from seeing the figures in the distance as automatons and then recognizing the humanity in the North Korean when he is confronted with it. This reversal seems to hint that the soldier is trying to pull back and deny the humanity of the figures in the distance, but the ending of the story is ambiguous, and the reader is left to wonder if the soldier will be able to forget the lesson that he has learned in the story and fire on these soldiers without recognizing their humanity.

In an effort to get the reader to recognize the humanity of the soldiers fighting on each side of the war, Kurtzman creates a variation of the trope of ascribing animalistic characteristics to the enemy. In "Bug Out!" in issue #24 of *Two-Fisted Tales*, Kurtzman tells the story of an American soldier in Korea whose squad is forced to scatter, or "bug out," when they are attacked by the North Koreans, and how the North Koreans sneak up on the squad when it has regrouped, and they kill most of the squad. The narrator is able to get away, and he later finds a North Korean camp. The narrator sees the four North Koreans huddled around a pot of rice, and he is so hungry that he sneaks up behind them and kills them "like an animal fighting for brute survival" (22). The narrator then eats the rice like a "hungry, wild-eyed dog" (23). In the middle of stuffing himself with the rice, he notices that American bombers are flying overhead, and when he sees that they are opening the bays to drop bombs in this location, he tries to "claw into the ground" like a "miserable wretched animal" (24). The scene then shifts to a hospital where the soldier is seen sitting in a wheelchair while one nurse explains to another nurse that there was "not a scratch on him" when he arrived at the hospital, and he contemplates "What happened to all [of his] fine civilized instincts" (24–25). The ending of this story emphasizes that the soldier has had some sort of psychological breakdown, which is probably Posttraumatic Stress Disorder, as a result of his experiences in the war. This ending significantly complicates the theme of shifting identity that also occurs in "Tooth and Nail." In this story the protagonist attempts to shift identities to his animalistic identity in a fight for survival, just as in "Tooth and Nail," but he is unable to shift back to his human identity once he is back in the relative safety of the hospital. This contradicts the idea in "Tooth and Nail" that an individual can neatly compartmentalize his identity. Instead, the ending of "Bug Out!" reinforces the idea that if an individual loses touch with his humanity, even temporarily, then he will have to deal with the consequences of his actions, and this may forever change the way he views himself as a human being.

3. "He Was a Living Breathing Human Being" (Field) 53

In his war comics, *Two-Fisted Tales* and *Frontline Combat*, Harvey Kurtzman resisted the cultural pressures of his era and attempted to provide truthful representations of war. Kurtzman's truth was that there were human beings with differing ideologies on both sides of the Korean War. In order to expose this truth, Kurtzman broke with the common tropes that his contemporaries used, such as portraying Asian characters as menacing, animalistic monsters in the "Yellow Peril" tradition, and instead chose to present a more realistic depiction of Asian characters. This was not a popular truth in a culture where it was easy to vilify North Koreans as a representative of quickly spreading communist ideals, and that largely advocated containing the spread of communism by whatever means necessary, so it is a testament to Kurtzman's skill as a storyteller that he was able to find and retain an audience during such a contentious time without major objections to his subject matter. The result of Kurtzman's search for truth is that his stories stand as a reminder of just how powerful a voice of dissent can be.

Notes

1. I want to express my sincere gratitude to Nancy Down at the library at Bowling Green State University for her assistance with researching elements of this article and to Edward J. Brunner at Southern Illinois University Carbondale for his feedback on earlier drafts and for his tireless encouragement throughout this process.

2. I mention this as an aside because I am sure that most readers are reasonably acquainted with the investigations of the House Committee on Un-American Activities in regards to communist influence in the entertainment industry and Senator Joseph McCarthy's attempts to expose communist influences in the government. These investigations took place at roughly the same time that Kurtzman was developing and writing his war comics titles, and they serve as reminders of how dangerous it was at that point in time to express any sentiment that might be construed as sympathetic towards either soldiers that were fighting to uphold the principles of communism or the actual principles of communism. For an extended discussion of censorship in the American press during this time, see Casey.

3. Kurtzman remembers: "When we started *Two-Fisted Tales*, or I did, it was going to be a slam-bang high-adventure book, and when the Korean War broke out, I naturally turned to the war for material" (24). In fact, it is not until the fourth issue of the series that it becomes completely devoted to war stories. See Benson, 21- 37, for the full interview.

4. *Two-Fisted Tales* replaced *The Haunt of Fear*, so the first issue features the issue #18, and the subsequent issues follow this same numbering scheme.

5. I limit my comparison to *War Comics* for several reasons. First, the beginning of this title's publication predates the beginning of Kurtzman's war comics by only a few months, which means that both *War Comics* and Kurtzman's comics are operating within and reacting to the same cultural landscape. Additionally, Atlas and EC were comparable in terms of their size and ability to distribute their products to their readers. Finally, and arguably most importantly, this title is largely representative of the same politically conservative point of view that many war comics of the time adhered to, which starkly contrasts with the more liberal leanings of Kurtzman's comics.

6. There have been numerous efforts to address Kurtzman's work in the past, from a number of different angles, but this is one of the first to offer a direct comparison with a contemporary

competitor. A couple of the more thought-provoking critical approaches to Kurtzman's work are the approach that Savage offers to provide context for Kurtzman's work, and Versaci's comparison of Kurtzman's work to films discussing the Korean War.

WORKS CITED

Benson, John. "A Talk with Harvey Kurtzman." *The Comics Journal Library Volume Seven: Harvey Kurtzman.* 21–37. Print.
Casey, Steven. *Selling the Korean War: Propaganda, Politics, and Public Opinion in the United States, 1950–1953.* New York: Oxford University Press, 2008. Print.
Hajdu, David. *The Ten-Cent Plague: The Great Comic-Book Scare and How It Changed America.* New York: Picador, 2008. Print.
Kurtzman, Harvey (w), Jack Davis (p), and Marie Severin (i). "Enemy Assault!" *Frontline Combat* Vol. 1. York, PA: Gemstone, 2008: 19–25.
Kurtzman, Harvey (w), Wally Wood (p), and Marie Severin (i). "Bug Out!" *Two-Fisted Tales Vol. 2.* Timonium, MD: Gemstone, 2007: 19–25.
Lopes, Paul. *Demanding Respect: The Evolution of the American Comic Book.* Philadelphia: Temple University Press, 2009. Print.
Ma, Sheng-mei. "Imagining the Orient in the Golden Age of Adventure Comics." *The Deathly Embrace: Orientalism and Asian American Identity.* Minneapolis: University of Minnesota Press, 2000. 3–37. Print.
"Midway." *War Comics* #26 (July 1954), U.S.A. Comic Magazine [Marvel Comics]: 25–30.
Nadel, Alan. *Containment Culture: American Narratives, Postmodernism, and the Atomic Age.* Durham, NC: Duke University Press, 1995. Print.
"The Prayer." *War Comics* #18 (April 1953), U.S.A. Comic Magazine [Marvel Comics]: 26–30.
Savage Jr., William W. *Comic Books and America, 1945–1954.* Norman: University of Oklahoma Press, 1990. Print.
Thompson, Kim, Gary Groth, and Mike Carton. "Harvey Kurtzman: The Man Who Brought Truth to Comics." *The Comics Journal Library Volume Seven: Harvey Kurtzman.* 83-125. Print.
"Tooth and Nail." *War Comics* #13 (Nov. 1952), U.S.A. Comic Magazine [Marvel Comics]: 1–5.
Versaci, Rocco. *This Book Contains Graphic Language: Comics as Literature.* New York: Continuum, 2007. Print.

4

"I Can Pass Right Through Solid Matter!": How the Flash Upheld American Values While Breaking the Speed Limit

Frederick A. Wright

Kaz Suyeishi, survivor of the first wartime use of a nuclear weapon, explains how the atomic bomb in Hiroshima, Japan, on August 6, 1945 began with a flash:

> Then suddenly there was a very, very powerful yellowish-orange flash — like when you're taking a picture and you use the flash — only a hundred thousand times more powerful.
> The flash was over in a second, and I was already on the ground.... Where the blue sky had been, there was only a grayish fog, and everywhere a red color — blood [qtd. in Jennings and Brewster 277].

The United States of America's use of nuclear weaponry effectively ended the Second World War, but the same use was the opening salvo in an even longer conflict: the Cold War, "a fluid, multinational conflict between western capitalist democracies and the communist regimes of Eastern Europe and Asia, led by the Soviet Union. It lasted 44 years and dominated the lives of Americans in both explicit and implicit ways" (Schwartz vii). Once the Soviet Union developed its own nuclear weapons, the Cold War derived its most central characteristic in the fear that should the conflict ever escalate, civilization, if not humanity itself, would be annihilated. Thus, the conflict would move at a glacial pace for the next half-century, restricted to an arms race, massive government expenditures into science, coded diplomacy, propaganda efforts, espionage, and proxy wars. In the American imagination, however, existed a desire to break free of such constraints and existential threats, and be assured that American values would triumph, and preferably quickly. In the mid–1950s, the fantasy world of popular culture met this desire by refashioning a superfast comic book superhero who had fallen out of favor, but whose name, immense power, and new red costume — the color of blood and Communism — pithily reflected the conflict and its stakes: The Flash. Indeed, even the character's nickname of the Scarlet Speedster reflected the desire of Americans to speed through the long and drawn out conflict with the "Reds," which was already over a decade long at the character's return in 1956.

This chapter explores the first five years of Flash's return (1956–1961), from his landmark appearance in the story "Mystery of the Human Thunderbolt" in *Showcase* #4, to the classic story that reintroduced his predecessor from the Golden Age of comic books back into the DC Comics universe in *The Flash* #123: "Flash of Two Worlds." The revival of Flash kicked off the Silver Age of comic books in the late 1950s and returned the superhero genre to prominence (Reynolds 9), but why did the revival meet with such success? One reason was the superb artistry of the Flash stories, but the character's success can also be attributed to how well he and his stories encapsulated American ideology of the time. The swift character allowed readers to fantasize being free of constriction while also containing anything else that threatened the status quo or what was taken to be the American way of life. Protecting his own Central City and the entire world from extra dimensional threats and science-misusing criminals, Flash used extralegal means to prevent deviance, much as the United States would engage in numerous covert and morally questionable operations during the Cold War. Birthed by a scientific mishap involving chemicals and lightning, Flash addressed fears of nuclear apocalypse by suggesting that even science gone wrong will work out in favor of the United States. In the early stories, Flash always forced a world out of control back into normalcy. Just as nothing could contain Flash — as he states in an early story, "The Pied Piper of Peril!" "I can pass right through solid matter!"— he made sure that everything else was contained (Broome, Infantino, and Giella 170).

Solving Problems with Science

By maintaining the status quo, Flash reenacted the containment strategy of the Cold War. Literary critic Alan Nadel, who explored the effects of Cold War ideology on high and popular culture in his book *Containment Culture:*

American Narratives, Postmodernism, and the Atomic Age, notes that "Containment was the name of a privileged American narrative during the [C]old [W]ar. Although technically referring to U.S. foreign policy from 1948 until at least the mid–1960s, it also describes American life in numerous venues and under sundry rubrics during that period" (2–3). The notion of containment provides an interesting lens through which to view the early Silver Age Flash stories. In the thirty-eight stories starring Flash during his first five years (not including the six solo stories of his sidekick Kid Flash, which have similar dynamics), the superhero contains threats to the status quo in twenty-five stories (usually criminals committing bank robberies or other disturbances), foils invasions and other would-be conquerors and destroyers in nine stories (Po-siden, of "The Man Who Claimed the Earth!," even has a very Stalinesque mustache), and in three stories he goes beyond containment of a threat to help liberate oppressed people. The remaining oddball story, "The Amazing Race against Time!," finds Flash assisting a superfast robot in a task of literal containment since "On the planetoid F203 near the center of the galaxy there is a weak spot ... where the terrible forces of another dimension threaten to break through! Every few years the barrier holding back those forces ... must be repaired or the galaxy will be destroyed" (Broome, Infantino, and Giella 197). Fortunately, Flash fixes the hole and saves the galaxy. This story can be viewed as an allegory for containing communism. Interestingly enough, of the thirty-eight stories, only one story, "The Secret of the Stolen Blueprint!," which follows the typical threat to the status quo plot, has Flash engage in the Cold War directly, tackling spies who steal the blueprint for a hydrogen power device.

Although Flash contained threats to what was construed as the American way of life, the character himself served as an exemplar of American exceptionalism since nothing, of course, could contain him. In the thirty-eight stories, he is shown breaking free of or through such items as a filmstrip, a comic book, the sound barrier, gravity, the timestream, an hourglass, ice, mirrors, a vibratory aura, the Earth itself to its center, machine traps, dimensional barriers, being shrunk, fate, giant boomerangs, ropes, brainwashing, and a giant atomic grenade, among other things. He can also run through walls; run on water including across the ocean; run on tightropes and wires even when one is falling; run up buildings; create whirlwinds and wind tunnels; leap from rooftop to rooftop or from cloud to cloud; run all the way around the world; melt metal, rocks, and snow using friction; out-swim a torpedo; ride a rocket; create explosive vibrations; dodge bullets, lightning bolts, and radiation blasts; set foliage on fire by speeding past it; forge handcuffs out of a nearby machine; run so fast as to be invisible; appear as both his alter ego Barry Allen and Flash at the same time; and even play tennis with himself, among other things. Indeed, the only thing that could seem to contain Flash at all was the imagination of his creators.

The speedy character initially emerged from the combined imaginations of M.C. Gaines, Sheldon Mayer, Gardner Fox, and Harry Lampert at All American Comics, and the first issue of *Flash Comics* was dated January 1940 (O'Neil 90; Daniels 50). The character was Jay Garrick, a college student who, when overcome with hard water in a botched chemistry experiment, gained super speed and took to fighting crime while wearing a winged Mercury hat and a blue and red costume festooned with lightning bolts (Fox and Lampert). Flash was popular enough to headline his own title for 104 issues in the 1940s, star in a solo book (*All-Flash*) for thirty-two issues during the same decade, appear in *Comic Cavalcade* for twenty-nine issues during the same period, and run with the Justice Society of America in *All Star Comics* until 1951 (Overstreet). But the declining fortunes of superhero comics in the postwar era caused Flash to run to a standstill (Dallas, "Jay Garrick" 8). As documented in David Hajdu's *The Ten-Cent Plague*, after the juvenile delinquency scare came to a head in 1954 with Senate hearings about comic books, the adoption of the Comics Code by publishers led the comics industry away from developing more adult stories in genres such as crime, horror, romance, war, and western back into more child-friendly fare to which the superhero seemed best suited. As a result, in 1955, when editors of National Comics (what DC was known as at the time and which had absorbed its sister company All American a decade earlier) met to decide what to put in the next issue of *Showcase*, someone suggested bringing back Flash, an idea editor Julius Schwartz accepted if the character could be revamped (Kingman 35–36). The combination of editor Schwartz, writer Bob Kanigher, and artist Carmine Infantino created police scientist Barry Allen and his world (Infantino 51), and the success of the *Showcase* appearances led to Flash getting his own title and picking up at the issue number his predecessor never reached: #105 (Overstreet 611).

Upon his return, the character was incredibly popular — Infantino claims his title was DC's best-selling comic at one point (Dallas, "Carmine Infantino" 53) — and inspired the revival of other superheroes (Daniels 117). What likely fueled the success of Flash was how well the character and his stories encapsulated their times. As Richard Schwartz, author of *Cold War Culture: Media and the Arts, 1945–1990*, observes, the ideology of the Cold War seeped into most of American life during the period, including "forms of expression intended for mass audiences" (vii), which would of course include comic books. Writing of Superman, Schwartz presents an analysis of the appeal of the superhero that also applies to the revitalized Flash:

His continued attraction for Cold War audiences lay at least partially in his identification with the innocent and his continued defense of American values at a time when the "American way of life" was again threatened, this time by communism. The superhero provided a certain level of wish fulfillment for audiences that were anxious about threats to their personal and national security, including the possibility of nuclear annihilation [2].

After all, in the age of intercontinental missiles, when only minutes existed between their launching and their landing, who could indeed save the world from nuclear annihilation but a hero such as Superman or Flash? In fact, the very first scene of the very first Silver Age Flash comic book shows the military operators of a radar station on the East Coast—surely part of the national defense effort against a possible Soviet attack—detecting Flash speeding by and being baffled (Kanigher, Infantino, and Kubert 22). Indeed, even the new character's costume seemed to reflect the Cold War. Whereas the original Golden Age Flash costume had featured red on the character's shirt and boots, the Silver Age Flash's costume seemed to symbolically represent the extent to which the Cold War defined 1950s America, as the color red now had spread throughout the character's costume, rising up the head on the new mask and cowl that replaced the previous Mercury helmet and bare face (a change also symbolic of the covert nature of much of the conflict) and down the legs into the previously-blue pants. Even the yellow lightning bolt on the original red shirt had been shrunk and divided up to smaller lightning bolts placed to accent the red, though some of it had gone into the boots, which had changed from red to yellow.

In *Our Gods Wear Spandex: The Secret History of Comic Book Heroes*, Christopher Knowles suggests that the more science-oriented heroes of the Silver Age, such as Flash, fulfilled a need in the early Cold War audience by drawing on "the *zeitgeist* of the atomic age and the rapidly approaching space age" (138). In this manner, Flash also relieved anxiety over science and the growing stockpile of nuclear weapons, since problems were always solved through science, American ingenuity, and Flash's super speed. Any worries over dangerous scientific accidents could also be mollified by reflecting on Flash's origin. If being struck by lightning and bathed in chemicals only gave one super speed, what was there to be worried about? Experiment away! Bob Rozakis comments on the appeal of the pseudoscience of the Flash stories to him as a child, writing, "When you're eight years old, there's a lot of science you don't know. As a result, much of the pseudo-science that appears in the issues of The Flash seems perfectly logical" (5). Even older readers found the stories appealing though, as the Flash series won several Alley Awards from the nascent comics fandom movement, led by science professor Jerry Bails (Schelly 52). Fundamentally, Flash demonstrated that the power of science

Flash's costume emerges from his ring. From [Robert Kanigher (w), Carmine Infantino (a), and Joe Kubert (i)], "Mystery of the Human Thunderbolt!" *The Flash Archives*, vol. 1. Ed. Bob Kahan. New York: DC Comics, 1996. 21–32. Print.

was firmly under American control. The iconic image of his costume emerging from the ring he designed is a powerful visual illustration of American scientific mastery. This image is evocative of the power of the atom and the atomic age. The fact that Allen can control the tremendous energy of Flash as represented by the costume suggested that Americans too could control the tremendous energies that their technological progress had unleashed.

However, the science in the stories doesn't hold up to scrutiny without a healthy helping of the suspension of disbelief — can a costume really fit into a tiny ring? — and neither does the whole decision by Barry Allen as to how he can "use this unique speed to help humanity!" (Kanigher, Infantino, and Kubert 22). Although Flash would seem to get along well with police officers and other authority figures (which of course the Comics Code mandated), and would certainly fend off invasions from other planets and dimensions, it is odd that as a police officer and scientist Barry Allen would don a costume and work outside the law as a vigilante. Though the secret identity motif has long been a staple of the superhero genre, Flash's double identity also replicates nicely the situation of Cold War covert operatives whose heroism must remain unheralded due to the clandestine nature of their activities. As Walter Hixson, historian and author of *Parting the Curtain: Propaganda, Culture, and the Cold War, 1945–1961*, states:

> By definition, the Cold War — a state of belligerency absent direct superpower conflict — established limits on overt American aggressiveness. Although Washington armed for war, it had no intention of starting a military conflict over Soviet hegemony in Eastern Europe. Even in the steps that it took short of war, the United

States refrained from overt warlike behavior. In the mutual recriminations that emanated from both capitals, limits had to be adhered to if formal diplomatic relations were to be maintained. Few such restraints governed the *covert* behavior of the East-West rivals, however [12].

Flash operated as a superb covert cold warrior foiling invasions from other dimensions. And, as conservatives and liberals fought the whether the United States should continue the containment policy or adopt a more aggressive "liberation" policy in fighting communism (21), Flash did both. Story after story show him containing threats to the status quo and liberating oppressed people. As Matthew J. Costello summarizes in *Secret Identity Crisis: Comic Books and the Unmasking of Cold War America*,

> the Cold War American was viewed as an individual who lived in the most virtuous political system in the world, as evidenced by American prosperity, and whose divine mission was to extend the benefits of that prosperity to all American citizens and promote the virtue of its governmental system around the world by defending against the evil forces of totalitarianism [32].

Flash's activities can certainly be viewed metaphorically as representative of those of the United States during the Cold War. Indeed, he extended the American way to other dimensions.

Domestic Threats

In addition to easing fears of an atomic attack or invasion from outsiders, Flash also provided comfort to readers worried about subversion by domestic enemies. This too was somewhat reflective of Cold War fears as, not surprisingly, many of the villains focused on robbing banks, literally stealing wealth, which, of course, metaphorically could be viewed as the capitalist fear of the communist system's redistributing the wealth. Many of Flash's villains, such as the Turtle Man in his first story, were threats to the social order in this manner, and Flash often has to find clever ways to defeat them, also reflective of the Cold War conflict. For example, a direct approach to catch the Turtle Man in the rowboat he uses to escape a bank robbery fails since all Flash does is push the boat forward by running after it. Like a good cold warrior, Flash learns to fight by not fighting directly, declaring "Since I can't capture the rowboat by running after it — I'll have to stop it by not running after it!" and running around the boat to stop it and the Turtle Man (Kanigher, Infantino, and Kubert 31).

Though the Turtle Man wouldn't become a prominent foe, Flash soon gathered one of the most colorful collections of reoccurring villains of any superhero. Appropriately enough, one of these Rogues, as they eventually would be called, is Captain Cold, who might as well have been named Captain Cold War since he typically attempts to freeze Flash or otherwise prevent his movement, just as the Cold War restricted the movements of America in foreign policy. Metaphorically, Cold, with his radiation powered gun, like many of Flash's foes, can be viewed as an embodiment of science gone mad. However, Flash always finds a way to outwit his foes, reassuring readers that science can overcome the dangers it creates and encounters. These storylines of Flash matching his scientifically granted super speed versus his foes' science weapons are representative of the arms and technology race of the Cold War.

Brainwashing and subversive activity were also common motifs in these stories and were reflective of Cold War fears of the effects of communist propaganda (Costello 51), such as when Mirror Master replaces a bank teller with his mirror image in "The Master of Mirrors!" While Mirror Master mainly just wants to get rich (and what could be more American than that, really?), another foe, Gorilla Grodd, uses his brainwashing mind power to infiltrate American society in order to conquer it and the rest of the world, leading an army of gorillas (Marxist guerrillas, anyone?) (Broome, Infantino, and Giella 160). When Grodd's effort in "Menace of the Super-Gorilla" fails, he turns to duping an innocent race of bird-people to use as a proxy force (one can insert a patronizing view of innocent third worlders oblivious to the dangers of communism here — Cubans work well) in "Return of the Super-Gorilla!"

Given the cleverness of his foes, Flash often devotes his energy to uncovering deceit and subversion; however, like the covert operatives of the Cold War, he has to disguise his identity — a form of subterfuge — in order to do so. In addition, Flash commits crimes and questionable acts in order to defeat the Rogues. He speeds (though he could argue that speed limits only apply to automobiles), trespasses, steals (at one point yanking a pogo stick from a clown to catch the Trickster in "Danger in the Air!" ([Broome, Infantino, and Giella 125–26]), spies on people including on his girlfriend and future wife Iris in "The Man Who Claimed the Earth" (Broome, Infantino, and Giella 129–31), and even uses one of the Mirror Master's gadgets to trick Iris into dating him again in "Return of the Mirror Master" (Broome, Infantino, and Giella 23–24). Similar to how American leaders defended the questionable covert activities of the Central Intelligence Agency which included "coups against undesirable governments and even assassination of foreign leaders" (Hixson 12), Flash justifies his actions by their role in the pursuit of the greater good. For example, after snatching an acetylene torch from some men in order to foil a plot of the Weather Wizard, he thinks, "They won't mind my borrowing it in an emergency like this!" (Broome, Infantino, and Anderson, "The

4. "I Can Pass Right Through Solid Matter!" (Wright)

Flash circles the globe. From [Robert Kanigher (w), Carmine Infantino (a), and Joe Giella (i)], "Around the World in 80 Minutes!" *The Flash Archives*, vol. 1. Ed. Bob Kahan. New York: DC Comics, 1996. 69–82. Print.

Challenge of the Weather Wizard!" 47). In the perfect American world of *The Flash*, no one seems to mind since at the end of each story everything is always set to right.

In "Around the World in 80 Minutes!" Flash has to foil crimes around the world while still making his date with Iris West (please note her surname and what it represented in the Cold War). Flash states, "How can I answer all these calls for help from all parts of the world — and still keep my date with Iris in Center [sic] City?" (Kanigher, Infantino, and Giella 69), which is also about as succinct an explanation of the plight of the USA once America decided to contain communism abroad while also maintaining prosperity at home. In reality, producing "guns and butter" at the same time was a bit challenging, but in this fantasy Flash does it all, foiling the criminal blackmailing Paris with an atomic bomb and his criminal counterparts around the world, and saving a damsel in distress each time. As one of America's goals in the Cold War was to woo countries to our side, Flash certainly does his part in this story with his good deeds around the world. However, he is no James Bond, and chastely leaves the women he has rescued to make his date with Iris, whom he would eventually marry. However, as he states in one story, "No one — Not even Iris — must ever know that Flash and Barry Allen are the same person" (Broome, Infantino, and Giella 127), so his tragedy in these early stories is that Iris cannot know that he is really the heroic Flash, and Allen must go unheralded.

However, if Allen went unheralded, it was all in the name of freedom, and Flash's discovery that he "can pass right through solid matter!" is suggestive of the belief that although America could contain communism, nothing could contain America, just as Flash could contain any threats to the status quo, but nothing could contain him (Broome, Infantino, and Giella

Flash passes through solid matter. From [John Broome (w), Carmine Infantino (a), and Joe Giella (i)], "The Pied Piper of Peril!" *The Flash Archives*, vol. 1. Ed. Bob Kahan. New York: DC Comics, 1996. Print.

170). Indeed, the three images reprinted here from the early Silver Age stories encapsulate neatly the appeal of Flash at that time. If the first two images are all about containment (the ring containing the costume, and Flash containing danger in the world and their metaphorical equivalents of American containing scientific dangers with greater science and containing communism around the globe), this final image is of liberation, as it shows Flash passing through everything in his path, an image of complete freedom (in fact, Flash "scorns obstacles in his path") (Broome, Infantino, and Giella, "The Pied Piper" 170). Such an image of freedom and unimpeded progress no doubt appealed to many readers mired in the stalemate of the Cold War.

Alas, The Flash is, of course, a fictional character and must bow to the realities of publishing. Barry Allen continued to be popular for many years, but the early years of his return were his most popular, likely a result of how closely he embodied the hopes and fears of his early Cold War audience. In fact, of the eleven Allen stories reprinted in the original *The Greatest Flash Stories Ever Told* collection, only two date from post–1964 (Gold). Nevertheless, even if his glory days were long behind him, Allen would outlast his predecessor by many years and reach issue #350 of his own series. However, when the politics of the Cold War became more complex and America's actions in it came to be more and more questioned by American citizens, Allen similarly lost his way. He eventually suffered the death of his wife, found himself on trial for manslaughter, and even had his face surgically altered in order to change his identity (what could be greater an identity crisis than not being able to recognize one's own face in a mirror?) (Bates). Just as his fictional world became less and less perfect, so did the publishing reality behind it, and in 1985 his title would be cancelled and the character himself would be killed off saving the DC universe in issue #8 of the *Crisis on Infinite Earths* series. Not coincidentally, the Cold War itself wasn't long behind him in exiting the world's stage. While other characters such as Wally West, the former Kid Flash occupied the Flash mantle in subsequent years, Barry Allen has recently been resurrected (Morrison and Jones 30; Johns and Manapul). Was he brought back because America is once again mired in a worldwide conflict, this time against terrorism, or was he brought back out of a sense of nostalgia for the comparative order of the Cold War conflict when compared to the uncertainties of the War on Terror? Whatever the case, one can only hope that Barry Allen will help speed America and the rest of the world through the worries of these times and that the only flash seen is not the flash of a dirty bomb being detonated but only The Flash speeding by to once again save the universe in the American popular culture imagination.

WORKS CITED

[Bates, Cary]. "The Final Flash Storyline." *The Greatest Flash Stories Ever Told*. Ed. Mike Gold. New York: DC Comics, 1991. 257–66. Print.
[Broome, John (w), Carmine Infantino (a), and Murphy Anderson (i)]. "The Challenge of the Weather Wizard!" *The Flash Archives*, vol. 2. Ed. Dale Crain and Michael Wright. New York: DC Comics, 2000. 38–50. Print.
[Broome, John (w), Carmine Infantino (a), and Joe Giella (i)]. "The Amazing Race against Time!" *The Flash Archives*, vol. 1. Ed. Bob Kahan. New York: DC Comics, 1996. 189–98. Print.
———. "Conqueror from 8 Million B.C.!" *The Flash Archives*, vol. 1. Ed. Bob Kahan. New York: DC Comics, 1996. 122–33. Print.
———. "Danger in the Air!" *The Flash Archives*, vol. 2. Ed. Dale Crain and Michael Wright. New York: DC Comics, 2000. 116–27. Print.
———. "The Man Who Claimed the Earth!" *The Flash Archives*, vol. 2. Ed. Dale Crain and Michael Wright. New York: DC Comics, 2000. 128–40. Print.
———. "The Master of Mirrors!" *The Flash Archives*, vol. 1. Ed. Bob Kahan. New York: DC Comics, 1996. 134–46. Print.
———. "Menace of the Super-Gorilla!" *The Flash Archives*, vol. 1. Ed. Bob Kahan. New York: DC Comics, 1996. 148–62. Print.
———. "The Pied Piper of Peril!" *The Flash Archives*, vol. 1. Ed. Bob Kahan. New York: DC Comics, 1996. 163–72. Print.
———. "Return of the Mirror Master!" *The Flash Archives*, vol. 2. Ed. Dale Crain and Michael Wright. New York: DC Comics, 2000. 12–24. Print.
———. "Return of the Super-Gorilla!" *The Flash Archives*, vol. 1. Ed. Bob Kahan. New York: DC Comics, 1996. 174–88. Print.
Costello, Matthew J. *Secret Identity Crisis: Comic Books and the Unmasking of Cold War America*. New York: Continuum, 2009. Print.
Dallas, Keith. "Carmine Infantino." *The Flash Companion*. Ed. Keith Dallas. Raleigh, NC: TwoMorrows, 2008. 47–54. Print.
———. "Jay Garrick." *The Flash Companion*. Ed. Keith Dallas. Raleigh, NC: TwoMorrows, 2008. 6–8. Print.
Daniels, Les. *DC Comics: Sixty Years of the World's Favorite Comic Book Heroes*. Boston: Bulfinch, 1995. Print.
[Fox, Gardner (w), and Harry Lampert (a)]. "Flash Comics #1." *The Golden Age Flash Archives*, vol. 1. Ed. Dale Crain and Michael Wright. New York: DC Comics, 1999. 8–23. Print.
Gold, Mike, ed. *The Greatest Flash Stories Ever Told*. New York: DC Comics, 1991. Print.
Hajdu, David. *The Ten-Cent Plague: The Great Comic Book Scare and How It Changed America*. New York: Farrar, Straus and Giroux, 2008. Print.
Hixson, Walter L. *Parting the Curtain: Propaganda, Culture, and the Cold War, 1945–1961*. New York: St. Martin's, 1997. Print.
Infantino, Carmine. *The Amazing World of Carmine Infantino: An Autobiography*. Ed. J. David Spurlock. Lebanon, NJ: Vanguard, 2001. Print.
Jennings, Peter, and Todd Brewster. *The Century*. New York: Doubleday, 1998. Print.
[Johns, Geoff (w), and Francis Manapul (a)]. "The Dastardly Death of the Rogues." *The Flash* #1 (June 2010), DC Comics. Print.
[Kanigher, Robert (w), Carmine Infantino (a), and Joe Giella (i)]. "Around the World in 80 Minutes!" *The Flash Archives*, vol. 1. Ed. Bob Kahan. New York: DC Comics, 1996. 69–82. Print.
[Kanigher, Robert (w), Carmine Infantino (a), and Joe Kubert (i)]. "Mystery of the Human Thunderbolt!" *The Flash Archives*, vol. 1. Ed. Bob Kahan. New York: DC Comics, 1996. 21–32. Print.
Kingman, Jim. "Julius Schwartz." *The Flash Companion*. Ed. Keith Dallas. Raleigh, NC: TwoMorrows, 2008. 35–40. Print.
Knowles, Christopher. *Our Gods Wear Spandex: The Secret History of Comic Book Heroes*. San Francisco, CA: Weiser, 2007. Print.

Morrison, Grant (w), and JG Jones (a). "Ticket to Bludhaven." *Final Crisis* #2 (Aug. 2008). DC Comics. Print.
Nadel, Alan. *Containment Culture: American Narratives, Postmodernism, and the Atomic Age*. Durham, NC: Duke University Press, 1995. Print. New Americanists.
O'Neil, Dennis, ed. *Secret Origins of the DC Super Heroes*. New York: Warner, 1976.
Overstreet, Robert M. *Official Overstreet Comic Book Price Guide*. 36th ed. New York: House of Collectibles, 2006. Print.
Reynolds, Richard. *Super Heroes: A Modern Mythology*. Jackson: University Press of Mississippi, 1992. Print.
Rozakis, Bob. Foreword. *The Flash Archives*, vol. 1. Ed. Bob Kahan. New York: DC Comics, 1996. 5–8. Print.
Schelly, Bill. *The Golden Age of Comic Fandom*. Rev. ed. Seattle, WA: Hamster, 1999. Print.
Schwartz, Richard A. *Cold War Culture: Media and the Arts, 1945–1990*. New York: Facts on File, 1998. Print.

5

Jack Kirby's *Challengers of the Unknown*: Establishing Order in an Age of Anxiety

Phillip Payne and Paul J. Spaeth

In 1957 Jack Kirby pitched a new book to DC Comics called *Challengers of the Unknown*. The book featured a team of four daredevils who survived a near-death experience. Standing in the wreckage of the plane crash that should have killed them, they dedicate themselves to accepting risks that others would refuse, reasoning that they are living on borrowed time. "The Challengers are a suicide squad," Kirby said. "They are the men who take the risks" (Kupperberg 7).

Challengers of the Unknown as fashioned by Jack Kirby was a pivotal comic book coming in the wake of World War II as the country faced the uncertainties of the Cold War era. As a team, the Challengers faced threats familiar to post-war American society and reflected the values and gendered expectations of that society. The book featured themes of contemporary unease about the trajectory of scientific accomplishments. Its action-oriented storylines drew in elements from past comic book history, while anticipating the return of the superheroes in the 1960s.

The theme of a new beginning (renewal in the face of disaster) must have appealed both to Kirby and to the comic book industry in which he had worked for almost two decades. The 1950s had not been kind to the comic book industry as congressmen and psychologists singled out comic books as a threat to the nation's children. Kirby himself, long an established comic book creator, had recently experienced professional setbacks. He was ending his long partnership with Joe Simon, with whom he had created many groundbreaking titles and characters, and Kirby and Simon's publishing company, Mainline Comics, had failed. In 1957 few could have predicted that the much-maligned comic book industry was on the verge of a renaissance or that Jack Kirby's new title would help point the way (Morrow).

The Challengers of the Unknown, as Kirby introduced them in *Showcase* #6, included Red Ryan (circus daredevil), Rocky Davis (Olympic wrestling champion), Ace Morgan (Korean War hero and fearless jet pilot), and Professor Haley (master skin diver). Although not superheroes, each of the members had a nickname that served to describe their distinct talents. In their second appearance in *Showcase* #7 June Robbins (as the series develops she is sometimes June Walker) joins the team as an "honorary member." She is the only woman in the group, and often the only woman to appear in a story. Rather than wearing military uniforms or the skin tight costumes of the Silver Age superheroes, the team wore purple jump suits somewhat like the suits of the early space programs. The Challengers emerged on the comic book scene just as the space race was on the horizon and at a time when there was building anxiety in the world over the destructive power of the atomic bomb. The Challengers represented a combination of Cold War technocratic expertise with the machismo of a World War II combat squad. In all of this, the Challengers served as a calming influence, restoring the status quo by managing the threats inherent in the changing, and challenging, world of the time.

The Challengers in the Kirby Years (1957–1959)

The team first appeared in four issues of *Showcase* and then ran for eighty-six issues under their own title from 1958 to 1978. Although the rotating lineup of *Showcase* started with conventional adventure stories, issue #4 introduced Silver Age Flash, usually thought to be the start of a new comic book age of superheroes. Two issues later, the Challengers were introduced.

Jack Kirby could be called the "director" of *Challengers* in much the same way that the director of a motion picture is regarded as an author, even though many people work on the film. Kirby had planned to do the Challengers with Joe Simon, but it was Kirby alone who brought it to fruition. As Mark Evanier has noted, "Kirby could do *Challengers of the Unknown* without Simon, and he did. A writer named Dave Wood provided scripts, which pretty much meant sitting with Kirby, hearing him spin off a plot, and then going home and typing it up. Jack rewrote whatever he was given anyway" (101).

Although credit lines do not appear in the original *Challengers* issues, the attributions found in the DC Archives and *Showcase Presents* editions reinforce Evanier's description of Kirby's role as the central creative person in a team. Dave Wood and other writers helped Kirby bring the *Challengers* to life, but the interesting and imaginative storylines take a back seat to the design of the individual panels on the page.

Kirby's art drove the narrative. The greatest motion picture directors are those who fashion the visuals while constantly revising the script. In these early issues of *Challengers* we see Kirby in this same role, not only being directly responsible for the visual content, but having created, or having reworked, the story content. This was the kind of synergy that existed between Stan Lee, Jack Kirby, and Steve Ditko when they created the Marvel Universe, and this style of collaboration would come to be called the "Marvel Method" when Marvel Comics exploded into popular culture in the 1960s. Kirby was already using this kind of creative method before coming to Marvel.

In fact, *Challengers of the Unknown* has often been talked about, and rightly so, as being an early version of the *Fantastic Four* which Kirby created with Stan Lee in 1961. Both groups had their start in a flight crash which set up the members as a team of vigilantes. Perhaps the most interesting point of comparison is in the story, "The Menace of the Invincible Challenger," from *Challengers of the Unknown* #3, in which Rocky obtains super powers upon returning from a space flight, a story that clearly foreshadows the origin story of the Fantastic Four. "The Menace" story would seem to establish the Challengers as a forerunner to the revival of the super heroes of the Silver Age.

Kirby's first three Challengers stories include the two major elements that form the themes which would be developed in the rest of the series. These elements are (1) technology, sometimes contemporary, sometimes ancient, sometimes alien, and (2) the occult, usually dealing with the notion of hidden knowledge that had been lost in ages past. There is no real distinction made between these two elements. They are both presented as a way to acquire personal power, and as a threat to those who do not share in that power.

In the Challengers' first appearance, "The Secrets of the Sorcerer's Box," we find the origin of the Challengers in the wreck of a plane. The team is brought together by this life threatening experience. In the story that follows, the Challengers have an established headquarters, and are being offered a million dollars to perform a task. At the start the team is not concerned with saving the world, or battling crime; these are elements that appear in subsequent storylines.

The sorcerer who has sent for the Challengers calls himself Morelian and says that he is a descendent of Merlin. They are given the task of opening a large four-chambered box, a "Pandora's Box," with each chamber holding a new danger. The first danger is a giant armored manlike creature that looks decidedly classical. The next two dangers are technological: one is a telepathic sun-like orb that freezes everything with which it comes into contact; the

5. Jack Kirby's Challengers of the Unknown (Payne and Spaeth) 71

other is a cylinder that shoots out a device that weaves entangling webs around things. Morelian sees to his own demise by misunderstanding what the ancients had written about the box when he hurriedly opens the last chamber himself. The technology that he thought promised him power and immortality instead brought him death.

The threats in this first story are ancient with classical overtones, featuring technology beyond the standards of the time. The background idea holding the tale together is the occult notion that if you can obtain knowledge of things long hidden you will gain great power. All the parts of the story end abruptly, and are fantastic. There is no character development, the stories are all action-oriented, and the various episodes within the story are driven by Kirby's drawings. There are a number of other stories in the series like this one. In "The Menace of the Ancient Vials" a group of criminals, being pursued by the Challengers, come across an archaeologist who has found a set of vials of liquid from an ancient civilization. Those who drink from them acquire a variety of strange powers. In "The Secret of the Sorcerer's Mirror" a medieval sorcerer has created a mirror to show the locations of a set of hidden orbs that, when connected in a certain way, summons up a giant genie. In "The Riddle of the Star-Stone" a meteor fragment is fashioned by the use of "mystic calculations" into an object that grants its owner the powers of a super-man. All these stories combine the macabre from the strange tales and horror tradition of comics from the 1950s, the super-powered beings of the Golden Age, and the technologies from ancient or alien sources that give a science fiction feel to the whole.

The second story in the series, "Ultivac Is Loose" deals with the dangers of contemporary technology, and is perhaps the best story of the Kirby issues. An ex-Nazi scientist named Felix Hesse builds a giant thinking robot that becomes self-aware and telepathic. Hesse, who had been imprisoned because of war crimes, had fallen in with a bank robber who had convinced him to design the robot for a get-rich-quick scheme. He contacts the Challengers to help him with his runaway invention. In this story June Robbins makes her first appearance as the director of a computer center. The Challengers are surprised to find a woman in charge, but accept it.

The robot (Ultivac) is at first threatening, but then becomes a sympathetic character, mainly through the relationship he develops with June. Ultivac brings together several points. The story arc shows the ways in which Kirby and his collaborators borrowed from other forms of popular culture. Ultivac assumes the role of the great ape in a story that clearly mimics that of *King Kong* (1933). This is particularly apparent when Hesse puts Ultivac on display in a way similar to Kong. Another echo of the movie is when Ultivac escapes, cradling June in his giant hand while fending off fighter planes. Ultivac calls telepathically to June for help, and June persuades Ultivac to work with people instead of against them. This clearly puts June in a traditional role of the female care giver and voice of the common good. June would, for the most part, assume that role through the rest of the series. When Ultivac makes a public appeal to work for the betterment of humankind, Hesse, the ex-Nazi, destroys his creation realizing that he cannot use the robot for his own profit. In the end, June is shown presiding over what is left of the computing capacity of Ultivac as it has become a benign unit mounted in the wall.

It is interesting to note that even in this parable of science and technology there is a touch of the occult. When the Challengers seek the help of June and her computer system, the computer spits out an enigmatic prophecy much like something one would expect from an ancient Greek oracle, "Ultivac will fall when a Challenger dies!" Also, the name of the robot is certainly fashioned after the name of the first commercial computer produced in the United States, UNIVAC.

A number of other Challengers stories feature similar themes about technology. "The Man Who Tampered with Infinity," from *Challengers of the Unknown* #1, features a scientist who turns to crime when, rejected by other academics, he steals and then perfects the research of others in his mad quest for power. "The Monster Maker" and "The Isle of No Return" focus upon criminals who have stolen technology to use for their own ends (Costello 6).

One of the most interesting of the technology stories is "The Wizard of Time" where an assistant named Darius Tiko completes his master's work on time travel. The story flows through ancient Greece, ancient Egypt, and late medieval Europe, ending in a far distant future. In the Middle Ages, the Challengers meet Nostradamus, a figure whose very name evokes notions of prophecy and mysticism, and whose mathematical formulations are found to be the basis for the operation of the time machine.

Tiko uses the time machine to steal technology from the future. When he and the Challengers are caught, all five of them are put on trial by a mechanical judge representing the "United Earth." All charges are eventually dropped when it is said that people of the late twentieth century were seen to be "motivated by antiquated conditioning." As such, they "cannot be held responsible for violating the existing [future] laws of a more rational society." Here we have a time-hopping action story that ends in a morality play.

Finally, there are the stories that deal with aliens that pose a technological threat either directly, or through a chance encounter. In "The Day the Earth Blew Up" the Challengers are called into action by the United States government to investigate the disappearance of two scientists in the Antarctic. The team finds an underground base the size of a large city, from which a warlike race of aliens called the Tyrans is planning a violent takeover of Earth.

5. Jack Kirby's Challengers of the Unknown (Payne and Spaeth)

Alien beings that possess superior technology and who use it to try to take over Earth is a familiar theme of science fiction films of the 1950's. The difference here is that the conception of the story can be on a much grander scale in a comic book than was possible in movies of the day. Movies were constrained by the technology of the day and budgets. Even the best special effects of late 1950s required a significant act of imagination on the part of the audience. Kirby did not face this constraint. His "special effects" could be as elaborate as he could imagine, requiring no more suspension of belief on the reader's part than any other section of the story. Kirby's famed kinetic style not only helped propel the plot forward but also helped readers bridge the gap between panels and pages, one of the challenges of the comic book form. In the end, the aliens are destroyed by their own devices. The world is made safe again through the efforts of the Challengers, while the government generates a cover story to explain the bombastic battles that have taken place.

Other alien encounter stories include "The Human Pets" where the Challengers are captured by a young, and enormous, alien for his private menagerie. When his parents get home, the alien is forced to return these little human creatures to their place of origin. This familiar type of story shows humankind as mere playthings in relation to the superior technology, and size, of the aliens.

In the three other alien adventures, the Challengers come to the aid of these otherworldly beings. In "Captives of the Space Circus," the Challengers are captured by aliens but then lead a revolt against the owners of the circus, liberating both themselves and other creatures. The Challengers end by pointing out the moral wrong to alien viewers who had taken pleasure in watching the antics of the captives. In "Beasts from Planet 9" the Challengers round up giant stray creatures from a zoo ship from space. And in "Prisoners of Robot Planet," the team is recruited to free an alien planet from the fascist rule of a race of robots that they themselves had created.

The Challengers in many ways represented a throw-back to the masculine combat teams of World War II comic books, like *Blackhawk*, that confronted bizarre enemies and strange situations. The more fantastic the menace, the greater the need to transform members of the team into superheroes, more fitting to the aesthetic of the Golden Age and later the Silver Age of comics. In defeating their enemies the Challengers risked transforming themselves into superheroes, a process they seemed to accept at times but not something they sought. This could be seen as a metaphor for the United States' reluctant transformation into a superpower.

The *Challengers of the Unknown* served as a transitional comic book between the industry's difficulties of the 1950s and the Silver Age of the 1960s. At first glance, as a team of adventurers without superpowers, the *Challengers of the Unknown* would seem to be running counter to the revival of comics during the Silver Age. However, a significant portion of the *Challenger* storylines include elements of science fiction and fantasy. The Challengers of the Unknown shared Showcase with the Silver Age Flash after the Flash's revival in 1956 and Challengers story lines increasingly resembled those found in super hero comics.

Kirby's Cold War

Jack Kirby's *Challengers* stories reflect the tensions of the Cold War culture in America. The book's historical elements featured cultural themes from the immediate post–World War II era, with images that often came from movies, television shows and cartoons of the recent past.

A prominent element in the series was the Cold War theme of a love/hate relationship with science. On the one hand science provided progress, while on the other it held the potential for oblivion. One creative way in which Kirby and his colleagues played with this ambivalent attitude was by often interchanging science and magic, whether it was ancient, modern or futuristic. The unease with which society viewed the modern marvels of science was seen metaphorically as the same way people looked at magic or the occult. Both technology and magic produced the same kind of anxiety.

In a similar way the past, with its secret and now forgotten ways, and the future, with its unseen horizons, represented the unknown. In an era when the Soviet Union and China could change from being allies to enemies, and when atomic power promised both civilian and military uses, the future was not only unknown but represented a challenge that was difficult to deal with. Americans found that their history was being rewritten in relation to future threats.

The group's motto, "We are living on borrowed time," served as a metaphor for the atomic age with its attendant anxieties. It foreshadowed President Kennedy's famous call for a new generation to take up the torch. Like astronauts or scientists, the Challengers, under Kirby's creative guidance, did not directly confront communism. The threats posed often came from familiar villains made dangerous by the power they obtained from science or mystical sources. Although themes of liberation abroad and conformity at home were evident, there were no Soviet spies or looming international crises present.

The *Challengers of the Unknown* functioned as a conservative, calming influence in this age of anxiety. The heroism of the Challengers reinforced the idea of a Cold War consensus by the very absence of any overt political debate. In a typical story from the series the arrival of the Challengers was a great relief. The Challengers fit the heroic narrative mode as described by Costello in this way, "The hero exemplifies the values of a society, his role is to defend those values, to maintain a given way of life against potential threats or to redeem it from a threat realized" (Costello 15). While the Challengers fit broadly within this paradigm, the actual operation of the Challengers remained a mystery. The Challengers are not government agents, but they often operate at the behest of a government agency. Neither do the Challengers operate as a business. Although in their first appearance there is mention of an agreed upon payment, for the most part the Challengers seem to work pro bono. The most common motive mentioned is a desire for risk. At any point where the Challengers could have brought the Cold War consensus into question, the story is left ambiguous.

Many authors have noted the influence of the Cold War on Silver Age comic books, particularly the explosion of characters created at Marvel Comics. Generally cited is the role of radiation as a *deus ex machina* in the stories, a theme we clearly see in some of the Challenger stories. Characters like the Fantastic Four, Spider Man, and the Hulk were exposed to and transformed by various types of radiation. It is also in the 1950s that Kryptonite first appeared as a dangerous radioactive substance, the only threat to Superman's ability to defend truth, justice, and the American way. In this way the fantastic and science fiction elements of the stories lent themselves to an indirect examination of Cold War themes.

The Challengers, as a group of men that confronts threats to the status quo, represent conservative, patriarchal values as the men defend the society. However, lacking the dual identity of superheroes, or the home front of soldiers, the Challengers do not return to a warm hearth or a traditional family. Their decision to become a team means severing ties to their former lives and living in a world where women and children are largely absent. Indeed, during the Kirby period no back story was provided other than their credentials as adventurers. The men of the Challengers were reduced to their job descriptions. Their purple jump suits where symbolically like the famous "grey flannel suit" that identified a generation of faceless business men working for large corporations. The Challengers protected a society that they by and large did not participate in; a place in which heroes often finds themselves.

The lack of social interaction can also be seen as a way of steering clear of the charges made against comic books as damaging to the morals of society, particularly the family unit. Kirby, as a creator, was familiar with female characters and audiences. His Mainline Comics published a variety of genres, including titles such as *Young Romance* and *Young Love*. While Mainline Comics failed, it demonstrated that Kirby did not see comic books as limited to superheroes, or as a medium just for boys. As David Hajdu writes, "That the romance books were, at first, seen as harmless — just love stories, only girl stuff — allowed them to flourish in an era when other comics were held in suspicion" (Hajdu 161). However, romance comics had fallen into the pattern of depicting bad boys and illicit loves, and so had moved away from seeming to be harmless. This may explain why Kirby's Challengers lacked any romantic elements.

Given Kirby's background and the Cold War context, the character of June Robbins as the only woman in the book is interesting. As Elaine Tyler May and others have noted, sexuality could be seen as dangerous. Joanne Meyerowitz summarizes this notion: "Various scholars have argued that the Cold War assault on communism reinforced the subordination of women and the suppression of sexuality. In the most common variant of this argument, the fear of communism pushed middle-class Americans to look to masculine strength and the patriarchal home as protective forces in a dangerous world" (106). Women's sexuality was in many cases considered to be dangerous, exemplified by such stereotypes as the femme fatale who, as a foreign agent, seeks to seduce young men.

Story lines that might open the Challengers to criticism on sexual or moral grounds were largely absent. June, in "The Traitorous Challenger" secretly sabotages a mission. However, when the Challengers discover the reason behind June's actions, she seems more maternal than threatening. June is no femme fatale. Like her male counterparts June is something of an empty suit; very little of her background or personality is revealed other than she is attractive and a scientist. The name change from Robbins to Walker suggests that either she married, or divorced, or that her character's background was not considered significant enough to consistently use the same last name. June begins the Ultivac story as the director of a prestigious scientific institute, but in another story she is an assistant to a scientist, and later, like the Challengers, seems to have no visible form of employment. The Challengers' treatment of June's role is notably different from the treatment of gender in the *Fantastic Four*, where Sue Storm was a romantic interest for Reed Richards and where a strong theme of family exists. June, like her male counterparts, seems to exist in a world without sexuality or even personality. June's journey from professional woman to helpmate reflected the rise of the feminine mystique.

June's status as the "unofficial fifth member" of the Challengers underscores this. In "The Sorceress of Forbidden Valley" we find that June's plane has crashed into an unmarked island where an unknown civilization exists. When the Challengers follow to rescue her, they find that June has become a princess with supernatural powers. In contrast to occasions when Rocky or other male characters in the series gain supernatural powers, June falls under the control of a male criminal. Rather than being empowered, June is subjugated. She regains self-control only with the loss of her powers. Like many things in the Challenger's world, June's power was destructive and needed to be either controlled or taken away.

Conclusion

Jack Kirby's work on the *Challengers of the Unknown* was brief but important. The series stands as a transitional comic book creating a link between the post-war era and the Cold War generation faced with a fight being played out on a very different kind of international battlefield. Reading Kirby's issues of the *Challengers* we can see the introduction of themes which were later brought into full bloom in the revival of comics during the Silver Age. In particular, the Challengers foreshadowing of the famous quartet he would later create with Stan Lee, the *Fantastic Four*. As a reflection of Cold War culture, the Challengers represented themes of security at home as the team dealt with scientific and supernatural forces that threatened to disrupt society. However, as champions the Challengers were, with the exception of their identity as skilled adventurers, almost completely disconnected from the status quo they worked to preserve.

WORKS CITED

Costello, Matthew J. *Secret Identity Crisis: Comic Books and the Unmasking of Cold War America.* New York: Continuum, 2009. Print.
Evanier, Mark. *Kirby: The King of Comics.* New York: Abrams, 2008. Print.
Hajdu, David. *The Ten-Cent Plague.* New York: Farrar, Strauss and Giroux, 2008. Print.
[Herron, Ed, and Jack Kirby (w), Jack Kirby (p), Wally Wood (i)]. "The Beasts from Planet 9." *Challengers of the Unknown* #7 (April/May 1959), *Showcase Presents: Challengers of the Unknown.* Ed. Bob Joy. New York: DC Comics, 2006. 260–272. Print.
_____. "The Prisoners of Robot Planet." *Challengers of the Unknown* #8 (June/July 1959), *Showcase Presents: Challengers of the Unknown.* Ed. Bob Joy. New York: DC Comics, 2006. 298–310. Print.
_____. "The Sorceress of Forbidden Valley." *Challengers of the Unknown* #6 (Feb./March 1959), *Showcase Presents: Challengers of the Unknown.* Ed. Bob Joy. New York: DC Comics, 2006. 249–250. Print.
[Kirby, Jack (w, p), and Marvin Stein (i)]. "The Human Pets." *Challengers of the Unknown* #1 (April/May 1958), *Showcase Presents: Challengers of the Unknown.* Ed. Bob Joy. New York: DC Comics, 2006. 121–130. Print.
_____. "The Traitorous Challenger." *Challengers of the Unknown* #2 (June/July 1958), *Showcase Presents: Challengers of the Unknown.* Ed. Bob Joy. New York: DC Comics, 2006. 132–140. Print.
_____,and Roz Kirby and Marvin Stein (i)]. "Menace of the Invincible Challenger." *Challengers of the Unknown* #3 (Aug./Sept. 1958), *Showcase Presents: Challengers of the Unknown.* Ed. Bob Joy. New York: DC Comics, 2006. 169–180. Print.

_____. "Secret of the Sorcerer's Mirror." *Challengers of the Unknown* #3 (Aug./Sept. 1958), *Showcase Presents: Challengers of the Unknown*. Ed. Bob Joy. New York: DC Comics, 2006. 157–168. Print.

_____, and Wally Wood (i)]. "Riddle of the Star-Stone." *Challengers of the Unknown* #5 (Dec. 1958/Jan. 1959), *Showcase Presents: Challengers of the Unknown*. Ed. Bob Joy. New York: DC Comics, 2006. 208–232. Print.

_____. "The Wizard of Time." *Challengers of the Unknown* #4 (Oct./Nov. 1958), *Showcase Presents: Challengers of the Unknown*. Ed. Bob Joy. New York: DC Comics, 2006. 182–206. Print.

Kupperberg, Paul. Foreword. *Challengers of the Unknown Archives* vol. 1. New York: DC Comics, 2003. 7. Print.

May, Elaine Tyler. *Homeward Bound: American Families in the Cold War Era*. New York: Basic, 1988. Print.

Meyerowitz, Joanne. "Sex, Gender, and the Cold War Language of Reform," *Rethinking Cold War Culture*. Ed. Peter J. Kunick and James Gilbert. Washington: Smithsonian Institution, 2001. Print.

Morrow, John. Foreword. *Challengers of the Unknown Archives* vol. 2. New York: DC Comics, 2004. Print.

[Wood, Dave (w), Jack Kirby (p), Bruno Premiani (i)]. "The Day the Earth Blew Up!" *Showcase* #11 (Nov./Dec. 1957), *Showcase Presents: Challengers of the Unknown*. Ed. Bob Joy. New York: DC Comics, 2006. 56–79. Print.

[Wood, Dave (w), Jack Kirby (p), George Klein (i)]. "The Menace of the Ancient Vials." *Showcase* #12 (Jan./Feb. 1958), *Showcase Presents: Challengers of the Unknown*. Ed. Bob Joy. New York: DC Comics, 2006. 81–104. Print.

[Wood, Dave (w), Jack Kirby (p), Roz Kirby and Marvin Stein (i)]. "The Secrets of the Sorcerer's Box." *Showcase* #6 (Jan./Feb. 1957), *Showcase Presents: Challengers of the Unknown*. Ed. Bob Joy. New York: DC Comics, 2006. 6–29. Print.

_____. "Ultivac is Loose!" *Showcase* #7 (March/April 1957), *Showcase Presents: Challengers of the Unknown*. Ed. Bob Joy. New York: DC Comics, 2006. 31–54. Print.

[Wood, Dave and Jack Kirby (w), Jack Kirby (p), Wally Wood (i)]. "Captives of the Space Circus." *Challengers of the Unknown* #6 (Feb./March 1959), *Showcase Presents: Challengers of the Unknown*. Ed. Bob Joy. New York: DC Comics, 2006. 234–248. Print.

6

Red Menace on the Moon: Containment in Space as Depicted in Comics of the 1950s

John Donovan

In the 1950s, the Eisenhower administration publicly declared that United States' policy towards space would be one of "space for peace" and "space for all mankind" (McDougal 194). Yet the comics of the 1950s portrayed battles in space and competition for control of the moon, in contrast to the stated national policy. These comics reflected an opposing view of how the United States should deal with our space race with the Soviet Union. This essay will show how comics made after the 1957 launch of Sputnik reflected an American desire for control of space and superiority over the Soviets. Comics made during the 1950s showed both nations building armed lunar bases while the Eisenhower administration continued to advance the concept of space for peace. One perceived resolution of this dichotomy, which appeared in some stories, was that while space would still be used as an extension of the Cold War, the nations could be allies in space and put their rivalry aside when they encountered an alien threat to mankind. Storylines from this period will be examined for how they reflect containment culture in preventing the Soviet Union from dominating space, and especially the moon, as well as citing examples where the "space for all mankind" ideal is upheld.

Imagining the Future

Within several months of the Soviets' successful launching of Sputnik on October 4, 1957, President Dwight Eisenhower sent a letter to Soviet

Premier Nikita Khrushchev through State Department channels on January 12, 1958, stating his position that "outer space should be used only for peaceful purposes." He emphasized his concern by writing:

> There are about to be perfected and produced powerful new weapons which, availing of outer space, will greatly increase the capacity of the human race to destroy itself. If indeed it be the view of the Soviet Union that we should not go on producing ever newer types of weapons which would use or, more accurately, misuse, outer space, now for the first time opening up as a field for man's exploration? Should not outer space be dedicated to the peaceful uses of mankind and denied to the purposes of war? That is my proposal [United States, Dept. of State].

In the post–Sputnik era, comic writers did not always use images and storylines that promoted the "space for peace approach" advocated by the Eisenhower administration. After 1957, comics did tend to focus more on the political Cold War aspects of conflict in space, but it was evident that in the years leading up to 1957, space was seen as a future battleground, populated with weapons and spaceships that extended mankind's predilection for warfare into the farthest reaches of space.

Starting with the science fiction-oriented comics of the 1950s (pre-Sputnik), storylines did not always take an obvious political direction or directly link bad guys to communism. Often it would be done in a metaphorical sense, as was seen in "The Lost World," a story that appeared in Fiction House's *Planet Comics* #51 (Nov. 1947). Set in the year 1977, thirty years in the future at the time, the Earth has been conquered by aliens from the Planet Volta. Reminiscent of the description of the aftermath of a nuclear war with the Soviet Union, the setting for the story proclaims that "San Francisco is reduced to shambles!" adding that "all other cities crumbled, too, before the chaos spread by the conquering planet, Volta!" While there is no actual planet Volta, there is a city in Western Russia called Volta. As would be expected if Soviet communists had conquered the United States, the Voltons have to deal with American resistance fighters who are intent on expelling what they refer to as the "Volta horde" from the Earth. The Voltons, who wear spiked Pickelhaube helmets resembling those used by the German military from the mid-nineteenth century through World War I, refer to each other as "comrade" in the story. They are depicted as ruthless killers who imprison or kill those who resist their rule. The American resistance fighters are depicted as brave, resourceful, and persistent men and women determined to regain their freedom from the hated Voltons (Herrick and Evans). This story from *Planet Comics* #51 is just one chapter in an ongoing "Lost World" storyline that ran in *Planet Comics* from issues #21 (Nov. 1942) through #69 (Dec. 1952). The Voltons were created during the time that America was at war with Germany, so it is understandable that their helmets would resemble those of the German military, but in the post–World War II years, the reader could also see the Voltons as a metaphor for the communist enemy (especially with the "comrade" references in the story).

As comic book writers of the early 1950s looked to the future, it was assumed that earthly military power and political systems would naturally migrate into the farthest reaches of space. An excellent example of this can be seen in a "Kenton of the Star Patrol" story from Avon Publications' *Strange Worlds* #1 (Nov. 1950). The hero, Dave Kenton, is a "star patrolman" of an Earth Federation police force called the Star Patrol, responsible for stopping piracy and crime throughout the "vast area of billions of miles of empty space." Set in the year 3750, Patrolman Kenton lives in a space age that had its genesis in the mid-twentieth century. The story's introduction states that the atomic bombings of Hiroshima and Nagasaki were "the opening thunders of the atomic era, culminating in 1962 with a rocket landing on the moon," followed by man stepping foot on Mars in 1977. By 2077, man had reached one of the closest star systems to our sun, the Alpha Centauri. Along with these technical accomplishments, the weapons of war used by the Star Patrol to enforce the law in space evolved to meet the demands of a space environment. In this episode of Kenton's adventures, "The Corsairs from the Coalsack," the Space Patrol tackles pirates who attack spaceships loaded with treasures acquired in the various planetary systems. Both the Space Patrol and pirates use "beam-guns" that can melt a man "into a blob of chemicals," as well as "grim ships of war" equipped with "exploso-rays" to blast other ships (Kubert). Space, while definitely a new frontier, was also expected to be just another avenue for the political and legal systems already established on Earth embracing the weapons and tactics of war so familiar to the history of mankind. This warfare also included the use of atomic weapons.

The November 1952 edition of *Atom-Age Combat* #3 proclaimed on the cover that its stories were "Stranger than Fiction." Well, this was definitely truth in advertising. In a story entitled "Intrigues of the Planet Smasher," an evil scientist working from a lab on Venus devises a plan to "enslave the Earth" by utilizing "atomic bombardment" from space and destroying mountain peaks on Earth with atomic energy. He states that "any man able to transmit atomic energy can rule the universe." The scientist's plot is discovered when a "Space Patrol combat pilot" (note the reference to war expertise) in a nearby "saucer detection outpost" sees a space freighter destroyed by "an atomic shell" in the Venusian sky. When the evil scientist is confronted by the Space Patrol official, another scientist who was forced by the renegade scientist to do his bidding tells the combat pilot that the evil scientist has "been shooting atom splitting energy into space like a madman!" The Space Patrol officer is able to eventually overpower the "criminally-bent scientist" and foil the atomic bombardment plot.¹ The reference to combat space pilots was definitely on the minds of comic writers that year, because the next month in DC Comics' *Mystery in Space* #11 (Dec. 1952), a story entitled "Rocketeer for Hire!" was centered around an out-of-work pilot who longed for the day when he flew a "battle rocket in space-war." He even thinks to himself: "I'll never be happy until I feel a battle rocket under me again! Space-war's in my blood — in my brain! It's my whole life!" (Broome, Infantino and Barry). From a science fiction perspective, it became standard in the comic industry to see the war aspects of space-age conflict. But even comics that tried to depict a contemporary and realistic portrayal of man's venture into space could not avoid addressing the potential of space for military purposes.

Walt Disney's critically acclaimed 1955 television programming, *Man in Space*, was adapted into comic form in 1956 under the title *Walt Disney's Man in Space: A Science Feature from Tomorrowland*. The purpose of the television program (and the subsequent comic) was to promote a realistic look at man's progress toward space, and utilized the talents of rocket scientist Wernher von Braun as a technical advisor for the series (Von Hardesty and Eisman). In a section of the comic that discusses a proposed space station (referred to as "the Wheel"), the plan is to have military personnel man the space station as "military reconnaissance experts, aided by powerful optical and radar telescopes, (who) can observe every spot on the globe." There would also be a telescope aboard the station that "photographs the surface of earth for the military reconnaissance experts ... bringing it close for careful study." This was, without a doubt, a realistic and achievable use of space technology that would be on the horizon in the years to come. With the launch of Sputnik the next year in 1957, it would become satellites and their possible use by an enemy to spy on or attack Americans that would drive depictions of space warfare in the comics.

Sputnik Hysteria and War in Space

Americans reading and wondering about the Soviet satellite Sputnik circling above them in the sky in late 1957 could only imagine what the spacecraft was capable of. Was its "beep" heard on radio sets around the world sending coded secret messages to Soviet spies? Was it taking photographs of American military installations, equipment and personnel? Was it capable of spying on American citizens? One comic released in early 1958 tapped into this fear with a very eye-catching cover using a parody of a famous painting. *Matinée de Septembre* ("September Morn") was completed in 1912 by French artist Paul Chabas. The painting featured a nude young woman standing in the shallow water of a scenic Swiss lake on a cold September morning. The young lady in the lake was described by *Time* magazine as drawing "her body into an instinctive pose of protection against the cold" ("Lady of the Lake").² The cover to *Humbug* #7 (Feb. 1958) shows a young woman standing in a lake in a position similar to "September Morn." Entitled "1958 Morn," the cover added three satellites that are very similar in design to Sputnik, flying low over the nude young woman standing in the water, with various sounds coming from the satellites. One satellite is broadcasting the familiar Sputnik-like "beep, beep, beep," while the second satellite emits a camera-like "click, click, click," with the third sending out an "arf, arf, woof, bow wow, yip!" Inside the comic, the *Humbug* writers described other satellites that would be launched soon to accompany Sputnik. Two examples include the "Peacenik," a satellite armed with 21 protruding gun and cannon barrels used for "Soviet peace enforcement," along with the "Frightnik," a huge "rubber balloon fake, calculated to throw us (Americans) into greater hysteria than ever" (18). How satellites would be used in warfare was definitely on the minds of comic creators in early 1958.

The same month that *Humbug* #7 was on the stands, St. John Publishing Corporation released an issue of *Atom-Age Combat* that also tied in with the interest in satellites. St. John Publishing originally released a version of the *Atom-Age Combat* series in 1952 and 1953 discussed earlier, but cancelled it after five issues. In the wake of Sputnik, the company obviously decided to cash in on the war from space "hysteria" by resurrecting the series. *Atom-Age Combat* #1 (Feb. 1958) proclaimed on the cover that "In this daring issue ... disclosed for the first time ... the Atom-Age wars fought from panel boards, Rockets ... Missiles ... Satellites ... Nuclear Weapons." The first page sets the tone by stating "The age we are now living in will go down in history as The Atom Age!" adding that mankind now lives in a time where, consistent with the Eisenhower commitment to using space for peace, "for the sake of global survival it is the common duty of all of us to work incessantly to prevent the suicidal thermonuclear holocaust of Total War in the Atom Age!" But, the editors point out that they will not be "ostriches, and bury our heads in the sands in the face of danger!" Wanting to assure their readers that the comic will not fail to deliver on the promise of the weapons of war from the cover, they state that they are "performing a significant service by presenting dramatic stories of limited thermonuclear battle!" With images of missiles and rockets flying through space above the earth, the editors emphasize that "these stories are not science fiction! No matter how fantastic the weapons, vehicles, and devices you are about to see in the following pages appear to be, they are authentic or based on fact!" The bottom-line from the editors is that "This is the Atom Age! The unbelievable has already begun to come true!"³ Just how unbelievable war using satellites could be would be seen in a story released a couple of months later by National Periodical Publications (DC).

Mystery in Space #43 (April–May 1958) featured a story entitled "Invaders from the Space-Satellites!" Set in a post-atomic war-ravaged world of 2150, the Earth has been turned into "a barren planet." A character in the story, Commander John Yardley, says that after the atomic bomb was dropped on Hiroshima, the "world lived in perpetual dread of atomic war!" adding that "Even after space was conquered and man reached the moon, the danger existed...." In a classic panel depicting man's first landing on the moon, one of the astronauts points towards Earth and states: "An atomic cannon aimed from here could destroy any city on Earth!" Commander Yardley recalls that "interplanetary travel only added to our troubles, for in every United Nations session, there was an argument" between representatives on who would claim the planets of the solar system that were now open to exploration. This was followed by a global atomic war that resulted in a "devastated world, with less than a million human survivors scattered over its surface" in dome-covered "city-forts." To change history and avoid the nuclear devastation, Commander Yardley is leading a "time-scanner" project called "Operation Nullo" that has successfully eliminated all "processes that led to the atom bomb's invention," thus preventing the war that killed millions of people. Commander Yardley extols the benefits of "Operation Nullo" by stating that "with no atom bomb there is no Hiroshima, no Korea conflict, no Cold War! Men learned to live in peace and friendship!"

The irony of the story is that without atomic bombs to defend themselves, Earth has now been surrounded by "a host of globes ... circling the planet— resembling the space-satellites launched in 1957! They are spaceships from another solar system!" The aliens are determined to bombard the Earth with missiles launched from the satellites that will explode and absorb all oxygen in the Earth's atmosphere to kill mankind, allowing them to exploit the Earth's "precious metals" without man's interference. Earth reverses the effects of "Operation Nullo," reacquires atomic capability and launches atomic weapons against the satellites. Unfortunately for humanity, the aliens are able to neutralize the effects of the atomic weapons, rendering them ineffective. To fight back, humans devise large steel arrows that can be launched against the satellites and pierce their metallic structures (therefore depriving the aliens of their breathing atmosphere on the ships). The arrows work, and the aliens flee the solar system. The story concludes with Commander Yardley commenting that "our experience has taught us that Earth cannot endure if we fight among ourselves! If we must wage war— let us join forces— against invaders from other worlds" (Fox, Infantino, and Giella 1–8). Not only did depictions of satellites being used to attack mankind appear in science fiction-oriented

6. *Red Menace on the Moon* (Donovan) 85

Commander Yardley observes the moon's potential in war. From [Gardner Fox (w), Carmine Infantino (p), and Joe Giella (i)], "Invaders from the Space Satellites," *Mystery in Space* #43 (April–May 1958). National Comics Publications [DC Comics], 1–8. Print.

stories such as "Invaders from the Space-Satellites!" but they were also used in a superhero storyline that next year.

In "The Satellite of Gotham City" (*Detective Comics* #266, April 1959), a criminal scientist has created a Sputnik-like satellite (approximately 10 to 15 feet in diameter) that can shoot destructive flames, project powerful force-fields and create fissures in the Earth. Batman and Robin encounter the satellite and are determined to stop it. Batman, realizing the serious danger this weapon poses, tells the police that the satellite uses "intricate guidance parts to function! We've got a flying metal menace on our hands, Commissioner Gordon!" The satellite's capabilities are demonstrated with panels depicting it using a high-powered flare to blast a hole in a bank wall, creating a "force field" that can move a ship into a reef so it can be grounded and looted, as well as using intense flame to melt police cars and the Batmobile itself (a scene which was used on the cover of the comic with Batman proclaiming: "We're helpless Robin! That unearthly machine is melting the Batmobile!"). When the scientist's plot to use his satellite of crime is foiled by Batman and Robin, the criminal tells Batman: "Bah! I could have ruled the city with my satellite!" (Finger and Moldoff, 1–12).[4] While the danger from satellites seemed to be a good plot for storylines in the wake of Sputnik's success, the real focus of concern in a Cold War context would be even more evident in stories predicting how man would utilize near-Earth space and the moon for political and military purposes.

Red Menace of the Moon

Exploiting the popularity of space storylines, Western Tales, Inc. (also known as Harvey Comics), released a new series called *Race for the Moon*. Even though it only lasted three issues (March to November 1958), *Race for the Moon* is one of the best examples of how the space race would be depicted in a Cold War context in comics in the wake of the Soviets' Sputnik success. The comic promised on the first page that it would provide "spine-tingling action and adventure where no man has ever been! A new concept geared to the dawn of the Space Age!" A story entitled "Lunar Trap" that appeared in *Race for the Moon* #2 (Sept. 1958) managed to promote both the militarization, as well as the cooperative use, of space. The story opens with the line: "The Cold War can get pretty hot on the Moon — especially when the Americans and Russians have nothing to do with it!" An American mineralogist exploring the Moon's surface has his foot caught in what appears to be a "bear trap" on the lunar surface. He is captured at gunpoint by two Soviet soldiers who escort the American prisoner to a Russian lunar base that has heavy transportation equipment, a camera and weapons on the site. The American is accused of being a saboteur belonging to an American "raiding party" responsible for damage to Soviet equipment and vehicles around the base, which he promptly denies. Taken by the Soviet lunar base commander (interestingly, a female colonel) and Russian soldiers in a roving vehicle to the scene of recent attacks, the group is attacked by what appears to be a large, hairy beast throwing huge lunar rocks and destroying the transportation vehicle. The group, including the American, fights back and pursues the beast. The American tells the colonel: "There's your rock-thrower, colonel! It looks like he's started a Cold War of his own!" He then comments to her: "It's definitely not an American! Are you disappointed colonel?" The colonel responds: "I suppose if life can exist on the Moon — it could be possible for hate to perish between us!" Hours later, the beast is driven away by a "Soviet rescue party." The American is allowed to leave the Soviet base on good terms. While the story does not provide an all-out battle for control of the moon, it is obvious that both the United States and the Soviet Union have established areas of control on the moon. The next issue's cover, *Race for the Moon* #3 (Nov. 1958), showed an American astronaut running on the moon's surface carrying a placard attached to a stake with the words: "This lunar territory claimed by the United States of America." The American is being chased by a long line of what appears to be Soviet cosmonauts with a gun pointed at the American (while there is no identification on what appears to be cosmonauts, the one with the gun looks very much like Joseph Stalin). While *Race for the Moon* gave the impression that space would be used as an extension of the Cold War

6. *Red Menace on the Moon* (Donovan) 87

Joseph Stalin on the moon. From [Jack Kirby (p)], Untitled, *Race for the Moon* #3 (November 1958). Western Tales [Harvey Comics]. Print.

conflict, a story like "Lunar Trap" also gave the reader hope that Americans and Russians could put their politics aside and focus on a common enemy of Earth. This is a theme that would be repeated several months later in an issue of *Atom-Age Combat*.

A story entitled "Third Element," from *Atom-Age Combat* #3 (March 1959), opened with a battle taking place on the moon. It doesn't specify a year, but it is described as a time when the "two major powers on Earth fought the battle of space with satellites, rockets, and finally manned space ships to the Moon!" The cover even shows rockets and satellites being used for war in outer space. Without specifically designating them as troops from the United States and the Soviet Union, the two warring forces are described as the "Democracies" versus "the other element from Earth," shown shooting guns at each other while hiding behind craters and ridges near where their respective spaceships have landed on the lunar surface. One of the "Democracies" soldiers thinks to himself: "Here on the Moon, we fought the power battle of Earth! Both sides knew that only one would survive! The question was ... which one?"

In the midst of their battle, the two warring factions are suddenly attacked by alien creatures carrying weapons. The soldiers combine their forces and fight back against the aliens in unison. A soldier from the "Democracies" describes the conflict by stating that the two forces "united as one in our struggle for survival." When the combined forces from Earth defeat the aliens, the soldiers hug and congratulate each other in victory. A soldier from "the other element from Earth" tells the group: "We both were determined to plant one flag here on the Moon ... and we will! We will not claim this planet for either of our sides." A soldier from the "Democracies" completes this sentiment by adding: "We will claim it instead for all mankind!" He also adds: "All differences must be forgotten for we face a common enemy! We have given mankind an example to live by!" The story ends when the soldier concludes that "I think mankind will always be grateful for that forgotten, and unknown, Third Element!" In retrospect, it's easy to understand the desire of comic writers and artists to promote the military aspects of war in space. Battle in space makes for an excellent graphic to hook the reader, and in the wake of Sputnik no one knew what to expect next in a Cold War conflict. Even comics that sought to provide an educational approach to the realistic uses of space provided a military focus.

Space for All Mankind

In January 1959, Gilberton World-Wide Publications, Inc., the makers of the famous Classics Illustrated comics, released an issue entitled *The Illustrated Story of Space* (officially part of their *The World Around Us* series, issue #5), providing the reader a comprehensive overview of rocketry and man's quest to understand space and go to the stars. In a section covering the future use of space in light of the Sputnik accomplishment, the comic has United States Air Force military personnel discussing a proposed American space station. An officer tells other military personnel that "on the space station you'll spend a month making photographs." He adds that "one of your first jobs will be to operate a TV camera. It will broadcast to Earth a picture of half the world from several hundred miles up." He's asked if the space station will be used "in time of war?" The officer replies: "During a war it would give us information on enemy rockets. In peacetime it will give us weather information" (*The World Around Us* #5, 59). It's evident that the writers were emphasizing the link between the military and space operations, but they were taking a more "space for peace" approach as espoused by the Eisenhower administration.

As the 1950s came to a close, a movie about the life of rocket scientist Wernher von Braun was released by Colombia Pictures Corporation. The comic, *I Aim at the Stars*, released by Dell Publishing Company, Inc., in 1960 (officially designated as *Four Color* #1148, no month specified), made from this movie also took the approach that space should be used for peace. In one panel, they quote Wernher von Braun as saying: "The great powers must ultimately be equal in space! It is this balance of power which will secure peace and allow mankind to reach the stars!" (32). In addition to the comics of the time, there was also an 88-card set called *Space Cards* released by Topps Company, Inc., to cash in on the interest created in products related to the space race. Card #36, "Conquest of the Moon," was extremely interesting in that it shows a group of astronauts landing on the Moon and raising not the flag of the United States, but a flag with an emblem of the United Nations. The following description is on the card's back: "Although the members of the crew come from different countries, here on the moon, they have the common bond of being earthmen. As they stand at attention in their space suits, the World Flag is hoisted and the Moon is claimed for all people on the earth." A moment that would not occur for another eleven years in reality was envisioned by the creators at Topps as a forthcoming milestone in the continuing pursuit of using "space for peace" (*Conquest of the Moon*).

The young men and women who were the primary audience for comics of the 1950s could not help but notice the recurring use of space as the Cold War battlefield of the future. The science fiction stories of the early 1950s consistently emphasized the used of weapons and battles in space. In the wake of Sputnik, the Cold War itself migrated into comic covers and stories. Despite the militarization of space in comics, writers also tried to show the reader that while warfare was a possibility, it was not the inevitable outcome of space exploration. As seen in a couple of stories, it is possible that politics could be put aside when mankind is confronted by an alien enemy from outer space. The Eisenhower administration's promotion of "space for peace" may have made for good platitudes for writers trying to send a moral message to their readers regarding the need for international cooperation, but it was the imagery of weapons, rockets and satellites used for conflict that seemed to generate the graphic images enjoyed by the comic readers of the 1950s.

Notes

1. Interestingly, the panel on page 2 of the story with the saucer detection outpost shows Venus having blue skies, craggy mountain peaks, clouds, birds flying in the sky, and people outside with no helmets on. Very unlikely on a planet that we now know has a surface temperature of up to around 470°C.

2. In 1957, the "September Morn" painting was put on display in New York's Metropolitan Museum of Art where it remains today.

3. The indicia states "Vol. 1, No. 1," despite the fact that this was actually Vol. 2.

4. Why a scientist who could create such an innovative invention for the space age would use his talents to rob banks and ground ships is probably one of the recurring mysteries regarding mad scientist types in superhero comics.

Works Cited

"Atom Age Combat." *Atom-Age Combat* #1 (Feb. 1958), St. John Publishing, 1–3. Print.
[Broome, John (w), Carmine Infantino (p), and Sy Barry (i)]. "Rocketeer for Hire!" *From Beyond the Unknown* #17 (June-July 1972), National Periodical Publications, 38–46. Print.
Callahan, David, and Fred I. Greenstein. "The Reluctant Racer: Eisenhower and U.S. Space Policy." *Spaceflight and the Myth of Presidential Leadership*. Ed. Roger D. Launius and Howard E. McCurdy. Chicago: University of Illinois Press, 1997. 15–50. Print.
Conquest of the Moon ("Space Cards" #36*)*, Topps, 1958 [2½ × 3½-inch trading card from 88-card set].
Finger, Bill (w), and Sheldon Moldoff (a). "The Satellite of Gotham City." *Detective Comics* #266 (April 1959), National Comics Publications [DC Comics], 1–12. Print.
[Fox, Gardner (w), Carmine Infantino (p), and Joe Giella (i)]. "Invaders from the Space Satellites." *Mystery in Space* #43 (April-May 1958), National Comics Publications [DC Comics], 1–8. Print.
[Fox, Gardner (w), Carmine Infantino (p), and Joe Giella (i)]. "The 60 Million-Mile Long Weapon!" *From Beyond the Unknown* #11 (June-July 1971), National Periodical Publications [DC Comics], 1–9. Print.
Hardesty, Von, and Gene Eisman. *Epic Rivalry: The Inside Story of the Soviet and American Space Race*. Washington, DC: National Geographic, 2007. Print.
[Herrick, Thornecliff (w), and George Evans (a)]. "The Lost World." *Golden-Age Greats, Vol. 12*. Ed. Bill Black. FL: Paragon [AC Comics], 1998: 17–26. Print.
"I Aim at the Stars." *I Aim at the Stars* [Dell Movie Classic] #1148 (1960), Dell. Print.
"The Illustrated Story of Space." *The World Around Us* #5 (Jan. 1959), Gilberton World-wide.
"Intrigues of the Planet Smasher." *Atom-Age Combat* #3 (Nov. 1952), St. John's,1–6. Print.
[Kirby, Jack (p)]. "Lunar Trap." *Race for the Moon* #2 (Sept. 1958), Western Tales [Harvey Comics], 10–14. Print.
_____. Untitled. *Race for the Moon* #3 (Nov. 1958), Western Tales [Harvey Comics]. Print.
[Kubert, Joe (a)]. "The Corsairs from the Coalsack." *America's Greatest Comics* #13 (2005), AC Comics, 1–8. Print.
"Lady of the Lake." *Time* 2 Sept. 1957: 56. Print.
McDougall, Walter A. *The Heavens and the Earth: A Political History of the Space Age*. New York: Basic, 1985. Print.
"1958 Morn." *Humbug* #7 (Feb. 1958), Humbug. Print.
"Sputniks!" *Humbug* #7 (Feb. 1958), Humbug, 18–19. Print.
"Third Element." *Atom Age Combat* #3 (March 1959), Fago Magazines, 7–11. Print.
"Walt Disney's Man in Space: A Science Feature from Tomorrowland." *Walt Disney's Man in Space [Four Color]* #716 (1956), Dell. Print.
United States Department of State. *Documents on Disarmament: 1945–1959*. 2 vols. Washington, DC: GPO, 1960. Print.

Part II
Containing Sexuality in the Cold War

7

Girls Who Sinned in Secret and Paid in Public: Romance Comics, 1949–1954

Jeanne Gardner

It's 1952 and a popular redheaded high-school girl named Gail Warren is strolling down the street with romance on her mind. It's the street the kids call "Pick-Up Boulevard," where girls wait on benches for boys in cars to roll up and take them for a spin. Gail's prudish best friend calls it "looking for trouble," but hot-blooded Gail sees it as an exciting adventure, a "lottery of love!" In the breathless voice of a romantic heroine, she explains to the reader, "I was tired of *tame, imitation love-making*, and dreamed of the day when someone's touch would light a *fire* in me that *polite words* and *conventions* weren't supposed to put out!" With that, Gail is off on a five-page journey to heartache in "Shortcut to Love," a story from the June issue of a comic book called *Hi-School Romance*. But why does this "comic" story end with Gail in tears? Why doesn't she get to meet a nice boy on Pick-Up Boulevard, get married, and settle down? Isn't love at first sight a staple of the romance genre?

Though advertised on the cover as a "True Hi-School Romance," "Shortcut to Love" is really a cautionary tale. Initially, Gail has good luck on Pick-Up Boulevard. She is joined by Don, "wealthy, poised, and handsome," who wafts her away to Hilltop Crest for several electrifying evenings of clandestine kissing in his parked car. But at the end of the story the "Prince Charming" of Gail's dreams rather churlishly refuses to acknowledge their relationship in public, considering her just an ordinary pick-up, a girl who would have offered the same degree of sexual license to anyone who came along. The moral of the story, bluntly speaking, is that those "polite words and conventions"

Gail Warren learns her lesson the hard way. From "Shortcut to Love," *Hi-School Romance* vol. 1 #15 (June 1952). Home Comics. Print.

matter, and that how a girl meets a boy is just as important as who the boy is. Girls reading "Shortcut to Love" were plainly meant to come away with the lesson that even their most passionate yearnings had to be corralled and channeled through socially acceptable means, or they would be perceived as immoral and therefore undesirable. That Gail's behavior in allowing herself to be "picked up" by Don indicates a general level of sexual promiscuousness is assumed, and that this renders her unworthy of not only his love but even his notice, is also a given.

But the reader knows something that Don doesn't: right before he met Gail, a creepy character in a loud checked jacket accosted her, a guy whose manners struck her as "cheap and insulting." When he seized her for a kiss without any preamble, she gave him a good slap in the mouth. Her unwillingness to participate in sexual behavior prompted his parting shot, "You're only a kid! So long, infant!" Contrary to Don's belief at the end of the story, Gail does *not* participate in "an ordinary pick-up," but rather reserves her kisses for someone who would realize she was "a *woman* yearning for *love* ... not a *thrill-crazy kid*!" However, Gail is not mature enough to convey her loving emotions to Don in any meaningful way — she "tries to appear lighthearted," in an attempt to seem sophisticated and adult, but realizes after his brusque brush-off that "our *lips* had met ... but *we hadn't!* I saw that he didn't know how terribly I *loved him*!"

The themes sounded by this slim episode — ambiguity surrounding Gail's mature or immature status, uncertainty as to what maturity means, the explicit connection between maturity and sexual behavior, and the implicit connection of sexual behavior to social class (the creep is "cheap," whereas Don, "Prince

Charming," is wealthy) — give some strong hints about the tension between expression of desire and fear that characterized female adolescent sexuality in the early 1950s. The stakes were high as girls maneuvered uneasily through this minefield of maturity, sex, and class. As historian Beth Bailey argues, at that time, class identification became flexible, less a matter of income and occupation, and more to do with participation in a culture that, by the postwar period, "claimed a middle-class consensus," (Bailey 11). Middle class mores "appeared as uniform conventions of a dominant culture," and transgressing the boundaries of "nice" or "well-brought-up" behavior imperiled a girl's reputation (Bailey 11).

Sexuality and Social Class

In a time when the juvenile delinquent was a figure of national anxiety, the public display of immoral or indecent behavior was an offense punishable by law (Caponegro 313). But there were subtler, though equally damaging consequences to a girl's wild behavior. It also shed a negative light on her whole family, excluding them from membership in the cultural middle class. The problem that this created for girls and their families is obvious. As literary critic Ramona Caponegro has pointed out, the definition of what constituted "delinquent behavior" was impossibly vague and extremely broad, especially in the adult-oriented media that considered everything from unruliness to murder a symptom of delinquency (314). In the absence of clearly defined boundaries, a girl's actions and, for that matter, her family's class status depended on the approval of others and conformity in the face of peer scrutiny (Riesman 48). For example, in his famous study of *The Levittowners,* sociologist Herbert Gans reported on the subtle behavioral cues that allowed neighbors to rank each other in the famously homogenous suburb: "Generally speaking, working class parents give their children freedom sooner than middle class parents do. They often expect the child to get into trouble by the time he reaches adolescence, and accept its occurrence fatalistically" (26). In other words, an overly independent but immature young person is not only expected to get into trouble, but his or her family is assumed to belong to a class outside the cultural norm.

In romance comic stories of the early 1950s, the negotiation of a girl's independence and maturity frequently took place in a sexual context, and nearly as frequently involved a question of class status. While this was often a key plot point of the story and involved dramatic interpersonal confrontations between a girl and her parents or a girl and her boyfriend, the repercussions could be much wider. A wider reading of romance comics indicates that

Gail, for all her heartache, got off relatively lightly. Her reputation is not shredded, and she doesn't end up impregnated or jailed. In short, her humiliation is private, and her future status is not hopelessly blighted by public exposure of her sexually errant behavior — the ultimate punishment dealt out to girls in romance comics whose sins include seeking too much and too early independence, conflating sexual activity with maturity, allowing love to overwhelm convention, or picking the "wrong" boy whose bad influence exacerbated all other character flaws.

Romance comics addressed the hazards, pitfalls, risks, and consequences of the chancy terrain that crossed adolescent sexuality and social class, often with greater frankness than we today might expect to find in early 1950s. The unwelcome advances made to Gail by the boy in the checked jacket are far from unique, but romance comics often gave the subject subtler treatment than just having hormonal hoodlums with pencil-thin moustaches show up to threaten the heroines and serve as foils for the heroes. The simple fact that romance comics often acknowledged the existence and the strength of adolescent female desire, portrayed with sympathy the frustration of girls' romantic dilemmas, and addressed the role that class status anxiety played in girls' fears surrounding mature sexual relationships makes them fascinating objects of study, despite the flaws that critics have used to condemn the genre from its inception in the late 1940s.

"Shortcut to Love" is a fairly unremarkable example of a romance comic story. The formulaic plot, the overwrought dialogue, and the anatomically dubious artwork certainly do not soar above the standards of the medium, but neither are they particularly awful. Like many romance comic stories, it adheres rigidly to an unimaginative six-panel layout and relies heavily on clunky expository text written in a first-person confessional style (Duncan and Smith 204). Besides "Shortcut to Love," the June 1952 issue of *Hi-School Romance* includes three other illustrated stories, some advertisements, an advice column, and a few more prose-only narratives — all available for a mere ten cents. At thirty-six pages long, haphazardly printed in four colors on cheap newsprint, *Hi-School Romance* is a typical comic of its time, with few formal or material qualities of distinction. Yet it is a relic of the era when romance comics made up a full quarter of the comic book market (Benson, *Romance Without Tears* 6). That market was reaching a staggeringly high percentage of American youth (Waugh 334).

For all their starry-eyed illustrations and dreamy content, romance comics were born of opportunism and savvy marketing. The romance comic as we know it was synthesized from the content of "true confessions" pulp magazines and the youth-oriented characters and settings of humorous teen comics such as *Archie*— both of which had enjoyed notable success among female readers prior to 1947. In that year, Joe Simon and Jack Kirby were astute enough to try to broaden the age range of the female comic book audience with a title called *Young Romance* that claimed to be "designed for more adult readers." The formula worked — *Young Romance* was soon selling over a million copies per issue, more than enough to inspire other publishers to come up with copy-cat titles — over 120 of them by 1949 (Waugh 334). During the peak years of their popularity, prior to the traumatic readjustment to the comics industry occasioned by the adoption of the Comics Code in 1954, romance comics were sold to girls and young women by the millions (Benson, *Romance Without Tears* 6). Sales were strong despite immediate criticism from the likes of Dr. Hilde Moss of the Lafargue Clinic (run by the infamous anti-comic crusader Frederick Wertham) who alleged in 1950 that romance comics offered a "distorted picture of love" (Hadju 169–70).

Of course, the early 1950s were remarkable for much more than the rise of the romance comic. At this time, a unique demographic group was coalescing, oriented around a youth subculture, promulgated by the mass media and targeted as an increasingly influential market: the teenagers. Historian Wini Breines has argued that "teenagers of all classes ... were able to function as group not only in market terms but self-referentially as well" (Breines, 98). Broadly speaking, their peers and their subculture were becoming ever-more important influences on American teens, and their sexual behavior was accordingly in a state of flux. Breines and other historians of the period have written about the practice of "going steady," which Beth Bailey has called "a sort of play-marriage, a mimicry of the actual marriage of slightly older peers," complete with the implication of "greater sexual intimacy" (Bailey 49, 51). Bailey argues that the stability of such relationships was a desirable thing for teens among the anxieties of the Cold War and a nuclear-armed world but asserts, "adult reactions to the practice were overwhelmingly negative" (Bailey 49, 51) Breines concurs, asserting that going steady "frightened parents because it seemed to invite sexual intimacy" (Breines 119). But in the 1950s parents were fighting a losing battle because "teenage culture was too much a part of consumer society, youth too separate, and daughters potentially too independent for control to be successfully reinstated" (Breines 119).

Parents and other older authority figures such as teachers, community members, and "experts" like etiquette columnist Anne Landers, faced stiff competition from teen culture in offering models and prescriptions for girls. To market directly to newly affluent teens with any hope of success, sellers (including comic book publishers) had to affect a level of understanding, compassion, and sympathy with their young buyers. Like all the other advertisers seeking the youth market, the artists, writers, and publishers of comic books had to flatter, cajole, create, and then satisfy the desires of their young audience. The best romance comic creators, like artist Alex Toth and writer Dana Dutch, treated their audience with respect. Toth worked hard to draw inspiration from other media, like movies and fashion magazines, to make his costumes and hairstyles interesting and his illustrations dynamic (Levin). Dutch and other above-average writers like Joe Simon strove to add elements of agency and dignity to the young characters who supposedly encountered situations similar to the ones their readers would experience (Benson, *Confessions* 16). But, though they were marketing a product that could be selected, purchased, and consumed by a teenager without the mediation (or even the knowledge) of an adult, the creators of comic books couldn't push the envelope too far beyond the bounds of the accepted without experiencing a backlash.

The disjunction between the directives of the older generation and the actuality of teenage dating practices was especially hard on girls, as is evident in Ann Landers' writing on teenage sexual behavior. It is worth examining Landers' "rules" at some length, since they were widely disseminated via her syndicated column and speaking engagements. Landers affected a sympathetic and chatty tone with her teenage readers, agreeing that it was "rockier" to be a teenager in the fifties than it was in decades past and allowing that some "necking" (defined as "an exchange of kisses and caresses, keeping both feet on the floor and all hands on deck") was "normal" (Landers 154–7). However, when discussing anything beyond necking, her rules for girls (and they were directed only to girls) were punitive and aimed at frightening readers into compliance. For example, Landers' list of the consequences of "petting" (defined as "roaming hands, passionate kissing, loose garments, feet off the floor) included making you feel guilty and ashamed, ruining your reputation, losing your boyfriend because he may decide you're cheap after he goes farther than he knows he should, getting pregnant, breaking your parents' hearts, and having an unwanted marriage or a child out of wedlock (Landers 158).

It was a girl's responsibility to avoid situations that would lead to all these horrible consequences. Landers directed girls to keep busy ("so necking doesn't become the number one sport") avoid "going steady," and especially to stay out of parked cars, or, as she called them, "portable bedrooms" (Landers 154–158). But, as some of the letters Landers received from teenage readers make apparent, this advice was less than helpful for girls already in steady relationships. One girl wrote, "How can I make a guy keep his hands to himself? I like him a lot and don't want to lose him, but he's been getting out of line lately" (Landers 154). Nor does this advice acknowledge female desire, as seen in another letter from a girl whose relationship of five months was becoming untenably frustrating: "We are trying to control ourselves but I don't know how much longer we will be able to manage" (Landers 154). As a study of *The Adolescent Experience* put it, quite bluntly: "The dating system, as we find it in the middle class, forces its participants to be their own executioners of impulse" (Breines 117).

"Experts" like Landers implied that nice girls should never even find themselves in such uncomfortable and frustrating situations demanding sexual negotiation, but obviously many did, and those episodes were at the center of many romance comics — perhaps the very situations that Joe Simon meant when he referred to striving for "realism" in the early 1950s (Hadju 159). They may not have done much to alter the social stresses and systems that were capable of causing anxiety and fear among teenage girls in the 1950s, but comic books extended to their readers a sense of understanding. In romance comics, those characters that ended up heartbroken made mistakes and poor choices in the name of love. They were flawed, but were usually not inherently bad. Romance comics might have tried to teach girls to cut off their most passionate impulses for the sake of propriety, but at least they acknowledged that it was painful and difficult to swing the axe.

Virtue and Femininity

Brunette Debbie Nichols "had always been brought up to be a lady," but at sixteen she's "oh so terribly *disgusted*" with her small town of Hastings ("Thrill Crazy"). What she wants is "the life I saw on my TV screen — the life of the big cities — fun, thrills, living fast and furiously!" She gets her wish in the thrilling person of John Falon, an orphan who flashes twenty-dollar bills in the school cafeteria and zooms around town in a red and white sports car. Within a day, Debbie has decided that Johnnie is "more of a *man* somehow — more confident and independent than anyone I had ever met!" Meanwhile, Johnnie casts his eye on Debbie and whisks her off to Lover's Lane.

The scene in Johnnie's car is painful. Debbie is nearly incoherent with anxiety and grasping at any argument to extricate herself from Johnnie's embrace, while being careful not to insult him: "I — I hardly *know* you!" "I — I've never *done* anything like this before!" "Please! It's getting late!" Johnny, meanwhile, manipulates Debbie by using both the carrot ("You're the first girl I've met here who I could really go for!") and the stick ("Don't be so cold!"). Despite this, the next image to catch the reader's eye is Debbie in her yellow negligee, tossing and turning in bed, not even able to admit to herself how much Johnnie's kisses have "*aroused*" her. From then on, Debbie eagerly participates in Johnnie's "big-time life," going to "a hundred places" and doing "a hundred wild things." From the images that float around their laughing faces, those things include dancing, swimming, and driving, but also drinking

A painful scene in Johnny's car. From "Thrill-Crazy." *Hi-School Romance* v.1 #17 (October 1952), Home Comics. Print.

Champagne. Debbie's grades suffer and her peers gossip behind her back, but she's "sick and tired of being a *little girl!*"

Debbie's thrills come crashing down around her head when she's plucked from her classroom by the principal and the police. Johnnie's rich, but shady, older brother Norm had had a business rival murdered at the very night club where Johnnie took Debbie the night before, and through this highly circumstantial chain of events Debbie is arrested, humiliated, and publicly shamed. The judge calls her an "innocent dupe," but also faults her for "delinquent behavior," while she sobs in her parents' arms that she has "disgraced" them. In the final panel of the story, Debbie stares out at the reader through tear-drenched eyes and says, "All the romance I can look for here in Hastings has ended!" Her romance with Johnnie resulted, she explains, from her "tragic mistake of being *thrill-crazy!*"

"Thrill-Crazy," from the October 1952 issue of *Hi-School Romance*, is a far more punitive story than "Shortcut to Love," not only because the heroine ends up heartbroken *and* under arrest. Her severe punishment doesn't result from anything she did, or even that her boyfriend did, but from the third-hand actions of her boyfriend's brother. But Debbie's assessment of her romance with Johnnie reveals what she, and the reader, are meant to consider her real transgression: wanting "thrills," or as it is presented, a lifestyle that is not domestic, but instead revolves around expensive, upper-class pursuits like going to night clubs, drinking Champagne, and racing sports cars. Johnnie's fast-moving and rather predatory sexual advances are of a piece with the "thrilling" but vaguely degenerate lifestyle that Debbie, and the reader, would recognize from movies, radio, and magazines. That amorality is contagious, as is indicated by Debbie's increasingly reckless disregard for the middle-class values of respectability and hard work in school. "Thrill-Crazy" is evidence that romance comics could look just as skeptically at the upper classes as they could at the lower classes, but also that to conform to the conventions of the cultural middle class, the spectrum of acceptable behavior for girls was remarkably narrow.

Comic book historian Bradford Wright brings an emphatically political perspective to the question of the social function of romance comics by suggesting that they emphasized middle class values and traditional gender roles as a "domestic containment policy" integral to the Cold War "home front" (Wright 127). The re-emphasis on domestic virtue and femininity was deeply intertwined with the rapid expansion of the American middle class, because, as we have seen, feminine behavior that fell within the range of the permissible was a public performance of correct upbringing that reassured individual families concerned about their social status. Furthermore, it could be argued that this "containment" reassured an older generation that the disruptions of World War II and the expansion of popular culture would not cripple the country's youth, and therefore its future (Caponegro 313). But that culture threatened girls with the loss of respectability (and acceptable futures) if they succumbed to its simultaneous encouragement to "pursue the sexual cues that assailed them"—in short, for girls, the "rules" were not rules at all; they were puzzles (Breines 87).

Until 1954, romance comics went some way towards acknowledging that, but trouble was brewing. A backlash against such "realism" in romance comics contributed to a storm of criticism among parents, newspapers, and legislators. As Bradford Wright comments, though the sharpest criticisms were aimed at gory horror and crime comics, even seemingly innocuous romances were deplored for their mushiness, false sentiments, social hypocrisy, titillation, and cheapness — all of a piece with anti-comic spokesman Dr. Frederick Wertham's claims that they "instilled in female readers feelings of physical inferiority and gave them a false image of love" (Wright 160). To deflect this outside criticism, the comic industry adopted an extremely strict code of self-censorship. The text of the Code of the Comics Magazine Association of America, better known as the Comics Code, set the standards of acceptability in post–1954 stories and artwork: "Respect for parents, the moral code, and for honorable behavior shall be fostered. A sympathetic understanding of the problems of love is not a license for morbid distortion" (Reitberger and Fuchs 248).

In practice, this directive meant that a "sympathetic understanding" of the problems of *girls* disappeared from romance comics. As Wright puts it, "the comic book industry had effectively forsaken its adolescent audience. By stripping away the freedom of writers and artists to depict the varieties of their readers' fantasies and concerns, the code confined comic books to a superficial, puerile level and enforced the very kind of conformity that millions of young people were beginning to reject" (Wright, 160).

Perhaps this puerility is what Breines had in mind when she spoke of "the dream of a single, true love won through appearances, of romance as the key to women's fortune," which required "an indefinitely suspended emotional life prior to the appearance of Prince Charming," for it is certainly true that romance comics did seem to endorse this "dream" (Brienes 104). Especially before the introduction of the code, romance comics also presented the pitfalls and problems that girls encountered along the way, often addressing the ways that girls' physical arousal, fear of social disapproval, and the desire to appear "adult" in interactions with boys clashed in situations that could be awkward, frustrating, or frightening. Though Breines has stated that "middle-class white girls' disaffection was barely discernible because no one thought to consider it and because its expression was often oblique," we have seen that romance comic plots often *did* address that disaffection, and did so sometimes bluntly, and often sympathetically (129). Success, in romance comics, means successfully negotiating the uncertain terrain of the boundary between adulthood, but that process of negotiation is portrayed as a sexual minefield to traverse as one matured, part of the process of outgrowing the unrealistic, naïve, or, simply, "foolish" period of childhood.

Works Cited

Bailey, Beth. *From Front Porch to Back Seat: Courtship in Twentieth-Century America.* Baltimore and London: Johns Hopkins University Press. 1989. Print.
Benson, John, ed. *Confessions, Romances, Secrets, and Temptations: Archer St. John and the St. John Romance Comics.* Seattle: Fantagraphics. 2007. Print.

_____. *Romance Without Tears*. Seattle: Fantagraphics. 2003. Print.

Breines, Wini. *Young, White, and Miserable: Growing Up Female in the Fifties*. Chicago and London: University of Chicago Press. 1992. Print.

Caponegro, Ramona. "Where the Bad Girls Are (Contained): Representations of the 1950s Female Juvenile Delinquent in Children's Literature and *Ladies' Home Journal*." *Children's Literature Association Quarterly* 34.4 (Winter 2009): 312–324. Print.

Duncan, Randy, and Smith, Matthew J. *The Power of Comics: History, Form, and Culture*. New York and London: Continuum. 2009. Print.

Gans, Herbert J. *The Levittowners*. 1967. New York: Columbia University Press. 1982. Print.

Hadju, David. *The Ten-Cent Plague: The Great Comic Book Scare and How It Changed America*. New York: Farrar, Straus, and Giroux. 2008. Print.

Landers, Ann. *Since You Ask Me*. New York: Fawcett. 1961. Print.

Levin, Bob. "The Mark of Tyrone Power: An Appreciation of Alex Toth." *The Comics Journal* 262 (Sept. 2004). Web. 14 January 2011.

Reitberger, Reinhold, and Wolfgang Fuchs. *Comics: Anatomy of a Mass Medium*. Trans. Nadia Fowler. Boston: Little, Brown. 1972. Print.

Riesman, David. *The Lonely Crowd*. 1961. New Haven and London: Yale University Press. 2001. Print.

"Shortcut to Love." *Hi-School Romance* vol. 1 #15 (June 1952), Home Comics. Print.

"Thrill-Crazy." *Hi-School Romance* vol. 1 #17 (October 1952), Home Comics. Print.

Waugh, Coulton. *The Comics*. New York: Macmillan, 1947. Print.

Wright, Bradford. *Comic Book Nation: The Transformation of Youth Culture in America*. Baltimore: Johns Hopkins University Press, 2001. Print.

8

Rebellion in Riverdale

Rafiel York

Archie Andrews was introduced in *Pep Comics* #22, which hit the newsstands in December 1941. John Goldwater, Archie's creator, explains that he recognized the proliferation of superheroes in the comic book marketplace, "I admit I went into it frankly because of Superman, Batman and all the other superheroes. They were catalysts. I thought of Superman as an abnormal individual and concluded that the antithesis — a normal person — could be just as popular" (qtd. in Uslan and Mendel 7). Goldwater's conclusion bore fruit, as Archie proved to be so popular that he was given his own book, and soon, many of his supporting characters were as well. Starting with issue #13 (cover date March-April 1945), and continuing until issue #68 (May-June, 1954), the covers of *Archie Comics* carried a banner declaring its star to be "America's typical teen-ager," and emphasizing the normalcy that Goldwater intended for his character. However, Archie's stories rarely include many of the normal behaviors of teenagers. As Bradford Wright observes, "America's 'typical teenager' never uses teen slang, never fights, never smokes or drinks alcohol, always obeys his parents in the end, and betrays only the vaguest hint of his libido. In other words, he is typical only of the kind of teenager that most adults want to have around" (73). The lack of any sort of "edge" in *Archie Comics* is not surprising, considering its primary audience was pre-teen girls. Wright recognizes this fact, writing, "[*Archie Comics*] offered an idealized, tranquil, and nostalgic vision of high school life primarily for boys and girls who had not yet experienced it." Wright then adds that the "tone of the series betrays the judgmental outlook of adult supervision" (73).

Adult supervision was exactly what many people felt teenagers needed during the 1950s, as concern with the perceived increase in juvenile delinquency ran rampant across the United States. This concern reached its apex when Senator Estes Kefauver chaired The Senate Subcommittee to Investigate Juvenile Delinquency in 1955. The Kefauver Committee sought to discover the cause of juvenile delinquency, and to control or eliminate that cause. Originally the committee focused on the media's contributions to the problem, but it also investigated "obscene materials, drugs, and local delinquency problems" (Gilbert 153). At the conclusion of the hearings, Kefauver decided, "that juvenile delinquency essentially stems from the moral breakdown in the home and community and, in many cases, parental apathy" (qtd. in Gilbert 153).

The declining morality of American society had been a concern for nearly a decade when Kefauver reached his conclusion. In 1946, George Kennan, the Deputy Chief of the United States Mission in Moscow, sent "The Long Telegram" to Secretary of State James Byrnes. In it, Kennan explains Soviet policies and practices, and offers his ideas on how the United States should deal with them. While much of "The Long Telegram" focuses on international policies, Kennan also offers his assessment that Americans can ward off the communist threat at home through morality, family, and self-discipline (Kennan).

In response, the federal government promoted an American lifestyle that was characterized by morality, the family, economic progress and personal fulfillment. The America that would best combat the communist threat was one where men went to work and earned enough money that their wives were able to stay home with the kids in a suburban house stocked with the latest appliances, while focusing on making themselves beautiful. It was an America where the people went to church on Sundays, and practiced the morality they learned there during the rest of the week. It was an America where people prided themselves on being "normal." It was an America where all teenagers behaved like Archie and the Riverdale gang.

In the introduction to the collection *Archie Americana Series: Best of the Fifties,* Victor Gorelick writes, "it's funny, but when people think of Archie, they think of the Fifties. Maybe that's because it was a time when families stuck together. School was fun, teachers were goofy and friendships were important" (5). Gorelick's description of the decade reflects what Grace Palladino refers to as an "adult-driven adolescent culture," one that "emphasized healthy growth, discriminating tastes, and mature acceptance of social conventions" (157). However, Palladino explains that the creation of rock 'n' roll presented teenagers with an option to the "adult-driven culture," the "rebel culture,"

> Thanks to rock 'n' roll and the rebel culture associated with the music, teenagers now had a choice of social identities, whatever their family background. They could see themselves as adults-in-training and use their high school years to hone their skills and discover their talents, as adults had been preaching for years. Or they

could join the fast-paced teenage-only world of (loud) music, (fast) cars, and styles that mocked the very notion of adult guidance [157].

Based on Bradford Wright's interpretation of the characters, it seems simple enough to conclude that Archie and the Riverdale gang see themselves as "adults-in-training," and choose not to participate in the rebellion fomented by rock 'n' roll. John Goldwater voices a similar opinion, stating, "In order to stay viable, we have to be contemporary ... Archie is a square at heart, and this will never change. The stories, however, have to remain relevant to the year we're publishing or we'll start losing readership" (qtd. in Uslan and Mendel 10).

But it is not that simple. James Gilbert explains that at least part of the reason juvenile delinquency seemed to be on the rise in the 1950s was that the definition of criminal behavior increasingly included "a shifting category of acts that sometimes considered criminal and sometimes not" (69). Grace Palladino adds, "The interpretation of delinquent behavior was in the beholder." She explains that many "respectable parents" had to deal with their own rebellious children, "whose delinquency ranged from talking back and refusing to share in household tasks to going steady, staying out late, and taking the family car across state lines in order to buy beer" (161). Juvenile delinquency became any act of youthful rebellion, any expression of adolescent freedom, or any behavior of which adults disapprove. When juvenile delinquency is defined in this way, Archie and the Riverdale gang, who regularly challenge the expectations of adults in the realms of dating, gender roles, and basic morality, begin to look less square.

Going Steady

In his first story, in *Pep Comics* #22, Archie attempts to impress his new neighbor, Betty Cooper, by performing various acts of balance, standing on a moving bicycle, walking the length of a fence while blindfolded, and finally walking a high wire at the "Big Carnival." During his daredevil act, Archie tumbles off the fence and destroys both a painting of Betty's father and a "priceless" vase. Archie's father begins to discipline his son, but changes his mind when his own father observes, "he was just showing off for a girl. He's a chip off the old block!" (*Pep Comics* #22). His grandfather's observation, and his father's decision to lessen Archie's punishment ("your punishment will be paying for that picture"), indicate that both of the adults view Archie's motivation, if not his actions, as falling well within the realm of the normal. They accept the idea that teen-aged boys show-off to impress teen-aged girls, and Archie's grandfather even goes so far as to advise Archie that, "women like men with courage." His grandfather's encouragement leads to Archie performing on, and falling from, the high wire at the carnival, and once again embarrassing himself in front of Betty's father. Archie behaves like the prototypical "adult-driven adolescent," by following his grandfather's advice, and by mimicking (however unknowingly) his father and grandfather's courtship routines. He challenges no authority, and only angers Mr. Cooper by accident. In fact, Archie's focus on just one girl is out of step with the practices and expectations of the time-period, but this problem would soon be rectified.

Noticeably absent from this story is Betty's rival for Archie's affection, the rich and spoiled Veronica Lodge, who would not make her first appearance until *Pep Comics* #26, in April 1942. She joined the Riverdale cast when Goldwater decided to incorporate what he considered a non-traditional love triangle, having two girls compete for a boy rather than vice versa, into Archie's stories. This love triangle may have been somewhat unusual as a story-telling device, but dating several different girls, and for the girls several different boys, was the common practice among teenagers in America in the decades before the 1950s. Beth Bailey explains that dating in the 1930s and 1940s was "primarily concerned with competition and popularity" (27). The way to become popular was to date several different people at the same time, and when at a dance, to cut in and be cut in on, Bailey goes on to say, "not being 'cut in' on—was taken quite seriously as a sign of social failure. Everyone noticed, and everyone judged" (28).

Dating practices changed suddenly and dramatically, so quickly, in fact that teenagers in the early 1950s "could be totally unaware of the former powerful convention" (Bailey 29). By 1950, the new measure of popularity among teenagers was "going steady," or dating one person exclusively. The new generation of teenagers readily accepted the shift in the dating ritual, as Grace Palladino explains, "They were chafing at the bit to move into [the adult world]—to get out of school, get a job, get married (which was, in the 1950s, the only legitimate way to have sex). What they rebelled against was an artificial adolescent culture designed to keep them 'innocent'" (164). Adolescents wanted to become adults, and "going steady" provided on opportunity for them to practice one of the cornerstones of adulthood: marriage. This was a cause of concern for many adults, who realized that, "going steady marked the beginning of the end of teenage life, since it started a couple's sexual clock" (Palladino 168). The sexual activity in Archie comics may have been limited to kissing, but that does not mean the Archie and the gang ignored what was going on in the world of teens. The idea of "going steady" made its way into Archie comics, and along with it came a hint of teen rebellion.

The 1956 story "Kiss and Kill" opens with Archie proclaiming "Boy! What a Mess!! Betty and Veronica both think they're my one and only" (35).

The predicament, as Archie explains it to Jughead, is that both girls think they are "going steady" with him, to which Jughead responds, "Just lie down — you're dead" (35). On the next page, Veronica brags to Betty that she is wearing Archie's class pin, which Betty counters that she is wearing Archie's ring. By giving these items to the girls, Archie has declared each of them to be his "steady," as the protocols of dating demanded that "to go steady, the boy gave the girl some visible token, such as a class ring or a letter jacket" (Bailey 29). It is at this point that the girls realize they are both "going steady" with Archie, and they storm to his house to confront him about his duplicity. As the girls are about to attack Archie, Jughead steps in and convinces them that, "you're both so gorgeous he couldn't resist one for the other" (38). The girls accept this explanation, but they also refuse to allow Archie to go steady with both of them, after all, "going steady" was all about practicing monogamy.

They decide to compete for Archie's affection in a kissing contest, upon which Jughead sets a three-second time limit, prompting Veronica to complain, "Only three seconds!! That's a very short kiss" (39). Veronica's desire to engage in a longer kiss indicates that she understands another of the protocols of going steady, "steady couples ... necked heavily as proof of their affection" (Palladino 112), and it was necking that served as a couple's declaration that they could hear the "sexual clock" ticking. Archie and Veronica slip away to a romantic spot for their kiss (with Jughead in tow as the judge), leaving Betty alone to wait for her turn. Betty mopes while she waits, realizing that she is the clear underdog in the contest, as "even one of Veronica's short kisses makes Archie's socks roll up and down" (40). Veronica is clearly the more seductive of the two girls, and it comes as little surprise that she usually emerges as the victor in the competition for Archie's affection. It also comes as little surprise that Veronica's father, Mr. Lodge, emerges as one of Archie's most frequent adult foils.

In a three-panel story entitled "Heart's Delight," Archie and Veronica sit dangerously close to one another on the couch, while hearts float around their heads. In the foreground, Mr. Lodge looks at his watch with an irritated expression. Attempting to separate the couple, he tells the couple, "In exactly ten minutes ... the lights in this house will be turned off!" The punch line comes in the third panel, when Archie responds by saying, "That's all right sir — we won't be reading!" In each of the three panels of the story, Archie and Veronica move closer together, until in the final panel they are about to kiss. The kiss is not shown, but the punch line, combined with their posture and an increase in the number of hearts floating in the air leaves little doubt that the two will soon be necking. Archie's brazen declaration of his and Veronica's intentions forces Mr. Lodge's expression to shift from irritation to fury, and

Archie and Veronica's intention is clear. From "Heart's Delight," *Archie's Joke Book* #40 (1959). Archie Comics. 1. Print.

it seems doubtful that Archie will be around when the lights go out. As an act of rebellion, the punch line of "Heart's Delight" seems innocuous, but Mr. Lodge does not take it as so, and that is exactly why it is an act of rebellion. That Archie and Veronica will neck at some point is a given, and Mr. Lodge knows he is all but powerless to stop it, but that doesn't mean he has to like it ... or Archie.

Gender Roles

While the characters in Archie comics rebelled against their parents in the 1950s by "going steady," they also regularly abandoned the traditional gender roles that became Richard Nixon's focus in the Kitchen Debate of 1959. Nixon argued that America's superiority to the Soviet Union "rested on the ideal of the suburban home, complete with modern appliances and distinct gender roles for family members" (May 245). In the story "Wiltin' Dilton," Betty and Veronica meet with Dilton Doyly, Riverdale High School's resident genius, for "help" with their homework, but of course, they allow him to do all the work. The story opens with the girls thanking him, and Betty says,

"Dilly you're sensational! It would have taken us hours to do all that homework!" to which Veronica adds, "And you did it in minutes!" (72) With so much free time on their hands, the girls decide to watch TV, but all they can find are "crime and horror shows," which they choose not to watch, because "crime and horror shows give [them] the creeps." Dilton assures the girls that there's nothing to be afraid of, and watches TV while the girls go to the kitchen to make candy. At this point, the characters are playing their traditional gender roles, Dilton is the brave and capable man, and Betty and Veronica are in the kitchen, but predictably, this changes.

The crime program gives Dilton the creeps, and when Betty invites him to pull taffy he becomes terrified and jumps out the window thinking she intends to strangle him. After the girls coax him down from the tree in which he's hiding, Dilton again becomes frightened, this time by a menacing kitty with a pink bow. He leaps into Veronica's arms and asks Betty to walk him home. In the second half of "Wiltin' Dilton," the gender roles are reversed. The terror Dilton feels when he encounters harmless everyday things like taffy and kitties places him on the level as the stereotypical housewife who stands on a chair shrieking when a mouse runs across the floor. Betty and Veronica move into the role of protectors, a job traditionally reserved for men.

Laugh Comics #83 contains a story entitled "Spoil Sport," in which Betty realizes that she always comes in second to Veronica when they compete for Archie's affection, so she decides to give up on boys altogether. Rather than replacing her pursuit of Archie with a feminine hobby like dressmaking or cooking, Betty decides to join the Riverdale baseball team. Jughead immediately points out to Betty that there is no girls' baseball team in town, but this does not deter her, as her intention is to join the boys' team. During her try-out

Betty challenges gender stereotypes. From "Spoil Sport," *Laugh Comics* #83 (October 1957). Archie Americana Series: Best of the Fifties, Book 2. Ed. Paul Castiglia. Mamaroneck: Archie Comics, 2003. 58–63. Print.

Archie observes, "She's a natural! She's better than any of the boys!" He then encourages the rest of the team to accept her as their new second baseman. When Reggie resists making the change Betty asserts herself and argues her way onto the team. The punch line of the story is that Archie *is* the second baseman who Betty is replacing, and he is more than happy to leave the team, as it gives him more time to spend with Veronica.

It is the situation, and not the punch line, that is important in this story. Betty Cooper, the quintessential girl next door, abandons the traditional gender role that she is supposed to play as a good American, and challenges the accepted belief that girls should not play sports with the boys. Early in the story she is shown wearing a dress, but when she decides to pursue baseball, Betty changes into a baseball uniform, which features pants rather than a skirt, as was worn by the players in the All-American Girls Professional Baseball League during the 1940's and 1950's. Betty also explains, as she tries out for the team, that she has "always been a tomboy at heart." This being the case, it can be concluded that her "girly" behavior (wearing dresses, chasing Archie) was merely an act, an attempt to meet society's expectations for her. Elaine Tyler May explains that during this era women did not "concern themselves with the affairs of men.... Rather they cultivated their looks and their physical charms." Joining the baseball team, and acting like a boy, places Betty in a similar position to women who entered the workforce in the 1950s — women who "were seen as un-American" and viewed "with suspicion" (May 246). Once Betty decides to turn her back on fitting in, eschewing her "girl next door image," traditionally masculine attributes like aggression begin to manifest. When Reggie balks at making her the new second baseman, Betty argues her way onto the team. For a woman to assert herself in the way Betty does in this story is contrary to the gender roles imposed by American society in the 1950s.

Morality

Archie Comics #72 opens with a story entitled "Teen Type" that is clearly intended as a public service announcement to help parents to identify juvenile delinquents, and to encourage children to avoid a path that would lead to them becoming juvenile delinquents. Archie's father becomes outraged when he reads an article in the newspaper about a group of boys who "beat up that old man just for the fun of it" (1). Archie attempts to calm his father by explaining that he knows how to identify "hoodlums," and what follows is a series of three diagrams with commentary detailing the average hoodlum's appearance. The first of these diagrams offers front and side views of a "Duck's

The "Duck's Tail" haircut, a sure sign of a J.D. From "Teen-Type," *Archie Comics* #72 (Jan.-Feb. 1955): Archie Comics, 1–3. Print.

Tail" haircut, which also includes the caption, "usually worn by teen age hoodlums." Next, Archie explains the hoodlum's casual outfit, which "usually includes a chauffer's hat,— black leather jacket,— tight fitting dungarees, and ankle high boots." The final diagram is of a "dressed up" hoodlum wearing a zoot suit. By focusing on appearance of the "hoodlums" first, Archie behaves similarly to many high school administrators across the United States in the 1950s. James Gilbert explains that high school dress codes attempted to control students by forcing them to wear clothing that met with the approval of adults, which would, in theory, force them to behave in ways that met with the approval of adults (16). Archie goes on to address several behaviors exhibited by hoodlums, and finally convinces his parents that most teenagers are "clean living kids." The final panel of the story is a group shot of the five primary characters in Archie Comics (Betty, Reggie, Archie, Veronica, and Jughead), and a speech bubble that reads, "There are two ways to do things — the right way and the wrong way! Let's do the things we know are right and shun the things that we know are wrong!" (3). This pledge rings hollow, though, as each of the characters pictured has a long history of immoral behavior.

Ironically, the same issue of *Archie Comics* also contains a story entitled "Gripe Sniper," in which Mr. Weatherbee, the principal at Riverdale High School, installs microphones under a bench on campus so he can hear the "gripes" the students have with the school. Orwellian as this may seem, Mr. Weatherbee actually installs the microphone with the best of intentions. He believes that if he can hear the students' candid complaints about the school he can "promote better harmony between the students and our faculty" (18). This plan goes awry when Archie and Jughead are the first students to sit on the bugged bench, and Mr. Weatherbee becomes "Big Brother." Jughead tells Archie that the weather forecast calls for freezing temperatures that night, leading Archie to conclude "that means ice-skating! The pond will be frozen," and they decide to "play hooky" the following day. Mr. Weatherbee plots to catch the truant students, but at the last minute, they change their plans, reasoning that the ice will be too thin for skating, and Mr. Weatherbee finds himself alone at the pond. When Miss Grundy, the teacher of just about every class at Riverdale High School, sees the boys at school she asks them, "where are your skates, boys?" to which they respond, "Not cold enough," and "the ice wouldn't be thick enough." As she rushes to notify Mr. Weatherbee of the boys' change of plans (arriving too late, as he has already fallen through the ice), Jughead observes, "you'd almost think she expected us to go ice-skating instead of coming to school!" (20). While the boys do not actually break any rules in this story, they fully intend to do so, only to be foiled by weather that is warmer than predicted. At no point in the story do they consider whether playing "hooky" is an acceptable behavior, nor whether it is the right thing to do. They want to have fun, and they do not care if they have to violate the school rules and societal expectations to do so.

In a story from 1952 entitled "Change Your Partners," Archie and Reggie are planning a school dance in Pop's Choc 'lit Shop, when Jughead complains that they should, "have something you can sink your teeth into, like a barbeque or a clambake" (17). He goes on to explain that he does not enjoy dances because he doesn't like "getting that close to a girl," which leads Betty to suggest holding a square dance. Archie gives himself the task of hiring a "hillybilly band" and assigns Betty and Jughead to spread the word about the dance. Betty's last stop is Veronica's house, where she simply says, "dance tomorrow night in the school gym," omitting that it is a square dance. Archie arrives to ask Veronica to the dance, which she accepts, then she taunts Betty, telling her she "can always go with Jughead." Without missing a beat, Veronica explains to Betty that she has just purchased a new gown, and had no place to wear it, but now she does. Betty begins to tell her that the dance is a square dance, and that proper attire for the dance is "hilly-billy," but she thinks better of it. Instead, she sets up Veronica, saying, "Don't you think it's a crime that we girls put so much thought into our clothes and the boys dress like tramps?" Veronica responds, "anybody who takes me out, dresses like a gentleman or else!" (20) When Archie shows up, dressed as a hill-billy, Veronica slams the door in his face, and he goes to the dance alone, where he dances with Betty, who has no date.

Veronica also acts deceitfully, as in the story, "Rhyme nor Reason," from 1956, in which she enters the "Deal Soap" poetry contest. Reggie points out to her that Betty wins all the poetry competitions, but he finds a way to guarantee that Betty will not win this one. The contest limits each entrant to one submission, so knowing that Betty will submit an entry on her own, Veronica and Reggie create a fake entry and put Betty's name on it. As she walks away from the mailbox, having just posted the fake entry, Veronica bumps into Archie who is on his way to the mailbox to drop off Betty's entry. Veronica escorts him, and when they place the postcard in the slot, Archie reveals that he had changed Betty's name on the entry to Veronica's. Veronica is disqualified from the contest for submitting two entries, and the fake entry that she submitted in Betty's name wins the five hundred dollar prize.

In each of these stories, Betty and Veronica stab one another in the back, Betty by withholding information, and Veronica through forgery. Reggie is also guilty of deceit, as he acts as the Svengali behind Veronica's ruse. Each of them has a different motivation for perpetrating her offense. Betty deceives Veronica in response to her friend's taunt; she avenges a wrong that has been done to her. Veronica forges Betty's contest entry simply because she wants to win. She doesn't even have a noble purpose for entering the contest, five hundred dollars would mean nothing to the spoiled girl. Veronica cheats for no reason, other than selfishness. Reggie's reason for helping Veronica is never stated, but when she thanks him with a series of kisses, he encourages her to continue thanking him, making his motivation evident. Despite their different motivations, the Betty, Veronica, and Reggie all behave dishonestly and deceitfully, actions that belie Victor Gorelick's contention that "friendships were important" in both Archie Comics and the United States in the 1950s (5).

It is probably safe to say, that Archie Comics did not intend to subvert the ideals of containment era America, as challenging societal norms would not project the wholesome, family-friendly image that Archie cultivated. The Riverdale Gang's forays into juvenile delinquency are presented as harmless teenage antics, but in the sanitized world of Archie Comics, seemingly minor offenses take on added gravity. Lying to a friend or necking are not the same as the heinous crime that outrages Archie's father in "Teen-Type," but as Russell W. Belk observes, "the *Archie* series is unique in even mentioning Jesus, God, and prayer in some stories (3 percent). This is one reflection of the very conservative, Christian and traditional values of the Archie series" (32). Archie and his friends violate these values with regularity, revealing themselves to be typical rebellious teens, if not borderline delinquents.

WORKS CITED

Bailey, Beth. "Rebels Without a Cause? Teenagers in the 50s." *History Today* 40.2 (1995): 25–31. Academic Search Premier. EBSCO. Web. 12 Nov. 2010.

Belk, Russell W. "Material Values in the Comics: A Content Analysis of Comics Books Featuring Themes of Wealth." *The Journal of Consumer Research* 14:1 (June 1987): 26–42. Print.

"Change Your Partners." *Archie's Girls Betty and Veronica* #6 (1952). *Archie Americana Series: Best of the Fifties, Book 2*. Ed. Paul Castiglia. Mamaroneck: Archie Comics, 2003. 17–21. Print.

Gilbert, James. *A Cycle of Outrage: America's Reaction to the Juvenile Delinquent in the 1950s*. New York: Oxford, 1986. Print.

Gorelick, Victor. Introduction. *Archie Americana Series: Best of the Fifties*. Mamaroneck, NY: Archie Comics. 4–5. Print.

"Gripe Sniper." *Archie Comics* #72 (Jan.-Feb. 1955), Archie Comics, 18–21. Print.

"Heart's Delight." *Archie's Joke Book* #40 (1959), Archie Comics. 1. Print.

Kennan, George. "The Long Telegram (Moscow to Washington) (February 22, 1946)." *The National Security Archive*. 27 Sept. 1998. George Washington University. Web. 14 March 2010.

"Kiss and Kill." Pep Comics #116 (1956). *Archie Americana Series: Best of the Fifties, Book 2*. Ed. Paul Castiglia. Mamaroneck, NY: Archie Comics, 2003. 35–40. Print.

May, Elaine Taylor. "Containment at Home: Cold War, Warm Hearth." *American Families: Past and Present*. Ed. Susan M. Ross, New Brunswick, NJ: Rutgers University Press, 2006. 244–255. Print.

Palladino, Grace. *Teenagers: An American History*. New York: Basic, 1996. Print.

Pep Comics #22 (Dec. 1941), *The Best of Archie*. Ed. Michael Uslan and Jeffrey Mendel. New York: Perigree, 1980. 18–23. Print.

"Rhyme Nor Reason." *Archie's Girls, Betty and Veronica* #27 (Nov. 1956). *Archie Americana Series: Best of the Fifties*. Mamaroneck, NY: Archie Comics. 30–33. Print.

"Spoil Sport." *Laugh Comics* #83 (Oct. 1957). *Archie Americana Series: Best of the Fifties, Book 2*. Ed. Paul Castiglia. Mamaroneck, NY: Archie Comics, 2003. 58–63. Print.

"Teen-Type." *Archie Comics* #72 (Jan.-Feb. 1955), Archie Comics, 1–3. Print.

Uslan, Michael, and Jeffrey Mendel, ed. *The Best of Archie*. New York: Perigree, 1980. Print.

_____.Introduction. *The Best of Archie*. Ed. Michael Uslan and Jeffrey Mendel. New York: Perigree, 1980. 7–13. Print.

"Wiltin' Dilton" *Archie's Girls Betty and Veronica*. #36 (May 1958), Archie Comics, 18- 21. Print.

Wright, Bradford W. *Comic Book Nation*. Baltimore: Johns Hopkins University Press, 2001. Print.

9

The Amazon Mystique: Subverting Cold War Domesticity in *Wonder Woman* Comics, 1948–1965

Ruth McClelland-Nugent

Writing in 1954, Frederic Wertham had little good to say about Wonder Woman. She was "a frightening image" for boys, a "morbid ideal" for girls. He suggested the character's female supporting cast were lesbians, saying that "the attractive Wonder Woman and her counterparts are definitely anti-masculine.... Her followers are the 'Holliday girls,' i.e. the holiday girls, the gay party girls, the gay girls." Not only did the character promote lesbianism, she subverted natural feminine innocence, because "[t]heir attitude about death and murder is a mixture of the callousness of crime comics with the coyness of sweet little girls" (193).

But Frederick Wertham was behind the times. Certainly, Wonder Woman had begun as a proto-feminist character, described in 1941 by creator William Moulton Marston as subversive "propaganda for the new type of woman who should ... rule the world" (qtd. in Daniels 22). In the years that Marston wrote Wonder Woman, his stories exhorted women to become physically and mentally strong, promoted paid female employment, and critiqued what Marston saw as over-masculinized aspects of American culture. But after Marston's death in 1947, new writer-editor Robert Kanigher refashioned Wonder Woman into a heroine as interested in heterosexual romance as in crime-fighting. He described his first script as "a real love story, with real people" (qtd. in Daniels 93). The Holliday girls vanished, and Wonder Woman's boyfriend, Steve Trevor, became more prominent. If Wertham had actually been reading the book in 1954, he would have been hard-pressed to find the hints of lesbianism he claimed to see in the original comic. Despite the makeover, Wonder Woman never became the ideal American Cold War suburban housewife. She consistently put her "career" (saving the world) ahead of marrying Steve. In fact, her "family" was not a nuclear, heterosexual one, but rather an all-female one headed by her single mother, the Amazon Queen. The comic also contained special features promoting female trailblazers in sports and medicine, as well as careers in business in the military. Despite the comic's retreat from Marston's radical vision, it remained possible for readers to see in it an alternative to 1950s domesticity. Will Brooker suggests that regardless of authorial intent, the Batman stories of the 1950s offered elements "upon which a gay teenager could readily have drawn his own meaning" (135). Similarly, while Wonder Woman comics were not overtly critical of the 1950s domestic ideal, they contained building blocks for individual resistance to it.

"Wonder Woman Is Helping America Win the War": from World War II to the Cold War

Throughout Marston's wartime scripts there runs a strong critique of "man's world," which is ruled by brute strength, and needs the loving, but strong, rule of women to achieve peaceful balance. Marston tied feminine valor to the context of the Second World War, explaining that the Amazons, led by Queen Hippolyte, served the goddess Aphrodite (and the United States) in a world torn by the masculine forces of Mars, which were embodied by hyper-masculine Fascism. Hippolyte's daughter, the princess Diana, left the island to aid the United States in its struggle against the Axis, in her guise as "Wonder Woman." As one editorial comment helpfully explained, "Wonder Woman is helping America win the War and if America wins, peace will return — the world will be ruled happily by the love and beauty of Aphrodite!" (Marston and Peter 11).

Exhorting women to strength and heroism made sense in the era of Rosie the Riveter and other wartime propaganda encouraging women to work in factories and join the military. But after the Second World War ended, Marston's vision became more problematic. In theory, women were supposed to emulate the suburban housewife. As wives and mothers, women made family "togetherness" possible; a suburban nuclear family was supposed to be emotionally and financially complete in its own bubble of backyard barbecues, family games, television watching and automobile vacations (Miller 393). This family ideal played a key role in the political rhetoric of the Cold War, as demonstrated by Adlai Stevenson at the 1955 graduation ceremony for all-women's Smith College. The prominent Democratic politician informed the graduates that their most important contribution "in a great historic crisis" would be to assume "the humble role of housewife" (qtd. in Horowitz 124). If the most elite women in the country were supposed to be focused on heterosexual romance rather than careers, it is little wonder that new editor Kanigher decided to make Wonder Woman follow suit.

Marston had already given Wonder Woman a boyfriend, the dashing Steve Trevor, Army pilot and military intelligence officer. In Marston's formulation, however, a mysterious Amazonian prohibition against marriage prevented their romance from becoming too serious. Kanigher, however, reworked this idea, arguing that Wonder Woman could indeed marry, but would have to retire from crime fighting to do so. In the 1954 story "Wonder Woman's Wedding Day," she assures Steve, "The moment I'm convinced my services are no longer needed to combat the enemies who threaten our American way of life—I'd be happy to marry you." She takes her job a little too seriously for Steve's taste, as he laments in another 1954 story, "I wish you'd forget who you are for a moment and think about romance for a change!" (Kanigher and Peter, "The Missing"). Even when shaken by failure, however, Steve remained optimistic, even belligerent: "My day will come, Wonder Woman! Just you wait!" (Kanigher and Peter, "Daily"). Marriage and career were so incompatible that criminals tried more than once to fake a peaceful world in order to trick Wonder Woman into retirement-by-matrimony. As Angle Man chortles in *Wonder Woman* #81, "Okay! I'm satisfied! Wonder Woman's married—-and retired from crimefighting! She gave her word! She won't go back on it!" (Kanigher and Peter, "Vanishing").

"*Your Eyes Shine Like Jewels!*" Wonder Woman's New Look

Kanigher changed the comic even further in 1958. The character's original artist, Harry G. Peter, left the book, leaving penciller Ross Andru and inker Mike Esposito to redesign the comic's visuals. They gave Wonder Woman a more distinctly hourglass figure, in line with postwar "New Look" fashion. With the curves came longer legs absent the muscle definition that had helped characterize Peters' Wonder Woman. Instead of Peters' strong, almost square jawline (reminiscent of a Gibson Girl), Andru and Esposito gave Diana a slimmer face, larger eyes, and softly arching brows. In her secret identity of frumpy Lt. Diana Prince, Wonder Woman lost her characteristic bun and instead sported a fashionable hairstyle and cat's eye glasses.

Story changes came with the new art. In May 1958, Kanigher introduced a new origin story for the Amazons. No longer did their opposition to Mars

H. G. Peters' Wonder Woman — her "almost square jawline" and muscular physique. From *Sensation Comics* #9 (September 1942). National Comics Publications [DC Comics]. Print.

form part of a cosmic gender balance, nor did the all-female Amazons worship a goddess of love. Rather the Amazons battled against generic "evil forces," under the patronage of chaste Pallas Athena (Kanigher, Andru, and Esposito, "Million Dollar" 10–11). In fact, the Amazons had once had husbands and lovers until they were killed in "terrible wars" (Kanigher, Andru, and Esposito, "Secret Origin" 194–5). The Amazon Queen, Hippolyta, was safely heterosexualized via a story showing her lamenting her long-lost lover, Prince Theno (Kanigher, Andru, and Esposito, "Wonder Queen" 392–7).

Kanigher also introduced new stories about Wonder Woman as a teenager, calling her "Wonder Girl" in this version. In these stories, she lived on Paradise Island and daydreamed about her future exploits. These stories also carried strong elements of heterosexual romance, in the person of Wonder Girl's would-be boyfriend, "Mer-Boy," who wanted to take Wonder Girl to undersea dances and to wear his fraternity pin (Kanigher, Andru, and Esposito, "Mer Boy's Undersea"). Mer-Boy later gained a rival in the form of a

9. *The Amazon Mystique* (McClelland-Nugent)   119

Andru's Wonder Woman and Diana Prince get modernized. From *Wonder Woman* #99 (November 1957). National Comics Publications [DC Comics]. Print.

winged "Bird Boy" (Kanigher, Andru, and Espositio, "Mer-Boy vs. Bird-Boy"). Kanigher also wrote more and more stories about the adult Wonder Woman's romance with Steve Trevor, which was now complicated by the grown-up Mer-Boy, "Manno." Stories like "Wonder Woman's Impossible Decision" turned on the drama of which suitor Diana would save from peril, indicating who she cared about most (Kanigher, Andru, and Esposito).

Despite the competition from Manno, Steve Trevor enjoyed a prominent role in Kanigher's stories. Sometimes his love for Diana played an integral role in saving the world. In "The Three Faces of Wonder Woman," Steve must pick out the real Wonder Woman from two equally super-powered robots, or else condemn the Earth to an invasion of extradimensional giants. Unable to distinguish his sweetheart by her strength or skill, Steve kisses each one and "recognizing the touch of [her] warm lips," finally picks the true

Amazon (Kanigher, Andru, and Espositio). At other times, Steve's romance returns to the familiar pattern of trying to trick Diana into marrying him. In the October 1958 issue, he tries to convince Diana that she could still help the world by taking take him on as her full-time project; he always needs help in his dangerous job as an Air Force test pilot. When she agrees to wed him if he needs her help three times in twenty-four hours, Steve triumphantly responds "You've lost, Angel! I've got so much testing to do in experimental planes tomorrow — that I'm sure to need your help thirty times — not just three!" (Kanigher, Andru, and Espositio, "Undersea Trap" 88). And in fact, Steve does need plenty of help — but the third time occurs fifteen minutes after the twenty-four hour deadline passes.

Steve's "tricks" are not unlike those of Lois Lane in the Superman comics of same era; both characters pursue super-powered love interests without knowing about their secret identities. Both try underhanded manipulation or games in order to learn more about their objects of desire, or to weasel their way into marriage. Yet Lois is explicitly punished for her manipulative actions. For example, in *Lois Lane* #14, Lois traps herself in the Fortress of Solitude in an attempt to snoop on her beau. Superman has one of his robots give her a "well-deserved spanking!" (Binder and Schaffenberger, 396). Even when Lois Lane uses her tricks for other ends — such as pursuing her career as a journalist, Superman disapproves and actively punishes her: "I'll have to teach her a lesson for using such tactics to get a story," he muses in *Lois Lane* #1 (Dorfman and Schaffenberger 138). Sometimes the ire at Lois' tricks seems counterproductive. When she does manage to scoop a story and simultaneously outwits one of Superman's attempts to punish her for snooping, it is her editor, Perry White who fumes, "Will anyone ever teach her a lesson?" (Coleman, Boring, and Kaye 447). Since White's paper is gaining an important story from Lois' daring "trick," his anger is not about her journalism. Lois Lane's schemes tend to challenge the authority of male figures, particularly Superman, and it seems no accident that in the stories referenced above, Superman calls in male allies (his own robot, Robin, Perry White, and Jimmy Olson) to punish her. Steve Trevor, by contrast, challenges a woman, and receives no "punishment" (other than failure) for his tricks.

Steve's schemes are more acceptable than Lois Lane's, but this does not mean that Wonder Woman never challenges him. Most frequently, Steve is chided by Wonder Woman for not appreciating a woman's character as much as her looks; she would prefer that he paid more attention to her "plain Jane" alter ego, Lt. Diana Prince. In *Wonder Woman* #126, as they laze on the beach, Wonder Woman praises her own alter ego's accomplishments: "Isn't Diana Prince the most intelligent girl you ever saw? Di can play the piano like a concert pianist! Di's in line for a captaincy ... she'll be a general soon!" Steve does not respond to Wonder Woman's conversation, instead praising her physical beauty, touching her face and leaning in for an attempted kiss: "Your hair is like silk! Your eyes shine like jewels! Your mouth is like a Cupid's bow! Meant to be kissed. " Frustrated, Wonder Woman rebuffs his advances, and muses "I've got to get him to start thinking about Diana Prince, for a change!" (Kanigher, Andru, and Esposito, "Unmasking" 234). In one of the few explicit references to punishing Steve for his boorish behavior, Wonder Woman decides she needs to teach him "a lesson in manners" after Steve jilts Diana Prince for Wonder Woman. With the help of a magic mirror, she makes her Wonder Woman persona appear physically altered—grotesquely fat or thin. Steve is so unnerved that he decides to seek out "plain" Diana Prince for a

Wonder Woman in the kitchen. From Robert Kanigher (w), Ross Andru (p), and Mike Esposito (i), "Wonder Woman's Surprise Honeymoon!" *Wonder Woman* #127 (February 1962); rpt. in *Showcase Presents Wonder Woman* vol. 2. ed. Peter Hamboussi and Sean Mackiewicz. New York: DC Comics 2008). Print.

date after all. He is surprised to find the lieutenant on Superman's arm; she jauntily turns him down, saying "I have other plans!" (Kanigher, Andru, and Esposito, "Mirage" 345).

Stories like this one suggest that Steve does not appreciate the true Wonder Woman, and suggest that women are justified in expecting more out of relationships. Another hint of Steve's blindness to Diana's true nature comes in "Wonder Woman's Surprise Honeymoon." In a storyline that turns out to be hallucinatory, Steve and Wonder Woman tie the knot, but the marriage does not put an end to her "career" of helping people. After she saves a plane from disaster while still wearing her wedding dress, she is mobbed by autograph-seekers, one of whom opines "Looks like you're going to combine marriage with answering distress calls!" In the next panel, Steve's face is contorted into a grimace as he thinks "Oh no! I can't go through this again! More autographs!" (Kanigher, Andru, and Esposito 260–1). When the couple finally escape the mob, Steve is again dismayed to find that Wonder Woman has given her wedding dress away to a poor bride who cannot afford one. When they finally arrive at a cottage, Steve relaxes on the porch while Wonder Woman bustles around the kitchen, a frilly apron worn over her costume. Steve muses "My first Amazon-cooked meal! I bet it will taste like nothing on earth!" Much to Steve's dismay, it does not: "This toast's burnt! The meat's raw! The jello's hot! The coffee's cold!" In the next panel, Wonder Woman slumps, apparently crying, holding a frying pan in her hand and sobbing: "Y-y-you n-never asked me wh-wh-whether I could c-c-cook!" Steve reassures her that he will do the cooking "...or we'll starve!" The panel presents Steve and Diana in the very picture of a domestic kitchen: dishes in the sink, coffee pot on the stove, and dinner still on the table. The only part of the picture out of place is Wonder Woman's costume, which functions as her badge of office, and reminds the reader that she is still not quite the ideal housewife of Steve's imagination (Kanigher, Andru, and Esposito 263–5). Nor is she likely to become one, as Steve occasionally seems to notice; in 1960 he plaintively asks Diana, "If I can't marry you as long as you're needed to fight crime and injustice — and as long as there's crime and injustice you'll be needed to battle it — then how can we ever get married, honey?" A smiling Wonder Woman enigmatically answers: "I guess that's another story!" (Kanigher, Andru, and Esposito, "Robot 360).

"Sister Amazons!" Wonder Family Togetherness

Even if Wonder Woman never quite managed to marry Steve, it did not mean she was bereft of home and family. But her family differed from the

Cold War American ideal. One of Wertham's sharpest criticisms of comic books was their lack of "ordinary home life. I have never seen in any of the crime, superman, adventure, space, horror, etc., comics an ordinary family sitting down at a meal. I have seen an elaborate charming breakfast scene, but it was between Batman and his boy, complete with checkered tablecloth, milk, cereal, fruit juice, dressing gown and newspaper. And I have seen a parallel scene with the same implications when Wonder Woman had breakfast with an admiring young girl, with checkered tablecloth, cereal, toast, and the kitchen sink filled with dishes draining in the background" (Wertham 236).

Wertham's swipe at the alleged homosexual content of *Batman* and *Wonder Woman* reveals that domestic scenes and family "togetherness" were, indeed, part of comic books, even if those scenes did not meet his expectations. In fact, superhero comics became more and more familial in the late 1950s and early 1960s, by way of new siblings, cousins, parental figures, and even super-pet characters. For example, in 1958, the *Superman* title introduced a new relative for Superman, his younger cousin, Supergirl. Rather than adopt her himself (a single adult man adopting an attractive teenager would not have met Wertham's definition of a "normal" family), Superman insists that his cousin live in an orphanage (Binder and Plastino). Supergirl longs for a nuclear family, and is overjoyed when Superman lets her go home with the Danvers family (Siegel and Mooney). Other comics included stories that showed heterosexual domesticity as part of alternative timelines or imagined futures. For example, in *Batman* and *Detective Comics,* Batman enjoyed an on-again off-again romance with Batwoman (Kathy Kane), while Robin gained a similar heterosexual romance interest in 1961 with the introduction of Batgirl (Betty Kane). In the imagination of Bruce Wayne's butler, Alfred, however, the romance went much further than occasional dating. In a series of stories described as "adventure[s] that might happen," Alfred chronicled a future wherein Bruce Wayne/Batman marries Kathy, and their son becomes the new Robin. Against Batman's wishes, Kathy Kane continues her adventures as Batwoman in these stories, but eventually gives it up as Betty Kane graduates into the Batwoman role. It is a rare picture of domesticity combined with superheroism. Yet it remains firmly outside the canonical storyline, although Batman muses, "You never can tell — maybe she'll be able to read it some day," implying that such stories might happen in future (Finger, Stone, and Paris).

It also took an imagined storyline, labeled "Impossible Tales," to tell family stories in *Wonder Woman.* The "Impossible Tales" included Wonder Woman, Wonder Girl (Wonder Woman as a teen), and Wonder Tot (Wonder Woman as a young girl) and Queen Hippolyte, often called the "Wonder

Queen." The three versions of Wonder Woman call each other "sister" and seem to function as independent characters; in fact, the confusion was so great that writer Bob Haney and artist Bruno Premiani apparently believed Wonder Girl was an independent character, and introduced her as such into the Teen Titans in 1965. The confusion was understandable; the characters referred to themselves as a family; covers like that of *Wonder Woman* #138 proclaimed they would feature "The Entire Wonder Woman Family!" and showed the four characters working together to stop some menace (in this case, the villain Multiple Man) (Kanigher, Andru, and Esposito, "Kite"). In "The Phantom Sea Beast," the family is shown sharing a sleeping quarters, each in her own bed. Kanigher, Andru, and Esposito frequently depict the Wonder Family working together, defeating menaces such as a sea-beast ("The Phantom Sea Beast"), giant versions of themselves ("Captives of Mirage World") or the wrath of the gods ("The Last Day of the Amazons"). Yet although the family worked together, it was clear that this was quite different from Wonder Woman's usual "work" that took her away from home. One might even argue that the Amazon's island was a sort of suburbia — if Wonder Woman's main sphere of "work" was the United States, then the Wonder Family tales clearly took place at the home to which she commuted: Paradise Island. A panel in *Wonder Woman* #140 provides striking visual evidence of this, as the Queen, Wonder Girl, and Wonder Tot stand on the steps of the palace pointing at Wonder Woman's plane. "Mommy look! Wonder Woman on time — like the sun!" Hippolyte, like a stay-at-home mother, seems excited by hearing stories outside her sphere: "I can hardly wait to hear what surprising adventures Diana has to tell us this time!" (Kanigher, Andru, and Esposito "Human Lightning" 60).

Yet since no man could set foot on Paradise Island, there could never be a father-husband to "complete" the household. In a 1965 story, "Wonder Girl's Mysterious Father," Kanigher posited this as a genuine emotional loss, showing Wonder Girl jealous of American girls who were enjoying "Father-Daughter Day." Her mother explains "I long to see your father too, Wonder Girl! But — you know — he was lost at sea!" (Kanigher, Andru, and Esposito 382–3). When an amnesiac man washes ashore on a nearby island, Wonder Girl is happy to pretend to be his daughter. But the situation is only temporary, as the man's real daughter returns (391–2). This story suggests that the all-female household is incomplete; both mother and daughter long for a male figure to complete their happiness. Against this, however, one must place the bulk of the "Impossible Tales," that show the "Wonder Family" as a happy, complete unit. It was not the only fashion in which the magazine communicated contradictory signals about heterosexual domesticity.

"Women of Distinction": Mixed Messages and the Feminine Mystique

Wonder Woman included a number of supplemental features in its pages, usually oriented to topics relating to women's lives. "Marriage a la Mode," for example, was a traditionally feminine feature, profiling marriage customs from around the world and doling out such tidbits as the fact that German brides received coins from elderly village men, while their Spanish Castilian counterparts must dance with any man who deposits a coin in the apple she holds. "Gems of Destiny," a recurring comic panel in a similar vein, touted superstitions about gemstones. Text-only columns covered feminine topics such as dolls, fashion, and housework. "Facts on Furs," for example, advised readers on how to select a good fur coat before concluding that "there remains only one more important step, and that is, how to convince daddy or hubby to add that item to your wardrobe."

Yet other features profiled female trailblazers and highlighted some very untraditional occupations. "Women of Distinction" profiled historic trailblazers in American history. This regular feature profiled some distinctly undomestic heroines: Blanche Stuart Scott, first woman to fly an airplane (*Wonder Woman* #126), for example, and Susanna Salter, the first woman mayor in America (*Wonder Woman* #81). And the text-only columns often veered far beyond furs and dolls into features that expounded more on the unconventional women of history. *Wonder Woman* #78 featured "Women Warriors," while *Wonder Woman* #101's "Samson in Skirts" profiled nineteenth century hospital reformer Louisa Schuyler. Elizabeth I, "The Fighting Queen," starred in *Wonder Woman* #108's text column, while *Wonder Woman* #110 examined a number of "The Women Who Won the West." These included Esther Morris, the first woman Justice of the Peace in America and Bethany Williams, a Western doctor, among others. Other features promoted challenging careers for women. *Wonder Woman* #96 encouraged girls to consider career choices in business, journalism, or the law ("It's a Woman's World), while # 77 celebrated "Women in Sports." A profile of "The Girls in Navy Blue" told the story of Navy WAVES, concluding that "[t]housands of Navy WAVES are filling many important assignments which are essential to the support of world-wide naval operations at sea.... Through the years, the Waves have earned their position in the Navy, as well as the high respect of the officers and men of the service."

The juxtaposition of these exhortations to feminine independence alongside features extolling marriage and fur coats may seem jarring. They also challenge the portrait of the American media of the 1950s as monolithic in its promotion of female domesticity. Famously, in her 1963 bestseller *The*

Feminine Mystique Betty Friedan harshly condemned American women's magazines for ignoring politics and careers; this analysis has been challenged by historians like Joanne Meyerowitz, who notes that many women's magazines of the 1950s prominently featured "feminine Horatio Alger" nonfiction features about women with notable successes in the world of business or politics. These publications mixed stories that celebrated domesticity with features about women's careers, education, and political involvement (232). Looking at the same period, Nancy Walker suggests that the apparent contradiction between domestic and non-domestic features in these magazines was "the product of negotiating a variety of often competing interests, and the result was a vexed but earnest, sometimes contradictory image of domestic America" (19).

The stories and features in Robert Kanigher's *Wonder Woman* point to a similar set of conflicting interests, expressed in the language of superhero comics. The book celebrated heterosexual romance, but offered readers an alternative vision of feminine independence and happy singlehood. It showed motherhood and sisterhood as positives, but featured only absent fathers and husbands, and those sparingly. Its features seemed to assume that readers wanted to know about marriage, grooming, and jewelry, but were also interested in women with non-traditional accomplishments. The magazine no longer offered up Marston's explicit critique of patriarchy, nor did it offer a systemic feminist critique of American society in the vein of Betty Friedan. Yet Marston's original vision of a strong Amazon warrior remained central to the comic, provided readers with a limited, but real, alternative to Cold War domesticity. One could be a loyal, even heroic, American woman while rejecting domestic life. The "Amazon Mystique" was no call to revolution, but it did offer a space of resistance for those who wanted — or needed — to find it.

WORKS CITED

Binder, Otto [w], and Al Plastino [a]. "The Supergirl from Krypton!" *Action Comics* #252 (June 1959). *Showcase Presents Supergirl* vol. 1. Ed. Bob Harras and Bob Joy. New York: DC Comics, 2007. Print.

Binder, Otto (w) and Kurt Schaffenberger (a). "Three Nights in the Fortress of Solitude!" *Superman's Girl Friend, Lois Lane* #14 (January 1960). *Showcase Presents Superman Family* vol. 3. Ed. Sean Mackiewicz. New York: DC Comics, 2009. Print.

Brooker, Will. *Batman Unmasked: Analyzing a Cultural Icon.* New York and London: Continuum, 2001. Print.

Coleman, Jerry (w), Wayne Boring (p), and Stan Kay (i). "The Amazing Superman Junior," *Superman's Girl Friend Lois Lane* #6 (January 1959). *Showcase Presents Superman Family* vol. 2. Ed. Bob Joy. New York: DC Comics, 2008. Print.

Daniels, Les. *Wonder Woman: The Complete History.* San Francisco: Chronicle, 2000. Print.

Dorfman, Leo (w), and Kurt Schaffenberger (a). "The Bombshell of the Boulevards," *Superman's*

Girl Friend, Lois Lane #1 (March-April 1958). *Showcase Presents Superman Family* vol. 2. Ed. Bob Joy. New York: DC Comics, 2008. Print.

"Facts on Furs." *Wonder Woman* #64 (February 1954), National Comics Publications [DC Comics]. Print.

"The Fighting Queen." *Wonder Woman* #108 (August 1959), National Comics Publications [DC Comics]. Print.

[Finger, Bill (w), Chic Stone (p), and Charles Paris (i)]. "Bat Girl—Batwoman II!" *Batman* #163 (May 1964). Print.

"The Girls in Navy Blue." *Wonder Woman* #71 (January 1955), National Comics Publications [DC Comics]. Print.

Haney, Bob (w), and Nick Cardy (a). "The Astounding Separated Man!" *Brave and the Bold* vol. 1 #60 (July 1965). Print.

Horowitz, Daniel. *Betty Friedan and the Making of the Feminine Mystique.* Amherst: University of Massachusetts Press, 1998. Print.

"It's a Woman's World." *Wonder Woman* #96 (February 1958), National Comics Publications [DC Comics]. Print.

[Kanigher, Robert (w), and Harry G. Peter (a)]. "Daily Danger." *Wonder Woman* #96 (February 1958) National Comics Publications [DC Comics]. Print.

_____. "The Missing Wonder Woman." *Wonder Woman* #66 (May 1954), National Comics Publications [DC Comics]. Print.

_____. "The Vanishing Criminal." *Wonder Woman* #81 (April 1956) National Comics Publications [DC Comics]. Print.

_____. "Wonder Woman's Wedding Day." *Wonder Woman* #70 (November 1954), National Comics Publications [DC Comics]. Print.

Kanigher, Robert (w), Ross Andru (p), and Mike Esposito (i). "Captives of the Mirage World!" *Wonder Woman* #142 (November 1963). *Showcase Presents Wonder Woman* vol. 3. Ed. Peter Sean Mackiewicz. New York: DC Comics, 2009. Print.

_____. "The Human Lightning!" *Wonder Woman* #140 (August 1963). *Showcase Presents Wonder Woman* vol. 3. Ed. Peter Sean Mackiewicz. New York: DC Comics, 2009. Print.

_____. "The Kite of Doom!" *Wonder Woman* #138 (May 1963). *Showcase Presents Wonder Woman* vol. 3. Ed. Peter Sean Mackiewicz. New York: DC Comics, 2009. Print.

_____. "The Last Day of the Amazons!" *Wonder Woman* #149 (October 1964). *Showcase Presents Wonder Woman* vol. 3. Ed. Peter Sean Mackiewicz. New York: DC Comics, 2009. Print.

_____. "Mer-Boy vs. Bird-Boy!" *Wonder Woman* #144 (February 1964). *Showcase Presents Wonder Woman* vol. 3. Ed. Peter Sean Mackiewicz. New York: DC Comics, 2009: 178–187. Print.

_____. "Mer Boy's Undersea Party." *Wonder Woman* #115 (July 1960). *Showcase Presents Wonder Woman* vol. 1. Ed. Peter Hamboussi. New York: DC Comics, 2007: 463–475. Print.

_____. "The Million Dollar Penny." *Wonder Woman* #98 (May 1958). *Showcase Presents Wonder Woman* vol. 1 Ed. Peter Hamboussi. New York: DC Comics, 2007: 10–11. Print.

_____. "The Mirage Mirrors!" *Wonder Woman* #130 (May 1962). *Showcase Presents Wonder Woman* vol. 2. Ed. Peter Hamboussi and Sean Mackiewicz. New York: DC Comics 2008. Print.

_____. "The Phantom Sea Beast!" *Wonder Woman* #145 (April 1964). *Showcase Presents Wonder Woman* vol. 3. Ed. Peter Sean Mackiewicz. New York: DC Comics, 2009. Print.

_____. "The Robot Wonder Woman!" *Wonder Woman* #111 (January 1960). *Showcase Presents Wonder Woman* vol. 1. Ed. Peter Hamboussi, New York: DC Comics, 2007: Print.

_____. "Secret Origin of Wonder Woman." *Wonder Woman* #105 (May 1959). *Showcase Presents Wonder Woman* vol. 1. Ed. Peter Hamboussi. New York: DC Comics, 2007: 194–195. Print.

_____. "The Three Faces of Wonder Woman." *Wonder Woman* #102 (November 1958). *Showcase Presents Wonder Woman* vol. 1. Ed. Peter Hamboussi. New York: DC Comics, 2007: 137. Print.

_____. "Undersea Trap!" *Wonder Woman* #101 (October 1958). *Showcase Presents Wonder Woman* vol. 1. Ed. Peter Hamboussi. New York: DC Comics, 2007. Print.

_____. "The Unmasking of Wonder Woman." *Wonder Woman* #126 (November 1961). *Showcase*

Presents Wonder Woman vol. 2. Ed. Peter Hamboussi and Sean Mackiewicz. New York: DC Comics 2008). Print.

_____. "Wonder Girl's Mysterious Father!" *Wonder Woman* #152 (February 1965). *Showcase Presents Wonder Woman* vol. 3. Ed. Peter Sean Mackiewicz. New York: DC Comics, 2009. Print.

_____. "Wonder Queen Vs. Hercules." *Wonder Woman* #132 (August 1962). *Showcase Presents Wonder Woman* vol. 1. Ed. Peter Hamboussi. New York: DC Comics, 2007: 392–397. Print.

_____. "Wonder Woman's Impossible Decision!" *Wonder Woman* #118 (November 1960). *Showcase Presents Wonder Woman* vol. 2. Ed. Peter Hamboussi and Sean Mackiewicz. New York: DC Comics 2008: 7–31. Print.

_____. "Wonder Woman's Surprise Honeymoon!" *Wonder Woman* #127 (February 1962). *Showcase Presents Wonder Woman* vol. 2. Ed. Peter Hamboussi and Sean Mackiewicz. New York: DC Comics 2008). Print.

"Marriage a la Mode!" *Wonder Woman* #108 (August 1959). Print.

[Marston, William Moulton (w), and Harry G. Peter (a)]. "The God of War," *Wonder Woman Archives* vol. 2. New York: DC Comics, 2001. Print.

Meyerowitz, Joanne. "Beyond the Feminine Mystique: A Reassessment of Popular Mass Culture, 1946–1958." *Not June Cleaver: Women and Gender in Postwar America, 1945–1960.* Ed. Joanne Meyerowitz. Philadelphia: Temple University Press, 1994. Print.

Miller, Laura. "Family Togetherness and the Suburban Ideal." *Sociological Forum* vol. 10, no. 3 (1995): 393–418. Print.

"Samson in Skirts." *Wonder Woman* #101 (October 1958), National Comics Publications [DC Comics]. Print.

Siegel, Jerry [w], and Jim Mooney [a]. "Supergirl's Secret Enemy!" *Action Comics* #279 (August 1961). *Showcase Presents Supergirl* vol 1. Ed. Bob Harras and Bob Joy. New York: DC Comics, 2007). Print.

Walker, Nancy. *Shaping Our Mother's World: American Women's Magazines.* Jackson: University Press of Mississippi, 2000. Print.

Wertham, Frederic. *Seduction of the Innocent.* New York: Rinehart, 1954. Print.

"Women in Sports." *Wonder Woman* #77 (October 1955), National Comics Publications [DC Comics]. Print.

"Women of Distinction." *Wonder Woman* #81 (April 1956), National Comics Publications [DC Comics]. Print.

"Women of Distinction." *Wonder Woman* #126 (November 1961), National Comics Publications [DC Comics]. Print.

"Women Warriors." *Wonder Woman* #78 (November 1955), National Comics Publications [DC Comics]. Print.

"The Women Who Won the West." *Wonder Woman* #110 (November 1959), National Comics Publications [DC Comics]. Print.

10

The Girls in White: Nurse Images in Early Cold War Era Romance and War Comics[1]

Christopher J. Hayton and Sheila Hayton

The nursing profession has long paid heed to its public image because the way the public perceives nurses is linked to recruitment levels, workforce retention, pay, working conditions, and quality of care (Fletcher 207–8). Media portrayals of nurses in film, television shows, novels, recruitment literature, but not comic books, have been studied extensively, and a history of particular stereotypes documented (Fletcher 208). Comic books, often written with heavy reliance on ideas culled from other media, act as windows into the mindset of society at the time of their publication (Hayton). Because comics tend to distill popular stereotypes for ease of communication with the reader, those within genres that purport to reflect real life especially can offer insight into prevailing public images and attitudes.

Classification of Nurse Media Stereotypes

Nursing pioneered first wave feminism in the nineteenth century, becoming the principle "acceptable" career for women outside the home (Hallum 14). By the early twentieth century the relationship between nursing and medicine had evolved into something resembling an allegory of Victorian middle class family life. The male doctor oversaw the patient's treatment, with most care provided by the female nurse. Likewise a Victorian father might dictate details of his son's upbringing, which was then largely carried out by his wife

(Hallum 93). Female-gendered nursing accepted a subordinate position relative to the male-gendered, scientific, rational medical profession, in exchange for limited autonomy (Hallum 20). During the early Cold War period stereotypical images that developed in nursing are related to the way women were viewed generally within what remained a male-dominated society (Fletcher 210).

While other systems exist, Jacqueline Bridges' simple four-category classification of the main images of nursing offers a useful framework for examination of nurse portrayals in comics. Bridges' four principal media images of nurses are:

1. The "ministering angel" is an idealized image of a good, young woman selflessly sacrificing time and energy to assist others. Rooted in the provision of care by nuns, the nurse uniform (from the nun's habit) and the term "sister" reflect this history. Angelic qualities include many characteristics attributed to motherhood. Public perceptions of early icons in nursing contributed to this noble, respectful image, which peaked in the first half of the twentieth century, but persisted through the early Cold War period (851). The nursing profession has sought to supplant the angelic image with one that reflects the educated professional (Gordon and Nelson 69).
2. The "battle-axe" is the woman who foregoes love, marriage, and motherhood for career advancement. Older, authoritarian, she wields considerable power, which is often undermined in the media by making her the object of ridicule (Bridges 851–2).
3. The "doctor's handmaiden" is a result of nursing and medicine being strongly gendered professions. It is also a result of the role developed for early nurses by Florence Nightingale. According to Bridges this is the media image that most closely reflects reality (851). The handmaiden is a version of the self-sacrificing angel in which the doctor instead of the patient is the object of devotion (Hallum 147).
4. The "naughty" or "sexy nurse" implies that young women in the nursing profession are available for exploitation by male patients and medical staff, in this image the nurse uniform becomes an accessory for titillation (Bridges 851). Although Kalisch and Kalisch assert that this was a relatively new image emerging in the 1960s and 1970s (270), it was certainly present in comic book Good Girl Art (GGA) with Marvel's *Nellie the Nurse* in the 1940s and 1950s. Its origin in comics also harkens back to pulp magazine covers of the 1930s and 1940s, which occasionally featured nurses.

Depictions of nurses in 1930s and '40s American comics tended to portray them as independent, adventurous, and, particularly, heroic women. Syndicated newspaper strip *Myra North, Special Nurse* appears genre-founding in this respect, with Myra's nursing activities eclipsed by international espionage (Coll and Thompson 2). Dell republished Myra's adventures in early comic book form in the late 1930s, while new wartime nurse heroes in the Myra tradition emerged in the 1940s. *Wings Comics*, published by Fiction House, featured *Jane Martin, War Nurse*, whose exploits followed Myra's pattern of departure from provision of care. As this series progressed Jane became embroiled in conflicts and secret agency. Pat Parker, a nurse in the "Girl Commandos" published in *Speed Comics* by Harvey, experienced a similar career (Vaughan).

The image of the heroic nurse evolved fictionally from the concept of the self-sacrificing angel conjured up by real life battlefield nurses such as Florence Nightingale, Clara Barton, and Edith Cavell. In keeping with the reverential view of nurses reflected in World War I nursing recruitment posters, and the importance and esteem associated with the role of women willing to place themselves in danger to assist in wartime, nurses were portrayed respectfully in these heroic tales. Nurses were, however, stereotypically women. Alongside the heroic nurse in the early 1940s the seed of the naughty nurse image took root in Marvel's *Nellie the Nurse*. The battle-axe senior nurse was present as a supporting character, Miss Witherspoon, in the Nellie stories. By the beginning of the early Cold War era, then, the heroic nurse (a version of the self-sacrificing angel), and the naughty or sexy nurse, were the two images of nursing predominating in comics, with the battle-axe sometimes present.

Love and War, 1946—1962

As the Cold War Era progressed, new genres of comics took birth in the industry's constant search for readership and sales (Wright 133). Nurse characters would find a home in several of them. Romance comics were pioneered by Joe Simon and Jack Kirby, their *Young Romance #1* of 1947 being considered the first true romance comic, although precursors and even rival claimants exist, such as Magazine Enterprise's *Romantic Picture Novelettes #1* of 1946 (Nolan 29). War comics substituted soldier heroes for doctors, and had wounded soldiers or civilians as patients. The nurse-war connection echoed the origins of the profession, and the self-sacrificing or ministering angel script, extended to accommodate the heroic nurse, survived in comics through the 1950s and beyond.

Comics featuring nurses were often a blend of both romance and war genres. In war contexts nurses usually remained heroic. However, in romance comics from the late 1940s and through the 1950s, nurses were frequently portrayed as romance-seeking husband hunters, on the lookout for a doctor or a handsome, wealthy patient as a potential mate. Professionally these nurses fell largely into Bridges' category of the doctor's handmaiden: pretty, white, subservient accessories to the male medical practitioner (852). With medical romance novels and television dramas gaining momentum throughout the 1950s and into the early 1960s (Kalisch and Kalisch 265–6), early Cold War era depictions of nurses in comics followed suit, with the flowering of the medical romance genre beginning in 1961 with Charlton's *Teen Secret Diary* #11 featuring Nurse Betsy Crane. Medical romance comics tended to present nurses in the doctor's handmaiden role, love-smitten young women playing a supportive role to a medical man. If not protagonists in the story, they were background to the activities of the doctor, as in EC's 1955 series *MD*, which was not a romance series. If they were older women, then they usually conform to some version of the authoritarian battle-axe spinster.

The Image of Nurses in Early Cold War Era Comics

The basic nurse image during this period is the young, pretty, white, feminine, heterosexual female. She is professional in appearance, wearing her smart nurse uniform and working in a hospital setting, helping a doctor in whom she is likely to have a romantic interest. In contrast to the incidence of red hair in the general population, she is nearly as likely to be a redhead as she is dark-haired, a brunette, or a blonde, suggesting a stereotype, perhaps associated with Irish women historically joining the ranks of the profession. Charlton's Cynthia Doyle is a classic example in this respect. By grouping elements identified during the reading of the comics studied, more detailed images emerge, including versions of the Bridges categories.

Nurses are commonly portrayed as self-sacrificing angels during this era. They are frequently shown as admirable and indeed admired and appreciated by the public in the comics studied, and worthy of that public confidence. Often shown as public servants, their self-sacrificing nature is likely to surface in emergency situations where they place others' well-being above their own safety. Perhaps the most striking example of this comes from a true story of a heroic nurse making the ultimate sacrifice in *New Heroic Comics* #44 published by Famous Funnies in September 1947 (Toth). The two-page short describes the night of Nurse Esther McElveen's death after she saved numerous patients from a fire that consumed the hospital. Nurse McElveen is shown as young and beautiful, professionally attired in her neat, starched, white uniform, and brave to the point of being willing to sacrifice her own life to save those of her patients.

Romance and war genre hybrids with nurse protagonists typically promote heroic versions of the ministering angel image. The Korean War afforded opportunities to explore difficulties faced by young lovers when one or both were taking part in the conflict. A fine example featuring nurses is found in *Young Romance* #78, the Aug.-Sept. 1955 issue of the Prize series, in a retrospective Korean War story "Army Nurse." Set in a Mobile Army Surgical Hos-

10. The Girls in White (Hayton and Hayton) 133

The self-sacrificing angel. From [Alex Toth (a)], "Nurse Without Fear," *New Heroic Comics #44* (September 1947). Famous Funnies. Print.

pital (M.A.S.H.) unit, the complex romance between Lieutenant Joyce Reed and Captain Roy Nelson unfolds, reaching a climax when Doctor Roy's chopper goes down and Joyce flies to his rescue, only to find him lying wounded and in the arms of her apparent rival. The important detail here with regard to the image of nurses is that, while men were drafted into the army, or could avoid the draft by volunteering in a medical capacity, women were not obliged to place themselves in danger. Nevertheless, many women did become nurses with the armed forces, sacrificing their own safety to help the fighting men.

Joyce's confession on the first page of the story provides the background necessary for interpretation of her reaction as she lands in the war zone: "Privately we nurses called Captain Nelson "Doctor Roy," and there was keen

Angels on the battlefield. From [Jo Albistur (p)], "War Nurse," *Young Romance #78* (August-September 1955). Prize Comics. Print.

competition to assist him with operations. Those of us that weren't in love with him at least admired his surgical skill. I both loved and admired him" (Albistur).

War zone romances inevitably have an element of suppressed feelings, however, because of the realistic need to remain focused on the conflict and its consequences. In "Army Nurse" two nurses, while brave and self-sacrificing, have an on-going romantic interest in, in this case, a doctor and a soldier, that persists despite the urgency of events. In the *Young Romance* image we see these self-sacrificing angels in blue army nurse uniforms descend on a Korean battlefield as injured personnel, including their lovers, are rescued.

DC featured army nurses several times in the late 1950s and early 1960s in its flagship war title *Our Army at War*. The cover story of issue #78 (January 1959) is titled "Battle Nurse" and features the romance of Stan and Jennie. Set in World War II, the tale involves Jennie's persistence in following her soldier boyfriend to Europe and then the Pacific by becoming an army nurse

10. The Girls in White (Hayton and Hayton)

The nurse in harm's way. From [Robert Kanigher (w), Ross Andru (p), and Mike Esposito (i)], "Battle Nurse." *Our Army at War #78* (January 1959). National Comics Publications [DC Comics]. Print.

(Kanigher, Andru, and Esposito). The cover and some of the story panels show perfectly the transformation of the doctor-nurse-patient relationship of the hospital or practice, discussed above, into the soldier-nurse-wounded soldier scenario applicable to the battlefield. In this issue Nurse Jennie shields a wounded soldier with her own body, while her man defends them against a fighter plane.

Several times DC's Sgt. Rock in *Our Army at War* found himself interacting with nurses in the European Theater of Operations. Characters like Rock, or later, Marvel's Sgt. Fury, were billed as tough, hard men, but occasionally their soft side would be revealed thanks to a nurse. Army nurses are usually portrayed as officers, and outrank the soldiers they find themselves treating. After a harrowing episode in "A New Kind of War" a nurse refuses to abandon a wounded Sgt. Rock when the Allied forces have to retreat. As Rock regains consciousness and sees the nurse looking down at him, he thinks he's looking at a pin-up. Her determination to protect her patient, demonstrated by her readiness to sacrifice her own life to save his, puts her in a different category. Rock is irritated that he can't rid himself of this superior and get on with the fight unencumbered, but at the same time his admiration for the nurse grows as they work together to thwart the enemy. The powerful attraction that is obviously there between the two, but which has to remain subdued, is allowed a brief moment of expression at the end of the story, causing Rock to have to 'eat' his earlier words when he had claimed that war and women don't mix. Pulling rank on Rock and flinging her arms around him, she says, "Stop squirming like a schoolboy when you're kissed for being a hero, Sergeant! That's an order!" (Kanigher and Kubert).

There's no doubt in early Cold War era comics that women were better suited to nursing than men. All the nurses depicted in the comics studied were female, and these women display multiple motherly qualities that add to their angelic stature. Only in Dell's *Linda Lark Student Nurse #1* (Oct.–Dec. 1961) was mention found of male nurses. In a single page text ad for nursing it states: "Though men also enter nursing, it is still primarily a woman's profession, and getting to the top is a great deal less difficult than in other professions where women are in the minority" ("Why Not").

In Cold War era comics nurses are comforting, compassionate, tender individuals whose mere interactions with the patient may demonstrate a therapeutic effect, especially if romantic inclinations on the part of either the nurse or both parties exist. They are usually dedicated to their work and have high moral values (there are exceptions), being respectable and taking seriously their role in putting the patient's well-being before their own. They are reliable, responsible, noble, and if given the opportunity to express it, patriotic individuals. They are often pure and innocent women, whose natural nursing propensities manifest when emergency situations arise, wherever they might be. They are often public-spirited individuals, and clearly public servants. Their self-sacrificing nature may even extend to fiscal generosity, and they are always ready to give their time and energy to those in need. While it contains elements of female subservience that the Women's Movement encouraged the removal of, in the context of the times this is a very positive image of nurses.

However, battle-axes often lurked in the background of nurse romance stories and other comics featuring nurses in the early Cold War period. They are usually career women whose sacrifice of love and marriage for the sake of nursing is indicated indirectly by others referring to them as "Miss." Because of the prevailing societal norms of the time, it can be inferred that they never married or had children. Their dedication to career has allowed them to achieve a senior position, usually in a hospital overseeing younger nurses. They may display military efficiency in their administrative role. While some are kind and matronly, others display the stereotypical battle-axe temperament, being punitive towards non-compliant younger nurses. As was the normal practice during the time in question, young nurses lived in hospital accommodation and the matron enforced rules such as curfews and refraining from romantic involvement with medical interns.

As most of the comics examined were of the romance genre, stories with nurses often involved secret liaisons between a student or young nurse and a young intern or a qualified doctor. Perhaps the archetype of this story line is demonstrated by "My Secret Marriage" in the June 1952 *Harvey Comics Hits #58*. This issue of the series was a compilation reprint of four romance stories featuring nurses, and was aptly titled "Private Lives and Loves of Girls in

White." In "My Secret Marriage" a student nurse living in a dormitory has to engage in clandestine meetings with her male friend; such fraternization is against the strict codes of conduct. The battle-axe in this story, whose job includes making sure the girls behave themselves, is atypically a married woman, but the name provided for her, Mrs. Frieze, captures the frosty nature of her interactions with her young charges. The young couple is inevitably found out, but the matron, who has sternly warned the young nurse about her behavior, ends up being very supportive. Typically, though, the battle-axe is a grumpy, gray-haired, bespectacled, older woman, who may be skinny or overweight but rarely of medium build. She is also most likely to be plain-looking or even ugly. While the young nurse represents temporary female independence and self-sufficiency, the battle-axe serves as a reminder of what she will become if she doesn't use the opportunity to find a suitable male provider.

The doctor's handmaiden is overwhelmingly the image of nurses presented in early Cold War Era comics. Nurses are doctor's helpers, less important than and subordinate to the usually male medical practitioner. Obedient executors of the doctor's orders, their place is most frequently at the patient's bedside. Presented as support workers, particularly in hospital contexts, such as in an operating theater, nurses are low-ranking participants. In "Prescription for a Broken Heart" from *Boy Meets Girl* #12 published by Lev Gleason in June 1951, for example, the nurse is comfortable following the doctor's orders. She is depicted as a competent team player in a drama-laden clinical setting, unhesitatingly entrusted with the anesthesia when in this case the leading surgeon has to leave the operating theater, finding himself unable to continue.

In romance comics of the period, nurses are frequently very supportive of a doctor, who may be experiencing some personal crisis or difficulty. The cover of Charlton Comics' August 1962 *Sweetheart Diary* #65, which introduces "Cynthia Doyle, Nurse in Love," exemplifies the handmaiden image, in this case with the love-struck Cynthia unrequited (Nicholas and Alascia). The cover depicts Doctor Ed Benson paradoxically smoking (not unusual for the time), while red-headed nurse Cynthia lovingly pours him a cup of coffee, having assisted him as his handmaiden all night.

Good Girls, Sex, and Deviance in Nurse Comics

The sexy or naughty nurse is an image the profession has sought to divest itself of. In modern times, despite the abandonment of the uniform in favor of gender- and even occupation-neutral scrubs, it remains, however, a persistent media concept. The nature of nursing care, in which the nurse has to sometimes access the patient's body in ways that are normally reserved for intimate relationships, appears partly responsible for its origins. It might also be considered natural for male mid-twentieth century soldiers, deprived of female companionship when in combat, to experience attraction for the nurses caring for them when they were wounded. It may be no coincidence, then, that in the age of the pin-up sweetheart of World War II, a sexy nurse by the name of Nellie should take the stage in mainstream printed popular media. As with the battle-axe, the sexy nurse may also be a means of power reversal, the interpretation being that the nurse is signaling her availability or vulnerability to the male patient, who can overturn the temporarily inferior position brought upon him due to illness or injury, and provide what the woman "wants" or "needs" (Bridges 852). Studies have linked this image to sexual harassment (Madison and Minichiello).

Beginning in 1942, Nellie started out as a sensible, young, pretty nurse serious about her profession but embroiled in mildly humorous situations. Nellie and Marvel's other career-girl humor comics (*Millie the Model, Tessie the Typist, Hedy DeVine*) became associated stylistically with the emerging Good Girl Art (GGA) trend. The border of Nellie's frilly petticoat would be ruffled by a slight breeze. Her uniform became tighter and figure-hugging, revealing an exaggeratedly shapely hourglass form. Nellie's naiveté and innocent sexuality became a source of visual exploitation for the male characters in the stories as well as, presumably, males amongst the book's readership. As a typical example, a one page Nellie short from the April 1952 *Nellie the Nurse #33*, drawn by Howie Post, illustrates an oft-repeated Stan Lee gag. Doctor Dingbat exploits the visually stimulating form of Nellie to determine a male patient's readiness for discharge from hospital. The male patient's predatory behavior is not only given acceptance and reinforcement as a norm but is also held up as a sign of his good health (Lee and Post).

Some nurses in romance comics appear sexy, to the extent that females generally in comic books of the period might assume idealized proportions and be clothed in shape-revealing attire. Apparently a norm for the period, nurses might be subject to what would nowadays be considered sexual harassment, from doctors, patients, and the general public. In "My Hospital Romance," from Harvey's *First Love Illustrated #6*, published in December 1949 and reprinted in *Harvey Comics Hits #58*, a doctor's inappropriate remarks are tolerated by a young nurse. Upon seeing her from behind, as she scrubs the floor while down on her hands and knees, he remarks, "Imagine *that* in a bathing suit!" His language thus objectifies her, and he proceeds to pursue her aggressively. The nurse's narration, however, indicates that she is excited by his unprovoked advances, and clearly this is the intent of the doctor. This kind of interaction appears to have been both normal and more-or-less

10. The Girls in White (Hayton and Hayton) 139

The sexy nurse. From [Stan Lee (w), and Howie Post (p)], *Nellie the Nurse #33* (April 1952). Atlas. Print.

acceptable in 1949, although another doctor witnessing the event does try to dissuade the first from harassing the probationary nurse. Also of note here are activities apparently typical of late 1940s nursing — scrubbing floors, preparing and serving meals, and conducting other menial tasks at the bedside, such as temperature-taking.

The sexy nurse image in comic books has clear precursors in sleazy pulp magazine bondage and damsel in distress covers that predate or are contemporary with the GGA trend. The Pulp Gallery holds examples that illustrate this point. The September 1940 issue of *Detective Tales* features a shapely, buxom, brunette nurse in a tight uniform, bound with ropes upside down by an insane doctor, being rescued by a heroic, manly detective. The December 1942 issue of *Spicy Adventure Stories* depicts a blonde nurse paddling furiously at sea in a dingy, with a torpedoed Red Cross ship sinking in the background. Her uniform is in shreds, revealing her ample breasts clad in a delicate pink brassiere, and her suspenders straining to hold on to the tops of her stockings. The culprits on the deck of a surfaced Nazi U-Boat are closing in with a long gaff, while the story title "Commando" suggests a rescuer not depicted, with the inevitable consequences left for the reader to deduce. These two pulp covers are typical of the way women generally were portrayed in such publications, and lack the specific emphasis on the nurse uniform as a sexual accessory that plagues post–Cold War media imagery of nurses. Nevertheless, from an evolutionary standpoint, the pulps and then comics exhibit examples that predate the previously presumed origin of the sexy nurse image.

Romance figures prominently in the stories featuring nurse protagonists, because of the genre to which the comics belong and the target readership (clearly evidenced by the ads in the books). In many of these stories nursing is inferred as a path to matrimony, and while most nurse characters have inclinations towards caring and dedication to work, there is inevitably some romantic interaction with a male patient or doctor, sometimes with another nurse or a female patient as a rival. Some nurses were stereotypically motivated by desires to find doctors or wealthy patients to marry. Vulnerable, liable to fall in love at any moment, their matrimonial exit from the profession was virtually inevitable. In order to achieve their romantic aims, some nurses are shown as manipulative and scheming. The implication of this image is that nursing is simply a bridge between school and marriage, and that nurses are ultimately self-serving rather than self-sacrificing, again undermining the more positive images of the profession.

While many positive impressions of nursing present themselves in comics, as "My Hospital Romance" cited above demonstrates, nursing can also be portrayed in unattractive terms. Besides having to do dirty work, nurses are often shown working long hours, having to tolerate bad working conditions, performing tasks that are physically demanding, and being overworked, suggesting that nursing is a low status occupation. In "No Remedy for Love" from *Great Lover Romances #13* published October 1954 by Toby Press, menial tasks encourage doubts about her career choice for a student nurse. The realities of the nursing job conflict with a young nurse's expectations. In addition to the menial work, an amorous intern makes his appearance and begins to flirt, but it is the student nurse who is scolded by the hospital battle-axe who has unexpectedly stopped by.

Most early Cold War era stories still describe nursing in more positive and even very positive terms. There are comic book nurses who find their work very rewarding, or communicate that nurses are in demand. Many stories are content-congruent with the very revealing message of this text from a nursing ad at the back of *Harvey Comics Hits* #58 from the Korean War period:

> You can be the most important young woman in the country today — a Student Nurse. On the skill you acquire now a whole community may one day depend — or the life of a soldier. Now that more and more graduate nurses are needed for our armed services, this year's high school and college graduates must prepare to fill their places at home. As a graduate nurse you can have the most satisfying career of service open to women ... in the armed services, your local hospital or industry. Later, as a wife and mother, your education will prove invaluable. Ask the Director of Nurses at your local hospital for further information, or apply to a collegiate or hospital School of Nursing.

In the 115 comics examined in this study, a variety of nursing careers were illustrated, although the hospital nurse was by far the most common. There were army, industrial, and community nurses. Some nurses engaged in research, although still assisting a doctor. Some were private nurses, while others worked for a doctor in private practice. There were dental and school nurses, and those who became administrators. Nurses were working in a variety of situations, and there was also the implication that nursing provided opportunities to travel and work in other places.

For the sake of plot-lines, nurses are sometimes shown engaged in unethical conduct. Prior to the introduction of the Comics Code in 1955, examples include stealing and taking drugs or blackmail. In "Dread Past" from Comic Media's *All True Romance* #14 (November 1953), a nurse is persuaded by her boyfriend to take narcotics from the hospital. The relatively low level of hospital security (by modern standards) makes stealing morphine easy for the nurse, who is rewarded with participation in drug parties. Coaxed into partaking of the stolen morphine, and into smoking marijuana available at the boyfriend's "tea parties," the nurse becomes a "wild-eyed, frenzied dope addict." In this same story the nurse and her drug user companions are arrested by the police. Upon completion of her sentence she moves away to start a

Nurse gone wild. From "Dread Past," *All True Romance #14* (November 1953). Comic Media. Print.

new life, and falls in love with a doctor. Marriage is on the horizon, until out of the blue her ex-boyfriend is brought into the hospital with severe injuries, and she ends up being his anesthetist. Knowing that he will reveal her sordid past and ruin her chance for happiness, she contemplates giving him an overdose of anesthetic! As she's hesitating, the patient dies (from internal bleeding), and she flees, thinking herself a murderer. In true romance comic fashion, the doctor goes after her and she ends up telling him her whole story, which leaves him unflinching in his love and resolve to marry her, and they live happily ever after.

In one of the two crime comics in the study, *Crime Does Not Pay* #132 published by Lev Gleason (March 1954), the cover (which appears to have been the inspiration for Marvel's much later *Night Nurse #3*), shows a nurse with a gun defending her underworld patient from a rival mobster! The nurse story inside, "A Fat Tip for Murder," not unusually has nothing to do with the cover depiction. Instead, a doctor murders a patient to get at his money, and the nurse deduces what has transpired and tries to blackmail the doctor. Not realizing the danger she's put herself in, she ends up dead as well. The doctor then disfigures her face and smuggles her body into the hospital cold room where cadavers are stored. Justice is done when the doctor ends up with "a date with the electric chair."

Such stories are the exception rather than the rule, and extreme misconduct disappears in connection with nurses following introduction of the Code. What does continue is the bitchiness and bickering between nurses, and the unethical or unprofessional romantic behavior between nurses and either patients or doctors. While kissing a patient when on duty is unprofessional and even unethical, in the context of the romance story it becomes excusable for the reader. A nurse may even go against doctor's orders in the interests of the patient, if she perceives that he has failed to see the real problem. Other less flattering images show nurses as dumb, incompetent, neurotic, or mean. The less desirable images tend to appear in the humorous adventures of Nellie the Nurse, in which the situation and characters are stripped down to the simplest form, their traits then exaggerated to provide the ingredients of comedy. Thus Nellie's rival Pam is envious to the point of insanity in terms of the schemes she dreams up to subvert the former's relationship with the heart throb intern. Nellie and most of the nurses become little more than mobile enlarged secondary sexual characteristics by the time Howie Post takes over the art in the early 1950s, displaying less intelligence as this evolution transpires.

Summary

Nurses featured regularly in American romance comics of the early Cold War era, during which they remained prominent examples of women with career aspirations. In these comics nurses displayed stereotypical female characteristics as well as those associated with their profession. While in many ways they embodied the independence sought by some American females, early Cold War comic portrayals of nurses support the re-domestication of women post–World War II, and restoration of male chauvinism. Positive images were counteracted with subversive devices that re-established the female as inferior and dependent, reflecting mechanisms of power reversal that undermine the independence of the working woman exemplified by the nurse. Overall, however, in the context of the times, the comic book images of nurses are positive and congruent with the messages being disseminated through contemporary nursing recruitment ads, which often appeared in the same book featuring a nurse romance story. The most prominent image present is that of the doctor's handmaiden, which evolved during the period studied and reached its zenith in parallel with the early 1960s explosion of medical romance in popular media, including comics. The introduction of the Comics Code had little impact on how nurses were depicted as women subordinate to men. In keeping with the Code's influence on morals and values presented in comics, however, depictions of situations in which nurses acted unethically or unprofessionally appeared to diminish.

Notes

1. In order to obtain a broad picture of the image of nurses portrayed in early Cold War Era comics, approximately 700 American romance comics, partly from the authors' collection and partly from the Digital Comic Museum (http://digitalcomicmuseum.com/), were examined for the presence of stories featuring nurses. Additionally, the entire series of DC's *Our Army at War* and *Our Fighting Forces* up to 1962, and EC's *Frontline Combat* and *Two-Fisted Tales* were skimmed for nurse stories. A few comics not of the romance or war genres but known to feature nurse stories were included in this study, especially a selection of *Nellie the Nurse* issues from different phases in the title's evolution. Nurses were featured in 115 of the comics. Due to the rarity and cost of the comics studied, this simply represents a convenience sample of material to which the authors had access.

2. A preliminary list of 98 components describing ways in which nurses have been portrayed in the media was derived from a complete reading of Julia Hallam's book, *Nursing the Image*. To this list were added new descriptors as the comics being studied were reviewed. Covers and/or stories featuring nurses were read and coded. Descriptors for any nursing ads present inside were added, to yield images of nursing presented by the book. In most cases stories studied were unsigned. Most are not indexed in the Grand Comics Database (http://www.comics.org/), therefore authors and artists of several comics referred to in this chapter are unknown.

Works Cited

[Albistur, Jo (p).] "War Nurse." *Young Romance #78* (Aug.-Sept. 1955), Prize Comics. Print.
Bridges, J. M. "Literature Review on the Images of the Nurse and Nursing in the Media." *Journal of Advanced Nursing* 15 (1990): 850–854. Print.
Coll, Charles, and Ray Thompson. *The Strange Adventures of Myra North, Special Nurse*. Greenfield, WI: Arcadia, 1987. Print.
"Dread Past." *All True Romance #14* (November 1953), Comic Media. Print.
"A Fat Tip for Murder." *Crime Does Not Pay #132* (March 1954), Lev Gleason Publications. Web [Digital Comic Museum].
Fletcher, Karen. "Image: Changing How Women Nurses Think About Themselves. Literature Review." *Journal of Advanced Nursing* 58 (2007): 207–215. Print.
Gordon, Suzanne, and Sioban Nelson. "An End to Angels: Moving Away from the 'Virtue' Script Towards a Knowledge-Based Identity for Nurses." *American Journal of Nursing* 105.5 (2005): 62–69. Print.

Hallam, Julia. *Nursing the Image: Media, Culture and Professional Identity*. London: Routledge, 2000. Print.
Hayton, Christopher. "Fantastic Giants: Charlton Comics' Monster Movie Adaptations." *SCAN Journal of Media Arts Culture* 6.2 (2009). Web. 28 Jan. 2010.
Kalisch, Philip, and Beatrice Kalisch. "Nurses on Prime-Time Television." *The American Journal of Nursing* 82.2 (1982): 264–270. Print.
[Kanigher, Robert (w), and Joe Kubert (p).] "A New Kind of War." *Our Army at War #104* (March 1961), National Comics Publications [DC Comics]. Print.
[Kanigher, Robert (w), Ross Andru (p), and Mike Esposito (i).] "Battle Nurse." *Our Army at War #78* (January 1959), National Comics Publications [DC Comics]. Print.
[Lee, Stan (w), and Howie Post (p).] Untitled. *Nellie the Nurse #33* (April 1952), Atlas. Print.
Madison, Jeanne, and Victor Minichiello. "The Contextual Issues Associated With Sexual Harassment Experiences Reported by Registered Nurses." *Australian Journal of Advanced Nursing* 22.2 (2005): 8–13. Print.
"My Hospital Romance." *First Love Illustrated #6* (December 1949), Harvey Comics. Print.
"My Secret Marriage." *Harvey Comics Hits #58* (June 1952), Harvey Comics. Print.
[Nicholas, Charles (p), and Vince Alascia (i).] "Cynthia Doyle Nurse in Love." *Sweetheart Diary #65* (August 1962), Charlton Comics: Cover. Print.
Nolan, M. *Love on the Racks: A History of American Romance Comics*. Jefferson, NC: McFarland, 2008. Print.
"Prescription for a Broken Heart." *Boy Meets Girl #12* (June 1951), Lev Gleason Publications.
The Pulp Gallery. 1 May 2008. Web. 17 April 2011.
[Toth, Alex (a).] "Nurse Without Fear." *New Heroic Comics #44* (September 1947), Famous Funnies. Print.
Vaughan, D. "Comic Book Care: A History of Nurses in Comic Books." *NurseWeek*. May 8, 2006. Web. 12 Nov 2010.
"Why Not Choose the NOBLEST Profession?" *Linda Lark Student Nurse* #1 (Oct.-Dec. 1961), Dell. Print.
Wright, Bradford W. *Comic Book Nation: The Transformation of Youth Culture in America*. Baltimore, MD: John Hopkins University Press, 2001. Print.

11

Horror Camp: Homoerotic Subtext in EC Comics

Diana Green

"Comic strips and graphic books have only recently been acknowledged as a serious art form, but in both mainstream and underground culture, they have served for decades as a powerful tool of satire and humor; and in their representation of GLBTQ people, they also serve as a barometer of shifting attitudes toward gay subcultures" [Theophano, "Comics..."].

In that context, re-examining EC Comics seems somewhat facile. The presumption of many would be that gay narratives in these books demean their subjects, if they exist at all. This presumption is based on the mainstream attitudes towards GLBTQ people during the 1950s. Many of these attitudes were born of ignorance and misinformation. As GLBTQ historian Eric Markus notes, "During this era, the general public rarely had a glimpse of the homosexual subculture and nascent gay rights organizations, and then only as a result of police actions"(2).

Same SexStories: Aliens, Deviance, and Homosexuality

Contrary to expectations, several EC stories deal with GLBTQ themes, and if not always in a positive light, with a seditious overtone. Chronologically, the first of these stories is "There'll Be Some Changes Made!" In this story, a damaged ship sets down on an alien planet. Encountering humanoid life, the crew effects repairs and accepts the hospitality of the natives. The captain falls in love with a native woman and elects to remain behind, becoming her mate. Six months later, his spouse cuts her hair. She begins to change physically. Exploring the area designated for giving birth, the captain discovers newborns emerging from shells. He realizes that the humanoids are a hermaphroditic species, like some Earth snails. Returning to his home, he discovers that his mate is now male. Upon seeing the captain, his spouse complains, "Arnold, baby! I wish you'd hurry up and change so things can be normal again!" (Feldstien and Wood).

This story uses the trope of gender confusion as metaphor for same-sex attraction. The notion that a species that changes sex would maintain rigid gender roles ("so things can be normal") is fallacious. Rather than thinking the issue through, it plays off the 1950s notions of gay sexuality equated with gender norms by presuming such a society would maintain a rigid gender binary. Gender roles based in sexuality were rigid during this time. The aberration of the norm was thought of as both laughable and menacing, as evidenced by Milton Berle in drag, mincing " I thweah I'll kiww you." This caricature of femininity, often called hag drag, reinforces the tired cliché of gay men having to role-play the femme to attract a man. However, the truth of same-sex relationship lies outside these roles, sometimes obliterating them, which can be a greater threat to those invested in such roles. As such, this story presages themes stated in Philip José Farmer's *The Lovers*, published the same year, and Theodore Sturgeon's *Venus Plus X*, published in 1960.

The seditious aspect of this story, then, is that it only plays to these clichés by inference. While the reader is arguably meant to infer a homophobic "joke" from a man being tricked into a relationship with another man, no such trick actually occurs. The captain's spouse, Luwanna, is neither a caricature of a male nor one of a female, and operates on his/her honest belief in the captain's sexuality and physiology echoing her own. More to the point, it can be concluded that same-sex relationships are not even human.

A more direct confrontation with gay issues occurs in the 1954 *Crime SuspenStories* tale "Standing Room Only" (Binder). The story beings with a smiling man holding a dress, sneering at a burned down house. The occupants of the house were his twin sister and her husband. He has killed them both and proceeds to take on his sister's identity to inherit her husband's fortune. Following the funeral, the brother dates his late sister's lawyer, but is caught when he inadvertently uses the men's room rather than the ladies.'

This story plays off notions of homoeroticism and gender aberration as fatal, concepts that are both implicit in Berle's menacing drag and that recur more overtly in noir writing and film. Indeed, one of Fritz Lang's final American films, the 1956 "While the City Sleeps," deals with a gender-confused teenage serial killer whose mind is warped by a domineering mother and by reading too many comic books! Along the same lines, a triangle of sorts is created in "Standing Room Only." This triangle is a mathematical anomaly, having two points that are really one: Carl, the brother, who assumes two roles, himself and Cynthia. However, Carl's Cynthia is a corruption of his actual sister. He acts out a misogynist's vision of femininity. Carl as Cynthia is venal, selfish, dishonest, destructive, and amoral, using "her" wiles to any self-serving end. By becoming his sister, he is competing with her and himself for the hand of her husband. In the short term, he wins the competition by becoming the infamous black widow of *film noir*: the woman who mates and then kills. As Gary Sweeny observes in *The Midnight Palace*, "The role of the femme fatale was to obtain, by any means, her darkest desires. She rarely held an ordinary job, but rather worked full-time as a deceptive siren. Sex was her most valuable asset, the prospect of which blindfolded the male conscience while she lured him into an unavoidable web."

It's also worth noting that Carl only comes into power through a drive for money, driven in turn by killing as a rite of passage from the masculine to the feminine. The feminine role he assumes is driven entirely by creature comforts, not by any of the emotions associated with femininity in mainstream consciousness of the 1950s. By dressing his sister Cynthia in his clothes before killing her, ostensibly to fool the authorities, Carl is "killing" himself as a man — a selfish, wasteful person — and assuming his vision of a woman — a caricature motivated by manipulative, venal and consumptive pleasure.

Both "Standing Room Only" and "There'll Be Some Changes Made" deal with unilateral same-sex relationships, and both imply deceit, or at best, misunderstanding. However, the Feldstein and Davis story "Operation Friendship" deals more blatantly in the territory of the noir triangle, albeit with science fiction trappings. Two lifelong friends, Andrew Hobart and Philip (whose last name is never given) enter into a blood brotherhood, which Andrew calls a "mating of mind." When Philip announces that he is engaged, Andrew tries in vain to talk him out of it. "Marriage is for others, not for us, with our wedded minds!" Over Andrew's protests, Philip enters into the marriage. Jealous and frustrated that Philip's wife seems only interested in his "physical attributes," Andrew plans to kill himself. When he is called away for "an emergency lobotomy," Andrew realizes another way. After two years of planning, he has Philip over for a game of chess. After trying in vain to convince Philip to leave his wife, Andrew tells him of his experiments in brain surgery, experiments leading to a successful seventy-five percent lobotomy. Andrew performs the operation on Philip, leaving most of his brain in a tank of liquid, connected to equipment that allows him to see the chessboard, to hear and to speak. Philip's body still lives with his wife, who seems oblivious to the change in him. For twenty years and presumably for the rest of their lives, Philip and Andrew live in secret in their "marriage of minds."

This story has pronounced echoes of the classic *film noir Gilda*. Arguably one of the most blatant gay relationships in noir, the relationship between *Gilda*'s male protagonists revolve around their love for one another and the interference caused by the introduction of a third party. The predominant fear of all sexuality, as is the case in the disembodiment narrative of "Operation Friendship," overrides all other concerns, even the true desires of one of the parties. As Andrew Spicer notes, "even after Mundson's apparent death, he controls Johnny, who marries Gilda so he can imprison and humiliate her for her disloyalty to his friend. The pleasure he takes from this is as perverse as it is masochistic, his own erotic feeling sublimating into a protracted punishment." So it is in "Operation Friendship." Andrew wants Philip to himself intellectually. As Andrew expresses little or no interest in sex of any kind, even turning down a girl in order to go to the movies with Philip. He imposes his standards on Philip by removing him from his body, taking the part he wants, Philip's intellect, for his own pleasure and absolute control. His "marriage of the minds" is unilateral, lacking any level of consent from Philip at the end. Philip's only alternatives are to speak his mind and be silenced or do as his "partner" demands. This can be seen as a reflection on constraints the nuclear family. Philip is assigned a specific role in the relationship, and his survival is contingent on carrying out that role. As reflected in the films of Douglas Sirk, many women in the 1950s felt constrained, if not trapped, by societal conventions around marriage.

"Operation Friendship" is another variation of the noir triangle, bisecting a person into the physical and the intellectual, so each of his loves may have the part they crave. Neither part is a whole person at that point, nor does it matter to the so-called lovers. Everyone has what he or she wants except the loved one.

New Worlds and New Trends

A more sophisticated and less threatening reading of the gay relationship is in Feldstein and Crandall's "Genesis." The story of humanity rendered sterile by radiation from atomic fission and man's subsequent colonization of Mars, "Genesis" offers a revolutionary vision of same-sex love. After discovering Martian rabbits that appear to be sexless, the Terran colonists begin to remake Mars in the image of Earth. The result is violent and destructive. After several decades, scientists realize that all Martian life reproduces by binary fission, like amoebas. Since humanity cannot reproduce by fission, the humans decide to return to Earth, to die on native soil.

The first of the settlers decides to stay, hoarding supplies as his comrades binge and destroy before leaving. Finally, the nameless first settler is left alone, the last man on Mars. He lies down, tears off his clothes, and becomes an amorphous shape. As his form congeals, a hand reaches down and takes his. It is his hand. He has succeeded in asexual reproduction. He and his brother/lover/self stand naked and silent, new Martians.

This story is compelling on several levels. The humans attempting sexual reproduction, presumably straight, are little more than barbarians with advanced technology. While the sexuality of the last Earthman, who is also the first Martian, is never explicitly stated, his revulsion at the destructive nature of his peers and his tender embrace of his new self/brother are implicit gay texts of a different sort. The eschewing of violent behavior and expressions of tenderness between people of the same sex are remarkable for their time. However, the narrative defies simple analysis as a solely gay text. The notion of fission implies a sexless relationship, one that could theoretically spread to create an entire society. However, the genuine affection expressed in the final two panels is the least threatening and most optimistic sentiment in the whole story. That this society can grow on another planet implies that it is sustainable without the interference of a society threatened by another form of reproduction, or another form of sexuality. This is an extension of the idea put forth by Foucault: "Homosexuality appeared as one of the forms of sexuality when it was transposed from the practice of sodomy onto a kind of interior androgyny, a hermaphrodism of the soul. The sodomite had been a temporary aberration; the homosexual was now a species" (43). This reinforces the notion of the Ledom, the artificial third sex in Sturgeon's novel *Venus Plus X*. In this text, the revulsion of the straight protagonist who finds himself stranded in this new societal model (Ledom is model spelled backwards) echoes the notion that heterosexuality, at least as it is commonly understood at this point in American culture, is both inherently violent and deeply suspicious and fearful of anything "other." Once again we have the idea that gay behavior is not human, but here the notion is that such behavior is preferable.

EC also overtly addressed gay issues in its title *Psychoanalysis*. The stories in this "New Trend" title were serialized over its four issues. Each serial was presented as a "case file," and the same nameless psychiatrist treated all four of the cases. The first case was "Case 101: Male: Freddy Carter." The young man in question, 15 years old, is a petty thief whose grades are failing. His worst crime is that he is a "mama's boy," preferring the arts and literature to sports and engineering, his father's profession. His father feared his son is becoming a "sissy," if he was not already at that point.

Over the course of four sessions, the psychiatrist reassured young Freddy that the arts are not inherently effeminate, that he need not steal to replace his relationship with his father with that of his friend, and that his good grades in art and literature are every bit as important as his poor grades in the sciences. The psychiatrist then took Freddy's parents to task for using their son as a weapon in their own power struggle (Feldstein and Kamen).

While the words "homosexual" or "gay" are not used in these stories, and no specific sex acts are described or alluded to, the implications of being a "sissy" in 1955 are clear, and will be discussed in more depth later. As this book was part of EC's "New Trend" line and bore the Comics Code seal, neither approval nor mention of homosexuality would be tolerated. As noted by Theresa Theophano, "The Code, established in the aftermath of United States Senate hearings examining comics as a cause of juvenile delinquency, reflected the era's attitude toward homosexuality and effectively barred the portrayal of overtly gay characters in mainstream comics"("Comics").

The specific provision with the Code falls under the general heading of Marriage and Sex. The specific text, Clause 7, the final clause of this section, simply reads, "sex perversion or any inference to same is strictly forbidden" (Comicartville). No further descriptor was seen as necessary. It seemed reasonable to the public sentiment at the time to paint homosexuals, necrophiliacs, pedophiles and fetishists with the same broad brush and to deny Code approval, and by extension most newsstand sales, to any comic that violated these tenets. In light of that threat, it is remarkable that *Psychoanalysis* offered this faltering step at dealing with issues of sexuality and gender roles, while keeping that valuable seal of Code approval.

The subtext of the narrative in *Psychoanalysis* is twofold. First, the psychiatrist breaks down stereotypes of masculine and feminine behavior and notions of gender-specific thought and emotional patterns. He convinces both Freddy and his parents that intellectual and artistic pursuits are not necessarily the sole province of the "sissy." His specific argument is that "many American men ... fathers ... think that their sons must improve their masculinity by indulging them in sports. It's their own over-reaction to a fear of their own femininity. But there's more to life than the worship of the virile athlete! This is not the cave man era! This is the 20th Century! We've come a long way. We've developed art ... music ... literature ... And you have a leaning toward these artistic pursuits! They're not feminine, Freddy! Your Father has made you ashamed of your talents because he hasn't got them himself!"

So the "rational man" of the 1950s can see past gender stereotypes in this narrative. However, in doing so, there is an indirect reinforcement of homophobia. The parents can relax, not because being an effeminate boy is acceptable, but because their son is not effeminate, not at risk. Within the 31 pages (and one cover) devoted to this story over four issues, the word "sissy" is used to describe Freddy ten times. Other descriptors used in this text include "effeminate drip," "whining, brooding mess," "a lily," "a baby (and later a "sniveling baby")," "a pansy," "a ninny," and finally, "our little lord Byron."

There is a great deal of discussion of whether or not it's fair to use these terms to describe Freddy, but little discussion as to why it's undesirable to have these descriptors apply to a 15-year-old boy. Simply put, Freddy never questions why it's bad to be these things. At one point in the narrative, Freddy equates being a "sissy" to being "like a girl," the closest the story comes to overtly recognizing the looming potential that Freddy might be gay, based on these dated preconceptions of masculinity and femininity. This story contends that those notions are antiquated, but does not go so far as to say that prejudices associated with them should also be eliminated.

As a sidebar, the child's name is suspect. "Freddy" is a diminutive of Fred, or Frederic. Could this boy, whose confusion over the arbitrary roles imposed by harsh parents and a harsher society, be a stand-in for Dr. Frederic Wertham, author of *Seduction of the Innocent*?

Such notions are not unprecedented. On September 9, 1951, a *Spirit* strip written by Jules Feiffer told of a Dr. Sigmund Schyzoid, who offered a highly erroneous account of a Spirit adventure, as the Spirit fought criminals via sound effects off-panel. Both Eisner and Feiffer demurred when asked directly about Dr. Wertham inspiring this character. At the time, *Seduction* had not yet been printed, and Wertham was best known for a handful of magazine articles on the subject. Still, it does establish that comic artists and writers responded to Wertham's attacks in the comics form.

And Dr. Wertham's attacks relate directly to the story of young Freddy. In *Seduction of the Innocent*, Dr. Wertham cautions of the power of cultural imagery in "creating" boys with gay tendencies. "Male and female homoerotic overtones are present also in some science-fiction, jungle and other comics books.... In many adolescents the homoerotic, anti-feminist trend unconsciously aroused or fostered by these stories is demonstrable" (190–1). Whether the naming of young Freddy is a subtle jab at Dr. Wertham or mere happenstance, this narrative serves to repudiate at least some of the ideas presented in the Doctor's much-discussed books. Most significantly, it calls into question the idea of gay behaviors as learned rather than ingrained, even if the narrative makes its point in an oblique way. Taken together with the other texts discussed herein, EC Comics present a complex, if ambiguous, image of homosexuality.

These stories are not perfect statements of any gay sensibility. Two of them convolute gay and transgender issues, and none deal with lesbian issues, plots or characters. However, as byproducts of the 1950s, a time that saw the beginnings of the Mattachine Society's founding in 1950 (Kaczorowski), the early meetings of the Daughters of Bilitis in 1955 (Theophano), and the sensationalism surrounding Christine Jorgenson's public sex change in 1952 (Stryker), these stories reinforce the words of Alan Moore, writing on gay history in that era: "Though harassed, we were still jubilant, the first rung of our climb achieved" (66).

Works Cited

[Binder, Otto (w), and Jack Kamen (a).] "Standing Room Only." *Crime SuspenStories* vol. 1, #22 (June-July 1954) [EC Comics]: 9–15. Print.
"The Comics Code Authority." *Comicartville* Web. 14 April 2011.
"Dr. Schyzoid." *Wildwood Cemetery: The Spirit Database*. Web. 14 April 2011.
Farmer, Philip José. *The Lovers*. New York: Ballantine, 1960. Print.
[Feldstein, Al (w), and Alan Davis (a).] "Operation Friendship." *The Vault of Horror* vol. 1 #41 (April 1954) [EC Comics]: 1–8. Print.
[Feldstein, Al (w), and Jack Kamen (a).] "Case File: Freddy Carter." *Psychoanalysis* vol. 1 #1–4 (April-Oct. 1955) [EC Comics]. Print.
[Feldstein, Al (w), and Reed Crandall (a).] "Genesis." *Weird Science-Fantasy* vol. 1 #29 (May 1955) [EC Comics]: 17–22. Print.
[Feldstein, Al (w), and Wally Wood (a).] "There'll Be Some Changes Made." *Weird Science* vol. 1 #14 (July-August 1952) [EC Comics]: 1–8. Print.
Foucault, Michel. *The History of Sexuality*. Trans. Robert Hurley. New York: Vintage =, 1980. Print.
Kaczorowski, Craig. "The Mattachine Society." *LGBTQ Encyclopedia*. 2004. Web. 14 April 2011.
Lang, Fritz, dir. *While the City Sleeps*. RKO Pictures, 1956.
Marcus, Eric. *Making History: The Struggle for Gay and Lesbian Equal Rights*. New York: HarperCollins, 1992. Print.
Moore, Alan (w), Villarubia, Jose (a). *The Mirror of Love*. Marietta, GA: Top Shelf, 2004. Print.
Spicer, Andrew. *Film Noir*. White Plains, NY: Longman/Pearson, 2002. Print.
Stryker, Susan. "Transgender Activism." *LGBTQ Encyclopedia*. 2004. Web. 14 April 2011.
Sturgeon, Theodore. *Venus Plus X*. New York: Pyramid, 1960. Print.
Sweeney, Gary. "Femme Fatale: The Black Widow of Film Noir." *The Midnight Palace*. Web. 14 April 2011.
Theophano, Theresa. "Comic Strips and Cartoons." *LGBTQ Encyclopedia*. 2002. Web. 14 April 2011.
_____. "The Daughters of Bilitis." *LGBTQ Encyclopedia*. 2004. Web, 14 April 2011.
Vidor, Charles, dir. *Gilda*. Columbia Pictures, 1946.
Wertham, Frederic. *The Seduction of the Innocent*. New York: Rinehart, 1954. Print.

Part III
The Problem of Consensus

12

"Dedicated to the Youth of America": Deviant Narration in *Crime Does Not Pay*

Chris York

On February 22, 1946, George Kennan, the deputy head of the U.S. mission in Moscow, sent his influential "Long Telegram" to then Secretary of State James Burnes. In it, he articulated his perception of Soviet power and the best strategy for confronting it. This communiqué would become a cornerstone for both the ideology of the Cold War and the rhetoric of containment. Toward the very end of the telegram, Kennan outlined his thoughts on how the United States should proceed in the face of the Soviet threat. At this point, his focus shifted away from foreign policy and toward domestic concerns. He wrote:

> Much depends on health and vigor of our own society. World communism is like malignant parasite which feeds only on diseased tissue. This is the point at which domestic and foreign policies meet. Every courageous and incisive measure to solve internal problems of our own society, to improve self-confidence, discipline, morale and community spirit of our own people, is a diplomatic victory over Moscow worth a thousand diplomatic notes and joint communiqués. If we cannot abandon fatalism and indifference in face of deficiencies of our own society, Moscow will profit — Moscow cannot help profiting by them in its foreign policies.

The response to such thinking amounted, essentially, to a policy of domestic containment. The moral and economic strength of our nation would be a bulwark against communism. To ensure that these defenses held, the nation would project the illusion of cultural consensus and encourage a culture of surveillance and suspicion. Communism would be kept at bay by the strong moral fiber of our nation and a vigilant attention to abnormal activities.

With so much riding on the moral integrity of the nation, it was doubly concerning for many of the vigilant to perceive an increase in juvenile delinquency during the second half of the 1940s, and many professionals and civic organizations began looking for the cause. One place they looked was in the emerging consumer culture, particularly those industries that targeted youth markets. Corporate capitalism and the consumer ideology on which it was built were unlike anything the older generation had seen before. As Bradford Wright notes, "Adults seemed to fear the young generation as the harbingers of a new and frightening social order, one transformed and corrupted by the media and consumer culture" (88). No component of that culture would receive more scrutiny than comic books.

At the end of the Second World War the comic book industry was in an unusual situation. No children's entertainment was more popular than the comic book, and, with the removal of wartime restrictions on paper, the comics industry was poised for massive expansion. But the late 1940s was also a time when the popularity of the superhero genre was waning. In fact, the creation of new superhero characters came to a halt during the war, and by the end of the decade many titles were being canceled (Wright 57). The genre that had ushered in the Golden Age of comic books found itself scrambling for both innovation and relevance in the postwar era.

In response to the declining interest in superheroes and the potential expansion of the industry, publishers began to diversify their product. In the decade between the end of the war and the beginning of the Comics Code, a variety of different genres would find their niche in the growing industry. While these genres seem, and in some respects were, quite diverse, Wright observes that despite the disparate subject matter, popular genres like teen humor, romance, superheroes, and jungle comics all could be read as endorsing mainstream values and beliefs. "All," he notes, "expressed moral certainty about American virtues, confidence in the nation's institutions, and optimism for a new age of affluence" (75).

By far the most popular genre in the late 1940s, however, was the crime comic book. Between 1946 and 1948 crime comics grew from three percent of all comic book titles to fourteen percent (Hajdu 87). The most popular title among them was *Crime Does Not Pay*. The first issues of *Crime Does Not Pay*, published by Comics House Publications (also known as Lev Gleason Publications) in 1942, sold around 200,000 copies each. By 1947, however, the readership had skyrocketed to a million copies for each issue. In fact, beginning in 1947 Charles Biro, the primary creative force behind the title, placed a banner across the top of each issue's cover that read, "more than 5,000,000 readers monthly." And considering that each issue circulated through several readers hands, the claim may even have been true (Hajdu 87).

While other genres drew upon the morals and values of a mainstream America, crime comics drew upon the rebellious, anti-establishment spirit that, in a sense, has always been very much American as well. Crime comics told the seedier side of the American Dream in which wealth and privilege were taken at gunpoint and the laws and norms of the society were cast aside in favor of chaos and violence. Make no mistake; crime comic books often paid lip service to more conventionally moral missions. In the first issue of *Crime Does Not Pay,* for instance, publisher Lev Gleason includes a letter on the inside front cover. He wrote that the comic is "dedicated to the youth of America with the hope that it will make better, cleaner young citizens" by showing them again and again that crime does not pay (Gleason). But while each criminal was punished at the end of each narrative, such punishment was generally confined to one or two small panels. The bulk of most stories portrayed criminals committing crime after crime, eluding the law, and enjoying the fruits of their ill-gotten gain. While the punishment of the criminal was often relegated to small panels at the end of the story, the benefits of crime were regularly portrayed in half-page splashes.

On top of the ambivalent portrayal of criminals, the moral philosophy of *Crime Does Not Pay* "was resolutely determinist: crime was not a relative or even a secular issue, but a simpler matter of the presence of evil" (Hajdu 65). In a society charged with improving its moral fiber and working toward cultural consensus in order to stave off the threat of communism, *Crime Does Not Pay* suggested to readers the illusive nature of these goals.

It is no surprise that such a comic, one that was both fantastically popular and a thinly veiled celebration of violence and criminality, would draw heavy criticism. At a time when experts perceived both a rise in juvenile delinquency and saw heightened ramifications in that delinquency, comic books became a serious threat to the moral order. By 1947 community-minded organizations around the nation were mobilizing against comic books, in large part due to the popularity of crime comics. Two watchdog groups began reviewing and evaluating comic books in 1947, The National Office of Decent Literature and the Committee on the Evaluation of Comic Books in Cincinnati (Nyberg 23). And in 1948 psychologist Frederic Wertham would not only speak about the negative influence of crime comics at the Symposium on Psychopathology and then at the Seventy-Eighth Annual Congress of Correction of the American Prison Association, but also published his condemnation of comics, "The Comics.... Very Funny!" in the *Saturday Review of Literature* (Nyberg 32–36). In it, he stated that "you cannot understand present day juvenile delinquency without understanding the pathogenic ... influence of comic books" (6). And though his evidence linking comics to delinquency was largely anecdotal, it was sensational and drew the attention of an increasingly anxious nation.[1]

Partners in Crime: Mr. Crime, the Criminal, and the Reader

It is easy to see why *Crime Does Not Pay* was startling to adults who read it, and why concerned civic organizations, church groups, and parents were so willing to take Wertham's claims at face value. Charles Biro took pride in the realism of *Crime Does Not Pay*. According to his artists, he wanted nothing to do with symbolism, chiaroscuro, or any kind of abstraction; he wanted a literal and detailed representation of the world, and he did not want his artists shying away from graphic violence. Readers needed to look no further than the cover of *Crime Does Not Pay* #22 to get the message (Issue #22 was the first issue of *Crime Does Not Pay*, which was formerly *Silver Streak Comics*). In the extreme foreground, a hand reaching for a revolver is pinned to a poker table by a knife. In the background, a gangster, grabbing a seductively dressed woman in one arm, tommy-guns a man across the barroom. Above them, two brawling patrons crash through the railing and fall toward yet another body sprawled on the floor below. At the end of the "Who Dunnit?" feature in the November 1943 issue, Biro himself appears, commenting that the story is "bloody ... but it's true! That's the important thing. We want our readers to see all the horror of the crooked path to crime" (Hadju 68–69).

As realistic (if gratuitous) as much of the violence was in the comic, the most insidious component of *Crime Does Not Pay* was a figure that strayed from the realism Biro embraced. Beginning with issue #24 in 1942, Mr. Crime, a ghastly figure in a top hat and a ghostly shroud, would usher readers through the featured story. For the first five years of his creation, Mr. Crime was present throughout the story, moving in and out of the narrative's action; at times he appeared to interact with other characters, and at times he turned and looked through the fourth wall to directly address the audience.

Mr. Crime's role was much more comparable to the chorus of Greek tragedy than a conventional narrator. In Greek tragedy, part of the chorus' function was as a narrator conveying to the audience legends, historical events, and actions that occur offstage. However, the dramatist used the distinctive characteristics of the chorus to influence the perceptions of the audience as well. As R. W. Burton notes, part of their role was "to awake definite intellectual, moral, and emotional responses in [the dramatist's] audience" (Burton 3). In essence, the role of the chorus was, in part, to signal to the audience how it should react to the action as it unfolded. But the chorus was also a character in the play with distinctive characteristics, and, through the leader of the chorus, it had the ability to advise, encourage, and sympathize with the other characters (Burton 5). The chorus, through its ability to work both within and outside the action of the drama, opened it up "to a variety of non-linear influences that a strict narrative can deny or inhibit" (Rehm 56).

Mr. Crime served a similar set of functions in *Crime Does Not Pay*. As a result, this sinister figure was the most immediate influence on the reader's moral and emotional interpretation of the action. Part of Mr. Crime's role was, indeed, to narrate the story. He introduced readers to the action in each story's opening splash, summarized essential backstory, and transitioned between scenes. In the 1945 story "10 Years of Terror: Vincent Piazzero," for instance, the opening splash shows Mr. Crime letting a growling criminal out of a cage. Mr. Crime says in a word bubble, "Ho folks! Close your windows, bolt your doors! I've turned the raging tiger loose! Heh, heh! Of course Vincent Piazzero is no animal, but he's just as deadly, yes, indeed ... and if you don't believe me, just ask the police! Heh, heh.... You'll soon find out!" (Palais).

But in this "true crime" narrative Mr. Crime was anything but an objective narrator. He commented on the action throughout, sharing with the audience his interpretation of the events and attempting to influence the perception of the reader. In the splash described above, for instance, Mr. Crime giggles furtively, inviting the reader to enjoy the spree of the violent criminal he has just unleashed.

As mentioned earlier, the stories of *Crime Does Not Pay* always ended with the incarceration or death of the criminal, but the body of the narrative often celebrated the criminal and left the reader with the impression that crime was thrilling and lucrative rather than doomed to failure. Mr. Crime's presence invites this reading. He transitioned between panels in a way that glorified the criminal. In the Vincent Piazzero story, for instance, Mr. Crime summarizes years of Piazzero's bootleg operation, commenting that, "[s]everal years passed and Vincent's business did prosper" and, with the police always one step behind, "Vincent in the meantime was blissfully on his way!" (Palais).

Mr. Crime went beyond slanting the tone of the narrative in favor of the criminal. He regularly undermined the authority and respectability of the law, often commenting on the cleverness of the criminal and the ineffectiveness of the police. In a 1946 story, for existence, Mr. Crime rode on top of John Dillinger's getaway car, ridiculing the police who were just emerging from the bank: "Heh, heh, Take your time boys! You'll never catch my Johnnie!" (Siege).

Similarly, in "King Killer of the Mountain," from *Crime Does Not Pay* #39, police hunt through the woods in search of murderer Ray Southerland. Mr. Crime hovers over the officers, taunting them as they approach a cabin where Southerland was last seen, "Step right in gentlemen and catch your killer! Ha, ha — if you can!" Later, as the manhunt continues, Mr. Crime mocks the officers, only now he addresses the audience through the fourth wall rather than the officers themselves: "Such a fuss! The sheriff had over five hundred men searching for my Ray! The fools — little did they realize what they were in for!" (Maurer).

Mr. Crime even questions the skill of the police during Southerland's apprehension. After a long manhunt one of the officers sees movement in a bank of bushes and fires blindly into them; "My Ray's bellow could be heard for half a mile as the sheriff's lucky bullets bit into his flesh!" (Maurer). This is hardly an admission that Ray had been outsmarted.

Mr. Crime is a spirit, and we are led to believe that, though he appears in panels with other characters, he is unable to communicate with them. Characters never interrupt his narration, they never make a reference to him, nor do they attempt to engage him in any way. In spite of that, Mr. Crime often refers to criminals as his students, and there are times when he speaks directly to them. In these instances, it is often unclear whether he is heard or not. In a 1947 story, "The Hoover Brothers," small timer Bud visits his estranged brother Don, a successful gangster, who takes him into the alley and beats him up. When Bud tries to get up and prolong the fight, Mr. Crime leans over his shoulder and advises him, "Hold it Bud. Your time will come" (Tuska, "The Hoover Brothers"). In the next panel, Bud complies with Mr. Crime's advice.

Over his first five years, such panels are common. Mr. Crime is often looking over the criminal's shoulder when he advises them, suggesting that he is in some way a part of the character — his subconscious or perhaps simply the presence of evil within the criminal. In issue # 53, Carlo Barrone, after serving a prison term, is unable to find Masselino, a criminal who he protected by going to jail. When he discovers that Masselino has resurfaced as a dress manufacturer, Mr. Crime advises Barrone, "You're not going to let that fat slob get away with it, after the rap you took for him?" Though Barrone never looks at Mr. Crime, his thoughts follow directly from Mr. Crime's comments, "So he's a dress manufacturer, eh? Better add a shroud to your line, Masselino!" The logic of the supposed conversation and even the reference to a shroud (like the one Mr. Crime wears) link the spirit with the man. Mr. Crime even grasps the hand strap on the subway, further suggesting his tangible presence in the frame. A panel like this blurs the line between Mr. Crime's narrative role and the action that he narrates. It suggests that there is a level at which he is able to engage the criminal.

One instance from 1947 would have been particularly disturbing to parents. In "The Devil's Diary," Mr. Crime watches the criminal development of young Denvil Dotson. Working as a soda jerk in a drug store, Denvil begins stealing from the till. When he finally gets caught, he sobs that his father will kill him if he finds out, and the drug store owner and the police officer let him go. Mr. Crime puts his arm around the boy as they walk away from the

162   Part III : The Problem of Consensus

Mr. Crime and the power of suggestion. From George Tuska (a), "Carlo Barrone: The Murderous Bully," *Crime Does Not Pay* #53 (July 1947). Lev Gleason Publications. Web.

scene. Mr. Crime comments, "Aren't people suckers?" The thought is echoed by Denvil, "Gee, I guess you can get away with anything if you know how!" (Tuska, "The Devil's") Certainly Mr. Crime personifies every fear that parents and other concerned citizens might have had. This evil spirit that seemed to be able to influence and "tutor" notorious criminals also spoke directly to the young readership through the fourth wall. Wertham crusaded against comic books in part because they lacked the regulation of other youth directed media of the era, and they could be, and often were, read without adult supervision (Wright 93). Mr. Crime's similarities to the Greek chorus suggest what a powerful conduit he was between young readers and the mayhem and evil of notorious criminals. For parents and critics who read *Crime Does Not Pay*,

Mr. Crime must have embodied all the negative influences they most feared in comic books.

From Crime to Common Sense

When crime comics came under attack in 1947 and 1948, Rudy Palais, a long time contributor to *Crime Does Not Pay,* noted that the criticism "didn't faze us — business was booming"(Hajdu 111). And there is some truth to that. Sales of *Crime Does Not Pay* were skyrocketing, so much so that Gleason Publications was in the process of launching another title, *Crime and Punishment,* that would debut in April 1948.

But there were signs that Biro was aware of the threat Wertham and others posed to the industry. Another contributor, Pete Morisi, thought the anti-crime comics crusade made Biro nervous (Hajdu 107), and the subtle changes to the comic book over the next several years suggest he was right. Whether inspired by legitimate concern or simply covering his bases, Biro responded to the anti-comics crusade by publishing a message on the inside front cover of the May 1948 issue of *Crime Does Not Pay*. Signed by Charles Biro and featuring a photograph of him with fellow editor Bob Wood and publisher Lev Gleason, the message was, in essence, a self-imposed code governing the content of Gleason Publications.[2] Of the twelve points outlined in the message, ten of them deal with the regulation of violent content, sexual content, and the proper portrayal of criminals and law enforcement.

While much of the code-making of the late 1940s was cosmetic and no substantial changes were ever instituted, there is evidence that there was a conscious effort to adjust the tone of Gleason Publications' crime comics. One of the directives Biro laid out in his message was that "[c]riminals must not be shown to enjoy the criminal act. This means no laughter or glee during the commission of a crime." Of course in every feature story since 1942 there had been laughter and glee during the commission of a crime — Mr. Crime's laughter. His malevolent presence and his encouragement and celebration of crime had played a significant role in creating the licentious tone of *Crime Does Not Pay* from the start. So it is no surprise that after this wave of anti-comics sentiment it was Mr. Crime whose role began to change.

Biro's letter had promised a positive portrayal of all law enforcement personnel, and there is clearly an attempt to comply with this directive. In issue #78, for instance, John Ross shoots an officer, leaving him for dead. But unlike stories in previous years, in which officers bungle arrests and prove ineffectual through most of the narrative, this officer is not finished. He rises up, steadies his aim, and shoots the fleeing Ross. Mr. Crime's comment: "Like all mad dog killers that stupid fool underestimates the courage and willpower of the police!" (Barry).

Similarly, in issue #79 a police officer makes an unofficial visit to Spike Spitz's fraudulent gold mining claim. In order to get a sample without being noticed, he asks Spitz for a drink of water and scoops a sample of his claim in the process. Mr. Crime declares, "Clever cop! He takes a drink and picks up a fistful of Spike's manufactured gold dust" (Tuska, "Spike Spitz"). In both examples, praise is doled out to the police, where it had formerly been reserved for Mr. Crime's pupils.

But other changes were in store as well. As part of this revamping, by the end of 1947 Mr. Crime's role began to shrink. He would continue to appear in the feature story until 1950. However, the occasions when he addressed the criminals directly and offered them advice or council diminished precipitously as did his visual presence. Rather than appearing within the diegetic framework as a character moving among other characters, more frequently his head began appearing near the top of the panel, where readers were accustomed to seeing the narrative text boxes. Consider one panel from "Link Gage," a feature story from 1949. Notice how being placed in the upper left-hand corner removed Mr. Crime physically from the action, and literally surrounded him with narration. In short, he no longer had the diverse responsibilities of a chorus which involved engaging both characters and audience; functionally and visually, he was simply a narrator.

Around the same time Biro began experimenting with other narrators. The 1950 story "Death House Blues," is a harbinger of the change. Mr. Crime, as had been customary, introduces the story in which District Attorney Leeds races against time to get a death house door confession. On the second page, however, Mr. Crime turns the narration over to Leeds. For the next three pages Leeds, not Mr. Crime, narrates a flashback of his ten-year involvement with the crime in question. Once the flashback is over, Mr. Crime resumes his duties, but this three page flashback signals a larger change in the comic. These stories will now be told from the law's point of view. Law officers, not criminals, are the clear protagonists in the comic book.

Mr. Crime would finally be replaced in *Crime Does Not Pay* #87. Though he would surface infrequently in secondary stories, he was no longer featured. Instead, Biro replaced him with "Chip Gardner, Private Eye," and while Gardner demonstrated a healthy disrespect for his superiors, like other hard-boiled detectives it was only because he believed that sometimes the law needed to be broken in order to see justice served. By 1950, *Crime Does Not Pay* had subtly evolved into a more benign comic. Once a comic celebrating the raucous life of criminals, its featured story now subjected criminals to the moral judgments of the detective protagonist.

By the end of the 1940s Mr. Crime's presence on the page and in the narrative are diminished. From George Tuska (a), "Link Gage," *Crime Does Not Pay* #78 (August 1949). Lev Gleason Publications. Web.

Visually, Gleason Publications' other crime offering, *Crime and Punishment*, moved even further to the side of the law. Though Mr. Crime appeared on the cover of the first issue, another character, Officer Common Sense, would play the role of narrator. Officer Common Sense first appeared in the May 1945 issue of *Crime Does Not Pay* in a story titled "The Cocksure Counterfeiter." The narrative begins with the origin of Officer Common Sense. He

166   Part III : The Problem of Consensus

was, in life, Officer John O'Shea. After apprehending two criminals and assuming that he had them subdued, he attempted to call in his report. O'Shea, however, forgot to frisk his captives and is murdered when one of them pulls a revolver and shoots him in the head. Sent to heaven, O'Shea requests from God, whom he calls "your honor," to return to earth as a spirit to help criminals realize that crime does not pay.

Officer Common Sense was not a frequent character in *Crime Does Not Pay*, and "The Cocksure Counterfeiter" illustrates why he is such a poor fit for the comic in 1945. On several occasions Officer Common Sense presents himself to the counterfeiter to try and convince him go straight. Despite seeing the apparition, the counterfeiter repeatedly succumbs to the lure of the criminal lifestyle. In the end, the "Judge in the Sky," represented by a cloud, asks if John's first mission was successful. He responds "No your Honor — I'm afraid I didn't do so well this time, but of course I'm rather new at it yet!" In comics committed to the criminal perspective, a moral narrator appears, at best, ineffectual and, at worst, foolish. The sloppy police work that leads to his death portrays O'Shea as well meaning, but incompetent.

Officer Common Sense was a much better fit under the new directives of 1948, when he became the featured narrator of *Crime and Punishment*. Now, instead of a ghoulish Mr. Crime speaking surreptitiously to the reader, an officer of the law encourages the reader to see the folly of the criminals throughout the story. In "Buck Kelly," from *Crime and Punishment's* second issue, Kelly buys a gun (which he refers to as his "great selling point") immediately after being released from prison. Common Sense comments, "Crooks are hollow men — empty of strength! That's why they buy physical strength!"

Under Officer Common Sense, the reader's perception is manipulated by a moral, law-abiding voice. From Bob Fujitani (a), "Buck Kelly: The Tough Guy," *Crime and Punishment* #2 (May 1948). Lev Gleason Publications. Web.

Later on the same page, Common Sense tries to get through to Kelly, "There's still time to think, Buck—you've done one stretch, but guns end up in the stretch that makes your neck longer! Throw that colt in the San Franscisco Bay, Buck—Do yourself a favor!" Unlike Mr. Crime's "conversations" with other characters, where it is unclear whether he is actually conversing with them, here there is no question that Office Common Sense isn't getting through.

Yet, unlike his first appearance, it is not Officer Common Sense who ends up looking foolish. Kelly's crime spree is pathetic. Officer Common Sense watches as hold up after hold up produces no substantial take for Kelly. Common Sense comments that "A shipping clerk's pay envelope boasted more money than Buck made with his 'great selling point!'"

This is not to say that Gleason's crime comics ever completely got on the good side of the critics. Despite claims the publisher would minimize the graphic violence and sexuality of the titles, such changes were inconsistent at best. In the end the changes weren't enough to keep the titles afloat, though given the pressure being exerted on crime comics it is likely that no amount of changes would have been sufficient. Though the Association of Comics Magazine Publishers and the in house codes of the late 1940s temporarily relieved some of the pressure exerted by civic groups and government committees, the anti-comics crusade was renewed in the 1950s. Furthermore, by the early 1950s crime comics were losing market share to romance and horror comics. The Comics Magazine Association of America's Comics Code, first published in October 1954, therefore, was more of a final blow than a turning point. But the legacy of *Crime Does Not Pay* extends beyond the controversy surrounding its graphic content. Mr. Crime was a unique figure in comics, and his choral qualities were innovative in their attempts to invest readers in the content of the narrative. In the years since, he has been often imitated, most famously in the narrators of the EC horror comics of the fifties: The Crypt Keeper, The Vault Keeper, and the Old Witch. It is, perhaps, more than a coincidence that the EC titles they narrated also drew heavy criticism from a concerned public.

Notes

1. Amy Kiste Nyberg gives a comprehensive account of the public outcry against comic books in her book, *Seal of Approval: The History of the Comics Code*.

2. In-house codes were a common response across the industry in the mid- to late '40s. In addition, some publishers joined together to form the American Comics Magazine Publishers (ACMP) which established similar guidelines to Gleason's for regulating content in comic books. In most instances, though regulations were in place, they were not rigidly adhered to. A lack of funding for the oversight of the regulations, and a lack of motivation given the lucrative

nature of the unregulated product, made the ACMP ineffectual. Again, Nyberg covers the ACMP in detail in *Seal of Approval*.

WORKS CITED

Barry, Dan. "John Ross: The Magician." *Crime Does Not Pay* #69 (Nov. 1948), Lev Gleason Publications. Web.
Biro, Charles. "A Message from Bob Wood, Lev Gleason, and Charles Biro." *Crime Does Not Pay* #63 (May 1948), Lev Gleason Publications. Web
Burton, R. W. B. *The Chorus in Sophocles' Tragedies*. Oxford: Clarendon, 1980. Print.
"The Cocksure Counterfeiter." *Crime Does Not Pay* #41 (July 1945), Lev Gleason Publications. Web.
Fujitani, Bob (a). "Buck Kelly: The Tough Guy." *Crime and Punishment* #2 (May 1948), Lev Gleason Publications. Web.
Gleason, Lev. Letter. *Crime Does Not Pay* #22 (July 1942), Comic House [Gleason Publications]. Web.
Hajdu, David. *The Ten-Cent Plague: The Great Comic Book Scare and How It Changed America*. New York: Farrar, Straus, and Giroux, 2008. Print.
Kennan, George. "The Long Telegram." *The National Security Archive*. George Washington University. 1995. Web. 18 March 2011. Web.
Maurer, Norman (a). "King Killer of the Mountain." *Crime Does Not Pay* #39 (May 1945), Magazine House [Gleason Publications]. Web.
Nyberg, Amy Kiste. *Seal of Approval: The History of the Comics Code*. Oxford: University Press of Mississippi, 1998. Print.
Palais, Rudy (a). "10 Years of Terror: Vincent Piazzero." *Crime Does Not Pay* #37 (Jan. 1945), Magazine House [Gleason Publications]. Web.
Perloff, Richard. *The Dynamics of Persuasion*. Hillsdale, NJ: Lawrence Erlbaum, 1993. Print.
Rehm, Rush. *Radical Theatre: Greek Tragedy in the Modern World*. London: Duckworth, 2003. Print.
Siege, Bob (a). "The True Story of John Dillinger." *Crime Does Not Pay* #45 (May 1946), Lev Gleason Publications. Web.
Tuska, George (a). "Carlo Barrone: The Murderous Bully." *Crime Does Not Pay* # 53 (July 1947), Lev Gleason Publications. Web.
_____. "Death House Blues." *Crime Does Not Pay* # 79 (Feb. 1950), Lev Gleason Publications. Web.
_____. "The Devil's Diary." *Crime Does Not Pay* #49 (January 1947), Lev Gleason Publications. Web.
_____. "The Hoover Brothers," *Crime Does Not Pay* #51 (May 1947), Lev Gleason Publications. Web.
_____. "Link Gage," *Crime Does Not Pay* #78 (August 1949), Lev Gleason Publications. Web.
_____. "Spike Spitz: A Killer Who Went Straight — to the Chair." *Crime Does Not Pay* #79 (Sept. 1949), Lev Gleason Publications. Web.
Wertham, Frederic, "The Comics,... Very Funny." *The Saturday Review of Literature*. May 29, 1948. Web.
Wright, Bradford. *Comic Book Nation: The Transformation of Youth Culture in America*. Baltimore: Johns Hopkins University Press, 2003. Print.

13

MAD's Guest Writers

Lawrence Rodman

As of the post–World War II era, a wild diversity of comic books crowded the newsstands. With the exception of movies, comic books were the only affordable option for visually dynamic entertainment. Upper tier companies managed to produce competent, or even superior features, but slipshod or shady publishers needed only a steady wartime newsprint supplier, or an idle press, to prosper. The popularity of superheroes had dropped off, but reader interest vacillated to various other genres in turn, war, Westerns, crime, and romance among them. The crime genre enjoyed a surge in the late forties to early fifties; the comics medium, with its roots in lurid pulp adventure, was especially adept at depicting such sensationalism. Lurid content sold well; the more sensational it was, the better. Entertaining Comics (EC), a group that was having a better time publishing crime books than it had with Bible stories and juvenilia under the name Educational Comics, got ahead of the curve by producing horror comics, in part based on creepy radio drama, and other extant source materials. EC's books became widely imitated. As various taboos were shamelessly flouted by craftsmen and opportunists alike, the ugliness came to a head.[1] The situation ultimately gave rise to congressional hearings and a subsequent industry crackdown. This was not the first culture war controversy over popular media by any means, and it was far from the last. Behaviorists are in continual debate over whether violent media actually influences similar conduct.[2] As for the violent, anti-social comic books of the 1950s, the alarm was officially sounded. Public opinion, taking its cue from cultural commentators and politicians, was swayed towards regulation, if not outright suppression. A great deal of material existed for right-thinking people to find objectionable. To the uninitiated — as was the case with that other fifties public nuisance rock 'n' roll — all horror comic books appeared to be the same aberrant garbage, making any qualitative distinctions beside the point.

170   Part III : The Problem of Consensus

In March 1955, DC Comics editor Mort Weisinger introduced the readership of *Better Homes and Gardens* to the Comic Magazine Association of America, a self-censorship initiative comprised of twenty four publishers. The association was to author and enforce the guidelines of the Comics Code Authority. "Just how much faith can you have in this seal?" he rhetorically queried of the Code's cover indicia, anticipating parental skepticism. "Is it a bona-fide guarantee of wholesome, healthy entertainment ... or a phony frill calculated to take the comic-book publishers out of the doghouse?" (58–9). Dell Publishing exempted itself from the association, as a family-friendly mega-concern, with already unimpeachable standards. The article also noted two other holdouts, Classics Illustrated and Entertaining Comics. The blood and guts in the Classics could have been justified as being true to their source (and they had a company tradition of pride in their educational value), whereas William Gaines, publisher of EC, had no socially acceptable excuse whatever. Weisinger clearly points a finger in Gaines' direction as one of the "conscience-less ... minority of unethical publishers" engaged in the production of "horror-type comics [containing] themes [such] as cannibalism, torture and grave robbing" (59).

While other publishing outfits were wiped out by the political fallout subsequent to the institution of the Comics Code, EC made a wan attempt to restructure. The forbidden horror and fantasy titles were replaced with adventure-driven ones that were watered down compared to EC's former standards. As it happened, EC also produced a nascent humor publication, *MAD*, which was opening comic books to taboo-breaking attitudes. To quote Maria Reidelbach, the author of *Completely MAD*, "Especially in the beginning, in the repressiveness of the McCarthy era, it [*MAD*] allowed people to thumb their noses and give a Bronx cheer to some of the more oppressive elements in society" (Levy B7).

Kurtzman and the Early MAD

MAD had commercial traction as well as bite. Having begun as a comic book in 1952, it had already been upgraded to magazine format as of issue #24, in 1955. As the dust settled for EC, and the compromised (unapproved) post–Code titles withered commercially, *MAD* became Gaines' sole viable title.

Interestingly, *MAD*—as a comic book and a magazine—is a singular publication in comics history in that it's in an active dialogue with the overall continuum of popular culture. Most comic books consist of a self-referential narrative, oblivious to matters beyond those in the medium's own formulaic ghetto. *MAD* began by jeering primarily at radio programs, comic strips, and

13. MAD's Guest Writers (Rodmen) 171

the pop ephemera that Gaines and his second-in-command, editor Al Feldstein, used extensively as the basis of their original New Trend (the popular, censorship-inciting) books.

Beyond publishing, the media of the day was an uneven mixture of old mainstays and raw novelties. Radio still thrived as an entertainment medium, featuring drama, comedy, quiz shows and musical programming, though it would not be fated to dominate the scene for much longer. Movies were entrenched, and that upstart, television, began to gain on everything else. *MAD* was in a position to take in and process all of it from its vantage in media-centric New York City. The comic book began by parodying its own form and that of all other media, with a voice — using the fundamentals of comics narrative — that was all its own. The founding editor responsible for that vision was Harvey Kurtzman. A gifted graphic artist, comedic auteur, and something of a perfectionist crank to work for, Kurtzman had been moving heaven and earth to produce the best and most realistic war and adventure comics on the market ... really slowly. Since pay rates, and therefore income, were tied to volume, he leapt at the opportunity to establish a humor comic book, something that could be put together quickly. His boss and patron, William Gaines, gave him that opportunity.

MAD was a new animal. While there had been any number of humorous comic books for kids, a satiric comic book capable of holding an adult's attention was unheard of (some newspaper comic strips had multi-generational appeal, but that was another matter). Comics professionals were a persecuted lot. Celebrated creator Will Eisner, until quite late in his life, related the story of being looked down upon at a cocktail party for telling a woman he "did comics" for a living. Even so, humor was the one genre that could be relied upon to get people to take them even less seriously than they already did. But *MAD* was Kurtzman's ideal vehicle of expression. No one would be spared from his native irreverence.

At this point, *MAD* was Gaines' only viable title out of his few remaining comic books, and Kurtzman was his only editorial asset. Aware that Kurtzman craved legitimacy beyond that afforded by lowly comics work, Gaines upgraded *MAD* to a twenty-five cent magazine. Kurtzman reformatted the publication from scratch, with new, improved production values more in keeping with the "slick" newsstand world that beckoned to him. This improvement also effectively placed *MAD* outside the jurisdiction of the Comic Book Code.

After a few issues of the new format, however, Kurtzman demanded a majority share of the magazine and was refused. He left EC, and moved on to greener pastures, under the auspices of magazine and nightclub mogul Hugh Hefner. Kurtzman was then replaced on *MAD* by his old editorial rival, the highly prolific and workmanlike Al Feldstein. What Feldstein lacked in visionary inspiration, as compared to Kurtzman's antic standard, he made up for in hard-bitten professional moxie. "He [Feldstein] liked the format and look that Kurtzman had created, but felt that the humor was too eccentric and lacked focus. Feldstein thought that these problems limited *MAD's* audience" (Reidelbach 40).

From "Too Eccentric" to "Slightly Impolite": Feldstein and His Guest Writers

Under Feldstein *MAD's* content boiled down to a cultural critique of America-at-large by creators from a vital subculture. "My writers — Larry Siegel, Stan Hart, Artie Kogan — were all Jewish boys from Jewish families in urban centers." He credits their facility with social critique to "a cultural awareness (an outsider attitude). It might even be in the genes, it might go back hundreds and hundreds of years of a certain kind of living in society. Trying to survive in that society" (Gluckson 72).

While Feldstein emphasizes his writers' marginality, his body of work with *MAD* displays the duality between rebellion and the desire for assimilation more typical of upwardly mobile Jewish professionals of the era. This particular tension was something that his more go-for-broke colleagues, Gaines and Kurtzman, didn't necessarily share. Who knew that you could make a good living editing a humor magazine, as opposed to, say, going into advertising? It was Feldstein's comparative assembly-line orientation that most characterized the fundamental contrast between his editorial style and his predecessor's. The artists most readily associated with the early individuality and artistic mimicry of *MAD*, including Will Elder, Jack Davis, and Wally Wood, would follow Kurtzman and defect (the latter two temporarily) to the Hefner-sponsored project. This wholesale change of the guard left it up to the editor to fabricate a sleeker model *MAD*, with an idea to what might actually sell.

Confronted with the requirement to turn out forty-eight (and ultimately fifty-two) pages of art and text bimonthly, Feldstein responded with customary pragmatism. Prior to his editorship of *MAD*, he had been shopping around a magazine conceived as a showcase for new talent. "I wanted guys like Lenny Bruce to have a place of publication. I went right out and got Ernie Kovacs, I got Bob and Ray, Jean Shepherd, "Jazzbo" Collins. I got Danny Kaye only because he gave me permission to do something off one of his records. But at least it was a nice name" (Gluckson 85).

From issues #31 to #55 (consistently at first, and then intermittently by the final issues of the run) a broad range of guest celebrity contributors were listed prominently on each cover. As EC was New York City-based, Feldstein also had access to the talent flowing through radio, nightclubs, and Broadway. Among the personalities he used or that gave him permission to reprint material to be rendered into comics magazine form were Orson Bean, Bob Elliot and Ray Goulding (Bob and Ray), Sid Caesar, Al "Jazzbo" Collins, Wally Cox, Andy Griffith, Danny Kaye, Ernie Kovacs, Tom Lehrer, Henry Morgan, J. Fred Muggs, and Jean Shepherd. This list, in itself, stands as something of a cultural artifact. It contains several renowned — if not legendary — showbiz personalities, a number of enduring cult performers, a few relative obscurities where entertainment history is concerned, and one animal: J. Fred Muggs, the simian mascot for *The Today Show*. The most familiar personalities are, naturally, those who've come down the decades to us from film and television. The most prominent men — and all were men, except for the non-human — on the list had (or indeed still *have*) careers that provide an occasion to study the nexus of the performing arts, commerce, and the particular cultural period from whence they arose.

Muggs, in fact, was a legitimate contributor. He painted the cover of issue #38 in March 1958. Inside that issue, in an uncredited feature entitled "*MAD's* Revised New Up-to-Date Alphabet Book," Muggs' work is put into critical perspective. "P is for Picasso, The king of modern art, Put his work next to J. Fred Muggs': You can't tell them apart."

Apart from the monkey, none of the contributors helped out on illustration. Feldstein's stable of artists brought each of the guest writers' intellectual properties into visual form. This is most notable in the case of Bob and Ray, who, although they had a modest network television presence, were first and foremost radio personalities (and, it might be said they had the faces for it). Acclaimed caricaturist Mort Drucker was a new EC hire just as the initial Bob and Ray script arrived. Drucker had come over from DC/National Comics, having done war titles, among other things, but he'd never attempted caricature. After the successful visualization of this first job, he was permanently matched with the comedy team, subsequently becoming an icon of the art form, a modern Daumier.

The scripts from Bob and Ray, as with most of the established performers, were originally written, at least in part, by their staff writers, making the actual provenance of the work fuzzy at best. According to Feldstein, "I was trying to get names into the magazine, like Bob and Ray, and Ernie Kovacs. Bob and Ray gave me some scripts of theirs to adapt. They agreed, and I got Tom Koch — his name was on the script — I called him up, and said, 'Do you want to write for *MAD*?' He said, sure!" (Gluckson 84) From the introductions given to specific articles, unless the source material is a self-evident reprint, as with a song newly accompanied by illustrations, it's very clear which were written (or can be *credited* as having been written) exclusively for *MAD*. Many of the personalities were essentially figureheads, representing the efforts of whole smoke-filled rooms of 1950s schtick-meisters.

A number of the *MAD Magazine* features starred sketch comedy star Sid Caesar, in one or several of his comedic personas. Apart from a heavy reliance on Ernie Kovacs' contributions, it's Caesar who carries most of the weight of name recognition over the course of these issues. In the text-heavy situational humor of the *MAD* piece, Caesar's protégé, writer Mel Brooks' authorial voice and Borscht Belt terminology comes through. It's evident that he had a hand in the contribution, however uncredited. In more general terms, it's an example of the extent to which Brooks, Caesar, and ethnic humorists at large had, by that point, imprinted their style upon popular culture. Whether the average national audience-member "got it" or not, however, *MAD's* faux-Yiddish routines and attitude became less of a function of actual satiric iconoclasm than a defanged representation of the Other — the weirdo or outsider. *MAD's* editorial voice was chronically self-effacing. It's an ironic voice, clearly belonging to a member of some group ("the usual gang of idiots," according to the masthead) that might benefit from playing dumb and being underestimated. To give Feldstein his due, *MAD Magazine* was no respecter of social orthodoxies, either of the right or left. But, as opposed to being actively subversive in nature, Feldstein's publication was more culturally entrenched by the fact of its very survival. It still dared to bite the hand that fed it, but not in the unregulated manner of the prankish, spitball-throwing comic book of yore.

Historic surveys of the American twentieth century consider the year 1945, denoting the period following the end of World War II, to be a clean break with the past. That's not to say that there weren't some old-school holdovers. In the tenuous early days of television, there was no formal consensus as to what programming should look like. The earliest TV stars came out of the vaudeville tradition to proffer comedic comfort food and thrown pies. Fifties television comedy, at first, was a phoenix risen from the embers of vaudeville, and to mash-up a metaphor, the accompanying old-boy comedy network was an ever-present animate corpse from an EC horror comic plot. Milton Berle appeared in drag, Ed Wynne in a fireman's helmet; old attitudes, old platitudes.

Into the void strode Ernie Kovacs, a multi-disciplinary comedic mastermind. His approach towards video production, a major facet of his varied career, was unique and well before its time. Unsurprisingly, he was a fan of the Kurtzman-era *MAD*, for its iconoclasm and riotousness. Kovacs and the early 1950s MAD staffers engaged in mutual admiration; he reading the comic, they watching him on the tube. From 1955 to 1958 and starting with #24, the first magazine-formatted issue, the Kovacs visage, with his massive head, moustache, and cigar, would grace mock ad campaigns, and his byline ("Ernie Kovacs Department") and photo were used prominently. He would be one of several comedic personalities that Feldstein pushed forward as his "icons," household names that would boost the magazine's standing and sales (Gluckson 85).

Among Kovacs' contributions was an article illustrated by Jack Davis, portraying Kovacs in his role as the poet Percy Dovetonsils. It was one of a number of *MAD's* topical jabs at effete long-hair culture (Sid Caesar and Al "Jazzbo" Collins also helped out with their observations and explications regarding the alien-ness of jazz musicians, a fifties bourgeois preoccupation). While the study of cultural repression as represented by the Comics Code would seem to be, in itself, a politically progressive act, MAD's rebellion was egalitarian. "Satire was important to MAD, but its real métier was iconoclasm. It was a pie chucked at the nearest face visible." Otherwise, for the most part, Kovacs scripted (with writer Mike Marmer) the series of *Ripley's Believe It or Not* parodies, "Strangely Believe It"(Walley 103). If the original Robert Ripley feature promised factual integrity, Kovacs and regular artist Wally Wood could do no less than turn the world on its head.

Ernie Kovacs' representation on the page, out of his native element — the television studio — seems somewhat diminished. However, Bob and Ray's imaginative multi-character world expanded as a result of the adaptation of their scripts into comics form. Their work originated on the radio, making timing and delivery of paramount concern, so the visualization of their set pieces would not necessarily have made much sense. Their early television shows were of the primitive, static-camera variety, and the comics versions vastly increased their visual range. The wit of the original text and Mort Drucker's expressive artwork make their comics effective. Their skits featured logic pushed-to-its-furthest-extreme sequences involving average, out-of-their-depth dupes, spokespersons for ridiculous, doomed causes, or profoundly spurious experts lecturing on pet topics. Their deadpan humor played on the disparity between society's often unreal expectations, and stark actuality. As Kurt Vonnegut, who wrote the introduction to their "best of" anthology, *Write If You Get Work; The Best of Bob and Ray* concluded, "Man is not evil, they seem to say. He is simply too hilariously stupid to survive" (vii).

The Bob and Ray world view was not without its post-modern sense of contradiction. They were at home in radio, but mercilessly ridiculed its passé storytelling conventions well into the eighties. They made fun of the duplicity of advertising — and the venality of human endeavor in general — but hired themselves out for radio ad campaigns, their main selling point being the attention-grabbing nature of humor.

Vonnegut also made the point in literature for The Museum of Television and Radio, considering Bob and Ray's extensive cast of characters, "third-raters all ... Mary McGoon, Wally Ballou, the McBeebee Twins, Kent Lyle Birdley, (and so on), not one of these, incidentally, is an ethnic stereotype." Ethnic ridicule would certainly not have been beyond the pale at the time; Sid Caesar and his heavy-weight writing team, including Mel Brooks, Woody Allen, Larry Gelbart and Neil Simon were master creators of 'crazy foreigner' routines. Caesar, during the rigors of his live broadcasts, might be called upon to assay German, French, Russian, or Japanese gibberish.

Caesar's *Your Show of Shows* and the various other productions in which he and his ensemble appeared were destination television shows. Over the course of ten years fronting variety series and specials, he presided over a Saturday night cult that expanded in direct opposition to the gradually reduced cost of television sets. Naturally, the stakes were pretty high both for Feldstein to secure Caesar's cooperation and scripts, and for *MAD* artists Wally Wood and Mort Drucker to somehow convey his artistry on the page. They were largely successful, as expressive caricaturists. One caveat over the transformation of his character work to comics has to do with the effect of dialect humor on the page as opposed to in performance. His character The Professor, for example, (who appeared in issue #47, June 1959) spoke in Brooksian Anglicized Yiddish. What would be an aural bombardment on TV is a something of chore to decode as text on the page, undercutting its humorous payoff.

Sid Caesar's spaced-out, malapropism-spouting character Progress Hornsby sent-up Miles Davis' brand of cool jazz in issue #48 (July 1959). Better yet, in issue #31 an uncredited member of the Usual Gang of Idiots asked the musical question "What's All This Jazz About Jazz," of actual cool cat and musician Al "Jazzbo" Collins, "one of America's foremost authorities on the subject of jazz." Whereas Caesar's Hornsby's goatee was "dyed flesh color so it does not interfere with the viewing of my immaculate chin" (Caesar), Collins' byline photo shows him thoughtfully stroking his own dark whiskers in anticipation of serious questions. Asked to supply a primer on musical matters for the benefit of the terminally square, Collins responds with comments on the order of, "the main thing I'd like to get across is that Jazz musicians ... I mean, these guys ... they have ideas. They like to play 'way out' ideas, you know. They try to get some new sounds ... some new creations. Just like a silversmith who works with all different materials, you know ... they're doing all these material things in a real etherial [sic] way." The interviewer is respectful, and Collins is eminently clear, in his way. But the article's splash page and accompanying panel illustrations, by a wigged-out, Dali-esque Wally Wood, show the drop-dead hip "Jazzbo" and some literally square, cubistic reporters, in a subterranean labyrinth, The Purple Grotto. Throughout the five pages of text, the illustrations get progressively stranger, somewhere stylistically between the set decoration and action of Stanley Kramer's 1953 Dr. Seuss flick, *The 500 Fingers of Dr. T*, and the detail from a Hieronymous Bosch painting. The furiously overcooked visuals are an apt oddball fantasia, but subvert the piece's stated purpose to aide in the enlightenment of jazz neophytes.

Feldstein's original intent had been to give un-housebroken anti-establishmentarian comics a newsstand berth. But, as the fifties wound down, Feldstein's slightly impolite stable, with their preemptive, self-effacing humor, dominated the publication's masthead. The "sick" (as in, essentially, politically conscious) comedians never quite showed up to the party, having mostly drifted into Hugh Hefner's orbit (as had Kurtzman). Lenny Bruce, to cite one obvious example, didn't make it into *MAD*, and Danny Kaye or Wally Cox (who, admittedly, were only represented in reprint form) didn't quite meet the definition of the 1950s rebel. An excerpt from Jules Feiffer's collection of cartoons from *The Village Voice, Sick, Sick, Sick*, ran in issue #41 (November 1958), though circuitously, by the acquisition of permission directly from the publisher, rather than through any desire on Feiffer's part to link himself to *MAD*. Feiffer's image of the materialist, neurotic, modern everyman was similar to that of Feldstein himself. As David Hajdu noted in The *Ten-Cent Plague*, in reference to Feldstein's lifestyle, "He took up golf and boating, and he bought a hi-fi set ... newer and fancier than Bill Gaines.' Feldstein was living the suburban ideal he subverted in the pages of EC comics" (Hajdu 194). At that point in time, the EC mission was less about challenging the status quo than about showing average Americans just how out-of-step they were with the evolving nature of their own culture.

The honest-to-god *sickest* humorist to come through the system was to be proto-yippee Paul Krassner, who was listed among the staff writers on several of the issues of *MAD* throughout this period, and, as of 1958 (simultaneously to his time at *MAD)* launched his more sophisticated — or at least more extreme — satiric journal, *The Realist*. With his forum for mingled factual reportage, satire and outright hoax, Krassner's publication was to become the link to underground comics, a distinction he shares with none other than the generally acknowledged god father of the movement, Harvey Kurtzman. In 1967, Krassner and Wally Wood ascended to hyper-satiric, sacrilegious glory, with their infamous "Disneyland Memorial Orgy" foldout, a tableau of obscenely entangled creatures from the Magic Kingdom.

With beat poetry, cool jazz, and juvenile delinquency on the one hand, and the consternation of the bourgeois confronted with these cultural signifiers on the other, the period was so ripe for satire that *MAD* would have to have been invented, were that not already the case. The *Mad* Signet paperback collections *Like MAD*, with Alfred E. Neuman as a beatnik on the cover, and

The Organization MAD, a play on William H. Whyte's *The Organization Man*, an influential sociological study of Eisenhower-era progress and prosperity, were both released in 1956. Combing through vintage *MAD Magazine* issues and checking out the articles representing the various comedic personalities of the day may be least convoluted way to acquire an understanding of the Cold War era, but it's undoubtedly the most fun.

Notes

1. EC was a singular force in comic book horror, however, the concept that Gaines and company *invented* the form was promulgated by Gaines himself (among others), through the fan press, to the point that it's become received wisdom. Historian and editor Greg Sadowski points to one-shots and continuing series being published as far back as the mid–1940s (296).

2. In a current situation analogous to that of *just before* the Frederick Wertham era of comics history, a recent issue of *The New Yorker* featured a review of contemporary video games by Nicholson Baker, who characterized one example as "a slasher movie.... It ... trick(s) you, or your parents (few families abide by the rating system), into tolerating a level of ... gore that would be otherwise impossible in a mass-market entertainment."

Works Cited

Baker, Nicholson. "Painkiller Death Streak." *The New Yorker,* 9 Aug. 2010: 52–59. Print.
Caesar, Sid. "For The Life of Progress Hornsby." *MAD Magazine.* July 1959. GIT Media Group. CD-ROM.
Gluckson, Robert. "Al Feldstein." *The Comics Journal.* July 2000: 65–85. Print.
Hadju, David. *The Ten-Cent Plague.* New York: Picador, 2008. Print.
Levy, Claudia. "Publisher William M. Gaines Dies; Founded the Satirical Magazine Mad." *The Washington Post,* 4 June 1992: B7. Print.
"Mad's Revised New Alphabet Book" *MAD Magazine.* March 1958. GIT Media Group. CD-ROM.
Reidelbach, Maria. *Completely MAD: A History of the Comic Book and Magazine.* Canada: Little, Brown. 1991. Print.
Sadowski, Greg. *Four Color Fear.* Seattle, WA: Fantagraphics, 2010. Print.
Vonnegut, Kurt. *Bob and Ray: A Comedy Sampler.* New York: Museum of Television and Radio, 1992. Print.
_____. Introduction. *Write If You Get Work: The Best of Bob and Ray.* By Bob Elliott and Ray Goulding. New York: Random House, 1975. Print.
Walley, David G. *The Ernie Kovacs Phile.* New York: Fireside, 1987. 103. Print.
Weisinger, Mort. "How They're Cleaning Up the Comic Books." *Better Homes and Gardens.* March 1955: 58–59, 254–255. Print.
Wood, Wally (a). "What's All This Jazz About Jazz?" *MAD Magazine.* February 1957. GIT Media Group. CD-ROM.

14

Beyond the Frontier: *Turok, Son of Stone* and the Native American in Cold War America

Chris York

By the 1950s the contemporary travails of the Native American were rarely on the popular radar. Rather, American Indians endured in the American consciousness almost exclusively through their portrayal in the Western genre, which was ubiquitous during the 1950s in television, film, and popular literature. In Carter Jones Meyer and Diana Royer's introduction to their anthology, *Selling the Indian: Commercializing and Appropriating American Indian Cultures,* they write that "[e]mploying stereotypes to characterize those we set ourselves in opposition to is the simplest way to deal with them" (xii). It has long been established that the reduction of cultures into one-dimensional caricatures make their dismissal both ideologically and physically a much easier task for the dominant culture. This is certainly true of Native Americans. Elizabeth Bird continues in a similar vein, noting that the Native American has been the quintessential "other" of American history, symbolizing the ideas and characteristics that served to reinforce the identity of white American culture in any given era (66). For Puritans, for example, the American Indians were servants of the devil. For Thomas Jefferson they were noble but doomed savages.

Within the deluge of western narratives, a peculiar case emerged out of Dell Publications, a comic book publisher known primarily for its comic books featuring Disney and Warner Bros. cartoon characters, in the form of *Turok, Son of Stone.* First appearing in *Four Color Comics* # 596 in 1954 and receiving its own title two years later, *Turok* defies many of the stereotypes inherent in the Western genre. Turok and his companion Andar, who are described as "Pre-Colombian Indians," find their way into a mountain valley during a hunting expedition in the American Southwest. They quickly discover that in this valley pre-historic creatures still roam the Earth. The premise of each story centers on the two Native Americans confronting pre-historic dinosaurs, mammals, and cavemen as they search for the way out of the Lost Valley.

In this early Cold War era Native Americans, true to their symbolic role as the quintessential "other," continued to serve as a metaphor for the nation's fears and anxieties. In the 1950s a number of different permutations of the Western genre rose to prominence. Among them were the cavalry Western and Indian Western. Both sub-genres featured Indians prominently and in both cases they served as symbols that represent the anxieties of the 1950s. Richard Slotkin, for instance, addresses specifically the cavalry Western as a means of rationalizing Cold War conflict and politics. Through the framework of the "Savage War," cavalry Westerns like *Rio Grande* addressed relevant Korean and Cold War issues like breeches in the chain of command and subversion of the democratic process. As in previous permutations of "otherness," the Indian is placed metaphorically into the role of the enemy aggressor. Indians in the cavalry Western served to "rationalize the development of the republican nation-state into an imperial Great Power" (353).

But the 1950s also saw the coming to prominence of Westerns that portrayed Indians sympathetically. Rather than rationalizing Cold War policy, films like *Devil's Doorway* and *Broken Arrow* contained within them critiques of United States policy and social conventions, particularly as they related to the emerging battle over civil rights (Slotkin 377). Within the Western, though, even sympathetic portrayals leave little room for Native Americans to move beyond stereotypes. Slotkin explains that "when an ideological issue or problem is projected into a Western movie setting, the range of possible and plausible resolutions is shaped by the rules and expectations that inform the mythic landscape of the genre" (350). This is clear, for instance, when we consider the frontier setting of the Western, which is both a geographic and symbolic borderland. It is here where eastern civilization and western wilderness, Anglo culture and native savagery, feminine decadence and masculine individualism all collide. The Indian emerges first as part of the wilderness, a savage standing in the way of progress. On the occasions when the Indian crosses over the ideological border he or she becomes a companion or sidekick who recognizes and chooses to exist within (if not necessarily embrace) Euro-American civilization. Even when we consider progressive-minded films of the fifties that portrayed Indians sympathetically, the borders to a large extent remain intact; the sympathetic Indian is often white in several ways. First, they are often white in the sense that they are played by white actors. More importantly, the Indian in sympathetic narratives has abandoned Native American culture for the more "civilized" pursuits of ranching or farming, or the Indian has in some way embraced or expressed his or her belief in the superiority of white society. Borders, then, remain intact. Native Americans are capable of civilization, but only by adopting Euro-American values and beliefs.

The Lost Valley and Vanishing Borders

Turok, Son of Stone defies the borders established by the Western, or at least escapes them, if only to create different ones. Quite literally, when Turok accidentally finds the Lost Valley, he steps out of the Western genre and into the realm of science fiction, where it is possible to get trapped in time. In this new narrative framework, the lost characters must work through conflicts, both internal and external to themselves, in order to find their way back to their own era. Important here is the elimination of the borders created in the western genre. There is no white civilization against which Turok and Andar must be defined. As a result, the Native American's conventional function as the symbolic "other" disappears. Turok and Andar are no longer identified exclusively through race. It is true that they continue to wear their readily identifiable Indian clothing (though not necessarily identifiable to any specific Native American nation), and they do possess traits that are stereotypically associated with Indians (they are, for instance, excellent hunters and trackers), but rather than falling into good Indian/bad Indian stereotypes, Turok and Andar fall into another generic convention, the hero and the sidekick.

Like the most recognizable comic book example of this convention, Batman and Robin, the sidekick is careless and impetuous. In the 1954 story "The Terrible Ones," for instance, Turok and Andar's attempt to form a friendship with a group of cave dwellers is met with hostility, and the two Indians have to dodge hurtling stones as they flee. Andar is outraged, "We ought to give them a taste of our arrows! That would change their song." Turok, however, is more diplomatic, replying, "No, it wouldn't! It would make them enemies for good!" (Dubois 53). In issue three, Turok and Andar again are pursued by cavemen. Upon reaching higher ground Andar draws his bow, "Now ... we can pick them off with our arrows, Turok!" But Turok again spares the cavemen, "Not so fast! We don't want to kill them — just teach them a lesson!" (Dubois 96). Though Turok and Andar are not differentiated in age in the narration (they are described at different times as "young men" and "Mandan youths"), visually, Turok appears older; he is taller and his face more mature. This visual differentiation along with their distinct personalities — Andar is impulsive and emotional; Turok is wise and rational — clearly places them within the conventions of the hero and young sidekick.

Like other heroes and their young sidekicks, Turok is not able to keep Andar's impetuousness completely in check. As a result, Andar's actions often provide the narrative conflict which the older, level-headed hero must resolve. In the 1958 story "The Monster of the Depths," for example, Andar laughs at Turok's premonition that camping near a stream is a bad idea, only to find himself taken captive in the middle of the night. In another story, "The Valley of the Vines," a misstep by Andar triggers a giant flesh eating plant that swallows both Native youths whole. In both situations, Turok must use his skill and ingenuity to free Andar and himself.

As a sidekick, Andar's haste and carelessness often generate conflict. From "The Valley of the Vines," *Turok, Son of Stone* #11 (March–May 1958). Dell Publishing. Print.

The hero and sidekick is a convention not unheard of in the western, of course. Even the pre–Western Leatherstocking Tales offer an early example with Natty Bumpo and his companion Chingachgook. Indeed, one of the most popular Western franchises in the 1950s was The Lone Ranger and Tonto. Tonto possesses many admirable traits. He's loyal, strong, skilled, compassionate, and intuitive. But "Tonto is always subjugated to the authority of the Lone Ranger. While the two men are supposed to be a team, the Lone Ranger ends up giving all the orders. There is no equality between the two men — there is only a member of a minority race doing the bidding for a member of the dominant culture" (Sheyahshe 43). Furthermore, Tonto, though clearly intelligent, still speaks in broken English. Michael Sheyahshe notes that, "When he speaks, his intentions are barely translatable and one is reminded of the meaning of his name when translated into Spanish: dummy." (43)

Dell, in fact, gave Tonto his own comic book in 1951, and though he is portrayed heroically, he is unable to completely shake the paternalism of his sidekick role. To begin with, the full title of the comic is *The Lone Ranger's Companion Tonto*. And though he is the featured character, he still suffers from the signifiers of savagery. Strangely, Tonto's thought bubbles and conversations are quite articulate in the presence of exclusively Indian company. These thoughts and dialogue, however, must have been viewed by the creators as translations from his native tongue, because when he speaks with white men he reverts to the broken English characteristic of most Indian characters of the time. In a story titled "War Feathers," for instance, a calumet is stolen from Chief Stone Bear's camp. The young braves want instant retribution on their enemy, but Tonto speaks before the tribe: "Stone Bear, I am certain this is the work of but a few braves! All I ask is a chance to track them down and try to retrieve the calumet without a bloody war!" Though his English is a bit stuffy, it is articulate. Yet, in the following story in the same issue Tonto speaks to a cowboy asking for water: "How! Day plenty hot! Canteen empty! Tonto like water for horse and for self!"

Turok and Andar's English is stiff and at times awkward, but in direct contrast to Tonto and most other Indian portrayals of the era, it is always clear and easily understood. There are no westerners against whom their language must be compared. As such, these articulate Indians are a powerful subversion of the savage stereotype. Furthermore, Turok and Andar's clear English often stands in contrast to the cavemen they encounter. Consider this example from the 1958 story "The Captive Hunters," in which Turok and Andar have been taken captive by cave dwellers who superstitiously believe that their leader, Lorl, can kill prey with his cave drawings. Turok and Andar have just been told that, as slaves, they are expected to hunt for the clan.

> Andar: Why can you not do your own hunting?
> Cave Dweller: We able kill only what Lorl draw!
> Turok: What Lorl Draws?
> Cave Dweller: If Lorl make picture in back cave —- we kill animal in picture! If Lorl not draw, we hunt but not kill any animal!

The contrast is clear (even if we choose not to read Turok's question as a didactic correction of the cave-dweller's poor subject-verb agreement). The absence of broken English, a time-honored signifier of savagery, points to a larger change. In the Lost Valley, the Indians shed the dehumanizing characteristics that persist in the western genre.

Andar's role as sidekick to some extent required him to be articulate. The comic book sidekick, in the tradition of Robin, the Boy Wonder, was prone to word play and sarcasm. Though not as gregarious as Robin, Andar had his moments. When Turok and Andar successfully hunt and kill a smilodon that had been terrorizing a group of cave dwellers, the community wishes to honor the heroes. Andar, however, has not eaten in days and has little patience for ceremony. Turok notes the honor being bestowed upon them, but Andar comments, "I like eating better, Turok! Honor is all right, but" (Dubois, "The Secret Place"). In a story titled "The Night Stealers" Andar even moves beyond proper English to engage in a bit of sarcasm. Escaping a rainstorm, Turok and Andar find what they think is an empty cave. When a spear lands at their feet, however, they look up to see a hoard of cave dwellers looking down on them. Andar turns to Turok and says, "They're not exactly welcoming us!"

The Cold War in the Lost Valley

In the Lost Valley, where the Western framework no longer applies, different conventions are allowed to enter the narrative. Turok and Andar are often portrayed as civilizers, a direct contrast to the western genre where they are juxtaposed to western civilization. In a 1956 story titled "The Secret Place," for instance, Turok had slain a dinosaur threatening a group of cavemen. Though he and Andar befriend the cave dwellers, he refuses to share with them the secret of his poison arrows with which they are able to kill giant dinosaurs with one shot. Turok tells them, "When it is safe for your people to have our arrow medicine, all shall have it! But that time is not yet!" Later, when Andar asks when they will share the secret, Turok elaborates: "When they have learned wisdom, Andar!... See, they are always fighting! Now their wounds will heal — but with our arrow poison, many would die!" It is, in other words, in the cave dwellers' best interest that they are kept ignorant, defenseless, and dependant on others.

What Turok articulates is a form of "benevolent assimilation," a term first used by William McKinley during the colonization of the Phillipines, but an ideology that has always explicitly or implicitly informed American imperial designs. The notion of benevolent assimilation suggested that American imperial designs were not about conquest and dominance. Rather, America, as the most civilized and democratic nation in the world, wanted to share the gifts of its culture and uplift uncivilized nations. Of course, the colonized country must be ready to accept these gifts. As Vincente Rafael notes, bringing civilization to the uncivilized "brought with it the need to enforce discipline and constant surveillance among the colonized population" (186). This colonial theme was common in Turok stories, and was revisited again in the 1960 story "A Cunning Foe" when a cave dweller, Gan, spies on Turok and Andar and learns their secret for making fire. Gan uses this secret to manipulate his fellow cave dwellers and assume for himself a position of power in the clan. Recognizing the threat Turok and Andar pose to his authority, Gan orders them burned at the stake. In a moment torn from the pages of Mark Twain, Turok fortunately recognizes the evidence of an approaching eclipse and, in predicting the oncoming darkness, proves that his magic is more powerful than Gan's. What is telling in both this story and "The Secret Place" is that Turok and Andar are the voice of civilization and progress, a voice that echoes American imperial rationalizations. When the United States determines that these countries have proven themselves capable of self-government and self-defense ("gained wisdom," as Turok puts it) the means of defense and development will be turned over to them. Until then it is in their best interest to submit to American authority. Turok and Andar, then are the colonizers rather than the colonized. This is nowhere more apparent than when Turok adopts the role of the Connecticut Yankee himself, Hank Morgan, one of literature's first time-travelers and most unapologetic colonizers.

In the end, although Turok and Andar get lost in time and escape the stereotypical constraints of the Western genre, they are unable to escape the rhetoric and paradigms of the Cold War. A 1962 story, "The Secret Cavern," for example, taps a popular fear and fascination with brainwashing that emerged during the 1950s. During their wandering, Turok and Andar come upon a group of cave dwellers who "act like sleepwalkers!" It turns out that they have been brainwashed and enslaved by other cave dwellers. While Turok investigates, he is taken captive and forced to take the "strange potion" that turns men into mindless zombies who obey only their master. Andar is, of course, able to find the antidote and rescue Turok, but the story taps into an anxiety concerning communist brainwashing that reaches back to the Korean War. After the war ended, there were reports claiming that American POWs had collaborated with their captors. While some saw this as a result of an

American military that had gone soft, others saw it as proof that communists had perfected psychological brainwashing techniques (Robin 164–65). Brainwashing stayed at the forefront of American anxieties throughout the fifties and into the sixties. The very year "The Secret Cavern" was published, John Frankenheimer released his film adaptation of *The Manchurian Candidate*, in which a Korean War POW is brainwashed and reprogrammed to assassinate a United States presidential candidate. So, while *Turok* is able to free itself from the restrictions of the Western, it is still very much in the grip of Cold War paradigms.

The anachronistic characteristics of the Lost Valley that dissolve stereotypes and shift borders did little to raise the popular awareness of the contemporary Native American. Like the western genre, *Turok, Son of Stone* defines the Native American as part of the past. With very little exposure to the Native American of the 1950s, it becomes easy to conclude that, if they do exist, there is no place for them in modern society. Certainly placing Turok in pre-history undermined any legitimate attempt at preserving historical accuracy. Dell prided itself on its educational content. At a time when the Comics Code Authority was demanding changes to the content of comics throughout the industry, Dell refused to align itself with the code. Dell wanted to distance itself from the publishers who had been pushing the boundaries of decency and offered instead a promise to parents that stated its comics were "clean and wholesome juvenile entertainment." The promise assured readers that Dell "eliminates entirely, rather than regulates, objectionable material." In *Turok* the wholesomeness stems, in part, from factual details concerning the featured animals in the comic book and information concerning pre-historic eras. In issue # 5, for instance, the mastodon is featured on the inside front cover. The text accompanying the illustration points out that the mastodon appeared "fifty-million years ago" and "mysteriously vanished" less than a million years ago. The rest of the comic book, however, portrays the two Native Americans co-existing with these giant cats. Considering the paucity of evidence in American popular culture that Indians continued to exist in 1950s America, the conclusion could easily be made by children reading the book that the American Indian, too, was extinct and therefore of no consequence in the modern world. Dell provided no educational content to disabuse its young readers of this notion.

In fact, there are moments where it could be implied that Turok and Andar are referenced in these anthropological entries. Issue # 4 featured the smilodon on the inside front cover, and the end of the entry observes that "no weapons in possession of human beings at that time could quickly have killed him — except by chance or unless they were poisoned" (118). While there may be some historical validity in this observation, it also foreshadows

Anachronism and the Lost Valley. From [Gaylord DuBois (w)], "The Smilodon," *Turok, Son of Stone* # 4 (June–August 1956). Dell Publishing. Print.

the second story in the issue, titled "The Smilodon," in which Turok and Andar are hunted by the giant cat but are ultimately able to kill it with their poison arrows. This subtle merging of anthropological fact and fictional narrative displaces the Native American, depriving them of any historical authenticity.

Furthermore, while Turok and Andar are clearly more technologically advanced than the cavemen they encounter, Turok and Andar's relationship to contemporary white men is ambivalent. In fact, creating this anachronistic dichotomy between the Native Americans, now civilized, and the cave dwellers, superstitious savages, suggests that an evolutionary continuum does exist. As a result, this new civilized/savage border validates the more conventional borders of the Western genre that Turok had escaped.

In the end, though *Turok, Son of Stone* takes a few ambitious strides beyond the conventional portrayal of Native Americans, the comic book was still very much a product of its time. Turok and Andar's adventures in the Lost Valley allowed them to shed the proscriptive elements of the Western genre. They were no longer set in opposition to the advance of Western civilization, and they were able to shrug off many of the characteristics of savagery. Furthermore, there were no white protagonists to whom they were subservient; Turok and Andar were the only featured protagonists. These are significant deviations from the conventional ways Native Americans were portrayed in 1950s popular culture. However, Turok's creators were unable to imagine any kind of civilization other than the one offered by 1950s America. As a result, the two Native Americans end up articulating an imperial ideology that is not far removed from the one used to rationalize the displacement and destruction of Native cultures across the American continent. In addition, displacing Turok and Andar into a world of dinosaurs and prehistoric mammals perpetuates the perception that Native Americans are not participants in 1950s society.

Works Cited

Bird, S. Elizabeth. "Savage Desires: The Gendered Construction of the American Indian in Popular Media." *Selling the Indian: Commercializing and Appropriating American Indian Cultures.* Eds. Carter Meyer Jones and Diana Royer. Tucson: University of Arizona Press, 2001. 62–98. Print.
"The Captive Hunters." *Turok, Son of Stone* #11 (March-May 1958), Dell. Print.
"A Cunning Foe" *Turok, Son of Stone* #18 (Dec.-Feb. 1960), Dell. Print.
"Dell Pledge to Parents" *Turok, Son of Stone* vol. 1. Ed. Randy Stradley. Milwaukie, OR: Dark Horse, 2009. 46. Print.
[DuBois, Gaylord, (w).] "The Exiled Cave Men" *Turok, Son of Stone* vol. 1. Ed. Randy Stradley. Milwaukie, OR: Dark Horse, 2009. 81–99. Print.
_____. "The Secret Place" *Turok, Son of Stone* # 5 (Sept.-Nov. 1956), Dell. Print.
_____. "The Smilodon." *Turok, Son of Stone* #4 (June-Aug. 1956), Dell. Print.
_____. "The Terrible Ones" *Turok, Son of Stone* vol. 1. Ed. Randy Stradley. Milwaukie, OR: Dark Horse, 2009. 27–44. Print.
"The Fight for the Watering Hole" *The Lone Ranger's Companion Tonto.* #13 (Nov.-Jan. 1954), Dell. Print.
"The Mastodon." *Turok, Son of Stone* #5 (Sept.-Nov. 1956) Dell. Print.
Meyer, Carter Jones, and Diana Royer. Introduction. *Selling the Indian: Commercializing and Appropriating American Indian Cultures.* Tucson: University of Arizona Press, 2001. Print.
"The Night Stealers" *Turok, Son of Stone* #13 (Sept.-Nov. 1958), Dell. Print.
Peweewardy, Cornel. "From Subhuman to Superhuman : The Evolution of American Indian Images in Comic Books." *American Indian Stereotypes in the World of Children.* Eds. Arlene Hirschfelder, Paulette Fairbanks and Yvonne Wakim Molin. Lanham, MD: Scarecrow, 1999. Print.
Rafael. Vincente. "White Love: Surveillance and Nationalist Resistance in the U.S. Colonization of the Phillipines." *Cultures of United States Imperialism.* Eds. Amy Kaplan and Donald Pease. Durham, NC: Duke University Press, 1993. 185–218. Print

Robin, Ron. *The Making of the Cold War Enemy*. Princeton, NJ: Princeton University Press, 2001. Print.
"The Secret Cavern." *Turok, Son of Stone* #28 (June-Aug. 1962), Dell. Print.
Sheyahshe, Michael. *Native Americans in Comic Books: A Critical Study*. Jefferson, NC: McFarland, 2008. Print.
Slotkin, Richard. *Gunfighter Nation: The Myth of the Frontier in Twentieth-Century America*. New York: HarperPerennial, 1993. Print.
"The Valley of the Vines." *Turok, Son of Stone* #11 (March-May 1958), Dell. Print.

15

East Europeans in the Cold War Comic *This Godless Communism*

Alexander Maxwell

During the Cold War, anxiety about the possibility of nuclear war combined with hysterical fear of communist subversion to generate xenophobia. Cold War rhetoric rarely did justice to the internal situation of either the Soviet Union or the countries of East and Central Europe under Soviet domination. Yet the didactic children's comic *Treasure Chest of Fun and Fact*, a lay Catholic magazine, combined crude ethnic stereotypes with an apparently genuine effort to inform its audience about the complex ethnic situation in the Soviet empire. Its ten-part serial *This Godless Communism*, a heavy-handed piece of anti–Soviet propaganda, sought to distinguish the peoples of Eastern Europe from their communist governments, and also from each other.

This Godless Communism appeared during the 1961–62 school year, as the Cuban Missile Crisis unfolded and Cold War tensions were escalating. Apart from one five-page story, each installment was six pages long. The ten episodes of *This Godless Communism* formed six major sections. The opening installment illustrated the comic's didactic nature, painting a dystopic picture of "the American family under Communism." Communists have taken control of trade unions, the radio, newspapers, and the family house. They dynamite the Washington Monument, teach atheism in school classrooms, seize private property, force both parents to perform physical labor apart from their children, and send the children to state-run nurseries. Strangely, they also shift the capital to Chicago. As the father learns he will be sent to fell trees in northern Wisconsin and see his wife only on weekends, he thinks to himself, "If I and my fellow Americans had only realized how horrible Communism really is" (Crandall).

The remaining nine issues comprised, in the words of Emily Clark, "an educational tool for children which contained a simplified history of communism" (17). The second installment described the life of Karl Marx. The third and fourth respectively describe Lenin's path to power and rule. Three further issues were devoted to Stalin: one looked at the collectivization of agriculture, another the purges and the Nazi-Soviet Pact, and a third the Second World War and subsequent Soviet expansion into East and Central Europe. Two further issues discussed Khrushchev; one covered his rise to power, the second depicted him crushing the Hungarian Uprising and fomenting communist subversion worldwide. The last issue discussed the various peoples suffering under Soviet communism, ending with an appeal for youth to be ready to struggle against the evils of communism: "pray hard and work hard, for the success of the battle may well be up to you" (Crandall).

The publisher and chief editor of *Treasure Chest* was George A. Pflaum Jr. By 1961, the Pflaum family, based in Dayton, Ohio, had been active in Catholic youth publishing for nearly a century. In 1885, George A. Pflaum Sr. had founded the *Young Catholic Messenger* (Fortin 226), which began printing black and white comics in the early 1940s (Borth). In 1946, Pflaum Jr. launched *Treasure Chest* as a full-color comic. *Treasure Chest* was rarely sold in stores; Catholic churches and religious schools ordered in bulk and distributed the comics to children.

When *This Godless Communism* appeared in 1961, Catholic comics had been appearing for over a decade, yet represented a relatively new trend in American Catholic culture. The American Catholic church had previously taken a hostile attitude toward comic books. Before the Second World War, several Catholic organizations had opposed comics for their supposedly dangerous ideas and lax morals. The National Organization for Decent Literature, founded 1938, specifically targeted *Sensation Comics*, best known for the character Wonder Woman (O'Conner; Clark 9). After the Second World War, however, Catholic organizations began using the comic medium to disseminate Catholic propaganda. In 1947, for example, Lewis Gates of Minnesota published around four million copies of *Is This Tomorrow: America Under Communism*, which described a small communist clique seizing power in the United States (Horowitz 115; Gabilliet 36).

Though Pflaum published as part of Catholic civil society, he also sought and received moral support from the United States government. Specifically, he declared his intention to publish an anti-communist story to J. Edgar Hoover, director of the FBI. Hoover made an improbable patron for Catholic comic books, not least because of his Protestantism: he had been raised Lutheran before converting to Presbyterianism (Ackerman 4). Hoover nevertheless respected the Catholic Church. By the late 1960s, Catholic protests against the Vietnam War would bring leftist clergy to the attention of the FBI (Rosswurm; Nepstad 51–52), but in 1961 the agency still enjoyed good relations with American Catholics. Hoover had supported the anti-comic book campaign of the early 1940s (Lent 11–12), but by the 1960s he had, like the Catholic Church, apparently concluded that comics could not be beaten and thus should be joined.

On March 13, 1961, therefore, Hoover wrote a letter for the readers of *Treasure Chest*, warning that "the responsibility of protecting and preserving the freedoms we cherish will soon belong to the members of your generation," and urging American children "to learn all that you can about it." After "pursuing the appropriate courses of study at your school," Hoover wrote, young people "will know and understand the nature of communism. This knowledge is most essential, for it helps us recognize and detect the communists as they attempt to infiltrate the various segments of our society." Pflaum reproduced the letter with letterhead and signature, and Reed Crandall drew a panel at the end of the first issue urging readers to "read the letter from the director of the F.B.I. at the beginning of this story." Both Hoover and Pflaum, therefore, consciously depicted *This Godless Communism* as a didactic effort.

Didacticism, Credibility, and Authenticity

Pedagogical ambitions inspired Reed Crandall, the artist who drew *This Godless Communism*, to make the narrative appear more factual and realistic than most of the fanciful or allegorical stories published in *Treasure Chest*. Crandall had previously drawn several comics incorporating political themes (Borth). After serving briefly in the U.S. Air Force, he worked for *Military Comics*, drawing several stories about the "Blackhawks," an ethnically diverse team of heroes fighting Nazi Germany and its allies around the world (Halperin 181; Gabillet 22). To give *This Godless Communism* an air of realism, Crandall drew several panels from photographs, including a picture of Lenin in his tomb and a portrait of Lev Kamenev. A panel showing the American declaration of war against Japan must also have been drawn or traced from a photograph; it depicts various press microphones in the correct order. Crandall nevertheless took some liberties for artistic reasons. A panel showing the Japanese surrender recognizably depicts the same table as a photograph of the actual event, but shortened the row of American officers witnessing the surrender. Another panel on the Berlin uprising of 1953 owes an obvious debt to a famous photograph, but Crandall enlarged the Soviet tanks. Perhaps he wanted to make the tanks appear more threatening, or perhaps he merely wanted to improve visibility. Crandall also added a worker's cap to one of the

15. *East Europeans* (Maxwell) 193

Crandall used photographs as templates for some panels, like this one from the Berlin uprising in 1953. From Reed Crandall (a), *This Godless Communism, Treasure Chest of Fun and Fact* (September 1961–June 1962). George A. Pflaum. Web.

stone-throwing protesters, and generally changed the layout of the street and buildings.

Crandall also drew several notable buildings in his backgrounds. Various panels depict Lenin's tomb with the Kremlin's wall and towers, Moscow's Cathedral of the Assumption, St. Basil's cathedral on Red Square, the Winter Palace, and the Admiralty building in St. Petersburg. One can also see Cyrillic lettering on various propaganda posters and shop signs. Working from his imagination in New York rather than drawing from life in Moscow, Crandall obviously fell short of perfect realism. One panel shows Stalin looking out a window at the line of mourners at Lenin's tomb; the perspective suggests that Stalin kept his office in the GUM department store. Nevertheless, detailed line drawings, or tracings, of Soviet landmarks also elevated the comic's visual quality. Images of Soviet landmarks arguably promoted the comic's pedagogical mission by exposing young readers to famous landmarks.

In keeping with its pedagogical objectives, *This Godless Communism* provided its readers with basic information about communism. Schoolchildren wholly unfamiliar with Soviet history would learn, for example, that Lenin used the slogan "land and bread," that his secret police was called the Cheka, that *Pravda* is a leading Soviet newspaper, that Soviet agriculture consisted of collective farms, and that Soviet industry was developed according to five year plans. Readers also received brief introductions to significant figures of communist history. The comic shows portraits of Engels, Trotsky, Kamenev, Zinoviev, Beria, Malenkov, Molotov, Zhukov, Bulganin, and Kaganovich.

When depicting communist ideology, the comic could most charitably described as "uneven." One panel in issue #6 explained Lenin's philosophy of professional revolution more or less accurately: Lenin explains to his followers "The larger a group gets, the more confused and weak it gets. The kind of group I want will be small, but every member will work without rest to destroy the present society" (Crandall). In the next installment, on the other hand, another panel depicting the Bolsheviks plundering a church has Red Army Soldiers improbably exclaim that the gold objects "can be used to worship the real god ... Communism"! Alice George concluded that American anti-communist propaganda "almost never encouraged children to reach a deeper understanding of the nation's adversary" (140). Despite Pflaum's didactic intentions, *This Godless Communism* probably contained too many inaccuracies to qualify as a proper educational text.

Nevertheless, Pflaum appears to have enjoyed some pedagogical success with at least one reader. James R. Barrett, a labor historian at the University of Illinois Champaign-Urbana, credited the comic with his "introduction to the Cold War" (120). On the other hand, Mike Benton seems to have exaggerated when he claimed that the comic "certainly did its job of indoctrinating millions of schoolchildren" (97). Freelance author Jeff Duntemann wrote that as a child he "rolled his eyes a little" at the religious overtones in *This Godless Communism*, concluding of *Treasure Chest* that "the comic ran the gamut from preachy (always) to silly (often) and the quality was very uneven."

Sympathetic Caricatures: East Europeans in This Godless Communism

If Pflaum sought to instill fear of communism in his American audience, he also wanted Americans to sympathize with East Europeans suffering under communist rule. *This Godless Communism* therefore tried to view the Cold

War from the other side of the Iron Curtain. It consistently depicted nations under communist rule, both in the Soviet sphere of influence in East-Central Europe and in the Soviet Union itself, as suffering from communist oppression. For example, issue #12 described the Katyń massacre in Poland and the deportation of Polish civilians, adding "the same thing happened in Estonia, Latvia and Lithuania" (Crandall). Issue #18 presents Greece, Korea and Tibet as victims. Even the relatively obscure Bessarabia is mentioned.

The plight of Hungary received special attention in issue #18. A panel on the failed 1956 Hungarian Revolution showed how "red tanks and guns crushed the Hungarian people, who were fighting for freedom" (Crandall).

The Communist Party did not represent all of the Soviet Union. From Reed Crandall (a), *This Godless Communism, Treasure Chest of Fun and Fact* (September 1961–June 1962). George A. Pflaum. Web.

Pflaum and Crandall particularly highlighted the persecution of Hungarian Cardinal József Mindszenty. Mindszenty, persecuted both during the Second World War by the fascist Arrow Cross movement and after the war by the Hungarian Communist Party, attracted considerable attention in the United States. Released from prison during the 1956 Revolution, Mindszenty sought asylum in the American Embassy in Budapest after the Soviet invasion. Denied permission to emigrate, he ultimately spent fifteen years in the American embassy building. The suffering of a prominent clergyman held an obvious appeal for the strongly Catholic *Treasure Chest*. Philip Jenkins wrote in a study of Cold War Pennsylvania that "the martyrdom of eastern European clergy became a central theme of Catholic writing on Communism" (173). Pflaum's comic suggests that Ohio Catholics shared similar concerns.

To distinguish suffering peoples from their communist oppressors, Crandall used a consistent series of visual clues. He used a woman in a headscarf to show an archetypical innocent civilian suffering from soviet injustice. Headscarf symbolism transcended national boundaries, appearing in panels on Germany, Poland, Ukraine, Hungary, and Russia. Only one non-communist woman from Eastern Europe appears without a headscarf: a Hungarian woman wears a hat to fight the Soviet invasion. A particularly telling panel depicts a kerchiefed woman unable to buy food, while the bare-headed wife of a communist functionary holds full grocery bags.

Though bare-headedness consistently implied wicked communist loyalties in East-European women, Crandall nevertheless depicted American women bare-headed as well. Crandall sometimes distinguished American women from communist women with an apron, signifying their domesticity, but also drew American women talking to their colleagues in the workplace, repeatedly symbolized with a water cooler. Bare-headed women, it seems, had become sufficiently "modern" to break with traditional gender roles. In this respect, Crandall implicitly conceded the modernity of Soviet Communists, and while he apparently acknowledged the Hungarians of the 1956 Revolution as "modern," he saw other East European non-communists as backward peasants.

Despite the Soviet Union's large Muslim population, furthermore, Soviet headscarves lacked any Islamic content. The only possible exception, a Kazakh headscarf, probably signified ethnicity rather than religion. While other Cold War critics of the Soviet Union found Soviet Muslims a rich source of material (Mende 1958; Kolraz 1961; Wilhelm 1971; Rywkin 1982; Bennigsen 1983), *This Godless Communism* ignored them. The Catholic mission of *Treasure Chest* apparently made a defense of Islamic religious freedom problematic.

Though a strident example of Cold War propaganda, *This Godless Communism* expressed a striking sympathy for ordinary Russians. The final installment asks its readers to consider: "What of the *people* of Russia? What kind of people are they?" The comic told its readers that Russians "are creatures of God with bodies and supernatural souls, even though their leaders say otherwise." Since only 8 million people out of a population 215 million have joined the Communist Party, the comic concludes that "we should remember that the Russians are our brothers in Christ. We should hate Communism ... but not the Russian people who are victims of it" (Crandall). Pflaum's apparently genuine sympathy with ordinary Russians reflected a general tendency in America's Catholic press to resist the conflation Russians and communists. Consider the Catholic press reaction to William Wellman's *The Iron Curtain* (1948), the first major Hollywood movie of the Cold War. *New York Times* reviewer Bosley Crowther noted that all Russian characters, apart from the defecting hero, were "granite-faced super-gangster types who, curiously, speak with heavy accents, while Mr. Andrews [the protagonist] does not." The Catholic journal *Commonweal* protested such caricatures, complaining that "these characters cease to be people and are merely symbols" (cited in Adler 252–54).

Pflaum's sympathy with Russian citizens stopped, however, when Russian national pride came into conflict with American national mythology. While describing Russians as a "patriotic people" who "hate Communism," the comic belittled two Soviet achievements central to Russian national pride. It dismissed Sputnik, suggesting "the Reds' 'Space-Race' lead proves *only* that they had a head start." It also downplayed what "the Russians" sacrificed to defeat Nazi Germany. One panel shows American soldier telling another that "they [Russians] ought to stop crowing and help us against the Japs" (Crandall). Given that Soviet casualties during the Second World War exceed American losses in Europe over a hundred times, Pflaum's implied moral equivalence between American and Soviet losses shows contempt for Russian life, considerable ignorance or both.

Yet ignorance may be the most likely explanation, since *This Godless Communism* elsewhere showed a certain lack of clarity about basic facts of contemporary Soviet geography. It seemed unsure, for example, about the difference between Russia and Ukraine. Issue #8 portrayed "Ukrainia" as a "state within Russia that wants to secede," so that Lenin's refusal to allow Ukrainian independence could demonstrate Bolshevik duplicity. Yet in a panel from issue #14 on the Second World War, in which "Hitler's soldiers were rapidly marching into Russia," a crowd greeted Nazi soldiers with the cry "Welcome to Ukrainia!" (Crandall). Crandall further described the great famine of 1932–33 as an event in which "millions of Russians starved to death," even though the Ukrainian diaspora in North America had repeatedly characterized it as a Ukrainian genocide (Pidhainy). Such ambiguities imply that Pflaum and Crandall intermittently saw Ukrainians as a sub-variety of Russians, rather than a distinct nation.

Tolerance and Multi-Culturalism in Catholic Anti-Communist Propaganda

This Godless Communism avoided any mention of East-European Jews, ignoring both Jewish victims of communism and the Holocaust. It briefly mentioned American Jews in the opening issue, which imagined "Jewish and Protestant ministers" as potential victims of persecution in communist America (Crandall), but non–American Jews living in Eastern Europe remained invisible. Perhaps Pflaum feared a discussion of Jews would confuse his main narrative about the global struggle between Christianity and atheistic communism. If so, Pflaum followed the example of more illustrious Catholic American intellectuals. One of America's most prominent Catholic thinkers, Jesuit political scientist Edmund Walsh, founder of the Georgetown School of Foreign Service in Washington D.C., in the words of his biographer, "minimized anti–Jewish persecutions with a surprising insensitivity" because of his "greater concern for the priests and Catholic Poles" (McNamara 124–25).

Yet if *This Godless Communism* ignored Jewish suffering, it conspicuously avoided Anti-Semitic imagery. The Jewish ancestry of leading Bolsheviks had been a central theme of anti–Bolshevik propaganda from the earliest days of the U.S.S.R. (Wolf 50; Kellogg 228–29). The bogey of Jewish Bolsheviks had featured very prominently in the interwar anti-communist crusade of Michigan priest Charles Coughlin. Coughlin liked to list leading Bolsheviks by nationality to show their Jewish origins and repeatedly called on American Jews to denounce the "atheistic Jews" of the Soviet government (37–38, 51–52, 62–63, 96; Gallagher; Fisher 86–88). By the 1960s, however, Nazi atrocities had made Anti-Semitism socially unacceptable, and *Treasure Chest* elsewhere acknowledged a Jewish contribution to the United States (Penowski 18–19). *This Godless Communism* therefore ignored the Jewish backgrounds of Trotsky, Kamenev, and Zinoviev. More remarkably, it avoided mentioning Karl Marx's Jewish ancestry even when discussing his family's conversion to Lutheranism; the comic attacked Marx as a Hegelian and materialist, but not as a Jew. Crandall misleadingly depicted Marx as an unwilling adolescent convert, though the Marx family actually converted before Karl was born.

While confused by Ukrainians and dismissive of Jews, *This Godless Communism* nevertheless broke from the general rule observed by Romanian-American media scholar Andaluna Borcila, who wrote that "during the Cold war, 'Eastern Europe' designated a world inhabited homogenously by Com-

Soviet ethnic diversity. From Reed Crandall (a), *This Godless Communism, Treasure Chest of Fun and Fact* (September 1961–June 1962). George A. Pflaum. Web.

munism" (43). The comic repeatedly highlighted distinct national communities in Eastern Europe, and if its ethnographic information contained several inaccuracies, it successfully introduced its readers to the magnitude of Soviet ethnic diversity. One striking panel distinguished the Caucasian, Ukrainian, Georgian, Tungus, Muscovite, Armenian, Kirghiz, Kazakh, and Uzbek. Most of these "types" were official Soviet nationalities: six represent constituent Soviet Republics; if Crandall's "Muscovite" represents the Russians ("Great Russians"), then the figure rises to seven. The only non-ethnic category, "Caucasian," encompasses several nationalities including Georgian and Armenian. Even here, however, Crandall might have confused "Caucasian" with "Circassian," a distinct nationality of the Northern Caucasus.

Crandall used folk costumes to show ethnicity, often resulting in inaccurate and inappropriate stereotypes. A panel from issue #4 showing Marx discussing Hegelian philosophy in the then–Prussian city of Berlin depicted his conversation partner wearing Bavarian Lederhosen. In issue #18 Crandall drew Greek Communists during the Greek Civil War in an equally stereotypical *foustanela* (a white kilt), with AK-47 rifles consistently drawn missing the pistol grip or trigger. A panel depicting Trotsky's assassination hilariously depicts a mustachioed attacker wearing a striped poncho and sombrero. Note that Ramón Mercader, Trotsky's Catalan assassin, was actually clean-shaven. Crandall undermined his pedagogical ambitions with such blunders, particularly in comparison to Ostendorf, the artist who drew another *Treasure Chest* serial, *America: the Melting Pot*. Ostendorf only used folk costumes when drawing the distant past.

Crude stereotypes like this one of Trotsky's assassin, Ramón Mercader, often undermined the pedagogical objectives of *This Godless Communism*. From Reed Crandall (a), *Treasure Chest of Fun and Fact* (September 1961–June 1962). George A. Pflaum. Web.

However crude the ethnic stereotypes in *This Godless Communism*, they nevertheless differed qualitatively from Crandall's depictions of Chop Chop, a Chinese character in the Blackhawk comics. Ma aptly concluded that Chop Chop's "prominent buck teeth, beady slanting eyes, protruding ears, bow legs, splayfeet [and] short stature" represented "racist stereotypes of orientalism" (164). Ethnic caricatures in *This Godless Communism*, by contrast, were not intended as comic relief. While Marx's Berlin classmates would not have worn lederhosen, nor Greek communists the *foustanela*, nor Mercader a sombrero, Crandall may have intended these costumes to serve the same function as noted landmarks in panel backgrounds: he probably hoped ethnic clothing would evoke foreign locations for juvenile readers. If Crandall gave Mercader a sombrero from the desire to add realism, however, the choice was counterproductive.

Crandall so frequently drew on popular caricatures that one childhood reader, Kathleen Marie Higgens, subsequently recalled the comic as promoting stereotypes not actually present in Crandall's art. Higgens, a philosophy professor at the University of Texas at Austin, read *This Godless Communism* as a schoolgirl, and retrospectively traced her interest in philosophy to panels explaining Hegel's influence on Marx: "the influential role of Marx's philosophy professor" intrigued her. As an adult, however, she remembered Hegel lecturing to "several blonde young men," while the young Marx was "distinguished from his fellows by a scowl as well as by his dark brown hair (223)." In fact, Crandall depicted all of Hegel's students with dark hair. Nevertheless, his art contained so many crude stereotypes that Higgens recalled additional ethnic caricatures.

Treasure Chest's attention to ethnic diversity reflected a genuine interest in showing respect for the various peoples of the communist world. *Treasure Chest* generally took a strong interest in bridging ethnic differences. It favored the civil rights movement, for example, and in 1964 published a series called "Pettigrew for President," which sympathetically described an African-American candidate (Reese). In the 1962–63 school year, furthermore, Merian Pehowski wrote a ten-part series on *America: The Melting Pot*; each installment covered an American ethnic group. Pehowski examined Irish, Italians, Germans, "Negro Americans," Greeks, "the American Indian," Poles, "English Americans" (which meant "British Americans," since the story included a Welsh miner), Spanish Americans (which included Mexicans and Puerto Ricans) and Jews. *America: The Melting Pot*, like *This Godless Communism*, combined pedagogical ambitions with factual inaccuracies: Pehowski's homage to Polish-Americans, for example, erroneously dated the partition of Poland to 1870. Both stories nevertheless show an apparently sincere desire to celebrate ethnic diversity and promote good inter-ethnic relations. By emphasizing ethnic diversity in communist world, therefore, *This Godless Communism* projected onto the Soviet Empire multicultural values developed for American domestic politics.

WORKS CITED

Ackerman, Kenneth. *Young J. Edgar: Hoover, the Red Scare, and the Assault on Civil Liberties.* Cambridge, MA: Da Capo, 2008. Print.
Adler, Les. "The Politics of Culture: Hollywood and the Cold War." *The Specter: Original Essays*

on the Cold War and the Origins of McCarthyism. Eds. Robert Griffith and Athan Tehoharis. New York: New Viewpoints, 1974. Print. 240–61.

Barrett, James "The Blessed Virgin Made Me a Socialist: An Experiment in Catholic Autobiography and the Historical Understanding of Race and Class." *Faith and the Historian: Catholic Perspectives* Ed. Nick Salvatore. Champaign: University of Illinois Press. Print. 117–47.

Bennigsen, Alexandre, Marie Broxup. *The Islamic Threat to the Soviet State.* London: Taylor and Francis, 1983. Print,

Benton, Mike. *The Comic Book in America: An Illustrated History.* Dallas: Taylor, 2007. Print.

Borcila, Andaluna. "How I Found Eastern Europe: Televisual Geography, Travel Sites and Museum Installations." *Over the Wall/After the Fall: Post-Communist Cultures through an East-West Gaze.* Eds. Sibelian Forrester, Magdalena Zaborowska, Elena Gapova. Bloomington: Indiana University Press, 2004. Print. 42–64.

Borth, Frank. Interview by Maria Mazzenga and Jordan Patty. Catholic History Research Center. 10 May 2006. Web. 8 May 2010.

Clark, Emily "Of Catholics, Commies, and the Anti-Christ: Mapping American Social Borders Through Cold War Comic Books." *Journal of Religion and Popular Culture* 21.3 (Fall 2009). Web. 10 April 2010.

Coughlin, Charles. *Am I an Anti-Semite? 9 Addresses on Various "Isms" Answering the Question.* Detroit: Condon, 1939. Print.

Crandall, Reed (a). *This Godless Communism. Treasure Chest of Fun and Fact* vol. 17 #2, 4, 6, 8, 10, 12, 14, 16, 18, 20 (Sept. 1961-June 1962), George A. Pflaum. Web.

Crowther, Bosley. *New York Times*, 13 May 1948, 21.

Duntemann, Jeff. "Treasure Chest and Obama as Pettigrew." *Jeff Duntemann's ContraPositive Diary.* 11 March 2008. Web. 21 April 2010.

Fisher, James. *The Catholic Counterculture in America, 1933–1962.* Chapel Hill: University of North Carolina Press, 1989. Print.

Fortin, Roger. *Faith and Action: A History of the Archdiocese of Cincinnati, 1821–1996.* Columbus: Ohio State University Press, 2002. Print.

Gabilliet, Jean-Paul. *Of Comics and Men: A Cultural History of American Comic Books.* Trans. Bart Beaty and Nick Nguyen. Jackson: University of Mississippi Press, 2009. Print.

Gallagher, Charles. "A Peculiar Brand of Patriotism: The Holy See, FDR, and the Peculiar Case of Coughlin, Charles E." *FDR, the Vatican, and the Roman Catholic Church in America, 1933–1945.* Eds. David Woolner and Richard Kurial. New York: Palgrave Macmillan, 2003. Print. 269–77.

George, Alice. *Awaiting Armageddon: How Americans Faced the Cuban Missile Crisis.* Chapel Hill: University of North Carolina Press, 2003. Print.

Halperin, James *Heritage Comics: Dallas Signature Auction Catalog* #817. Dallas: Heritage Capital, 2005. Print.

Higgens, Kathleen Marie. "The Good, the True and the Beautiful." *Falling in Love with Wisdom: American Philosophers Talk about their Calling* Oxford: Oxford University Press, 1993. Print. 223–25.

Hoover, J. Edgar. Letter. *Treasure Chest of Fun and Fact* vol. 17 #2 (Sept. 1961) George A. Pflaum.

Horowitz, David. *America's Political Class Under Fire: The Twentieth Century's Great Culture War.* London: Routledge, 2003. Print.

Jenkins, Philip. *Cold War at Home: The Red Scare in Pennsylvania, 1945–1960.* Chapel Hill: University of North Carolina, 1999. Print.

Kellogg, Michael. *The Russian Roots of Nazism: White Émigrés and the Making of National Socialism, 1917–1945.* Cambridge: Cambridge University Press, 2005. Print.

Kolarz, Walter. *Religion in the Soviet Union.* New York: St. Martin's Press, 1961. Print.

Lent, John. *Pulp Demons: International Dimensions of the Postwar Anti-Comics Campaign.* Madison, NJ: Fairleigh Dickinson University Press, 1999. Print.

Ma, Sheng-Mei. *East-West Montage: Reflections on Asian Bodies in Diaspora.* Honolulu: University of Hawaii Press, 2007. Print.

McNamara, Patrick. *A Catholic Cold War: Edmund A. Walsh, S.J., and the Politics of American Anticommunism.* New York: Fordham University Press, 2005. Print.
Mende, Gerhard von. *Documents: Soviet Russia's Anti-Islam Policy in Turkestan.* Düsseldorf: Forschungsdienst Osteuropa, 1958. Print.
Nepstad, Sharon. *Religion and War Resistance in the Plowshares Movement.* Cambridge: Cambridge University Press, 2008. Print.
O'Conner, Thomas. "The National Organization for Decent Literature: A Phase in American Catholic Censorship." *Library Quarterly* 65.4 (1995): 386–414. Print.
Penowski, Marian (w), Lloyd Ostendorf (a). *America: the Melting Pot. Treasure Chest of Fun and Fact* vol. 18. #1, 3, 5, 7, 9, 11, 13, 15, 18, 19 (Sept. 1962-May 1963), George A. Pflaum. Web.
Lloyd Ostendorf (i). "Let Freedom Ring." *Treasure Chest of Fun and Fact* vol. 14 #2 (25 September 1958), George A. Pflaum. 15–21. Web
Pidhainy, Semen. *The Black Deeds of the Kremlin: A White Book.* Toronto: Ukrainian Association of Victims of Russian Communist Terror, 1953, 1955. Print.
Reese, Barry (w), Joe Sinnott (a). "Pettigrew for President!" *Treasure Chest of Fun and Fact* vol. 19, #11–20 (30 January-4 June 1964). George A. Pflaum. Web.
Rosswurm, Steve. *The FBI and the Catholic Church, 1935–1962.* Amherst: University of Massachusetts Press, 2009. Print.
Rywkin, Michael. *Moscow's Muslim Challenge: Soviet Central Asia.* New York: M.E. Sharpe, 1982. Print.
Wilhelm, Bernhard "Moslems in the Soviet Union: 1948–1954." *Aspects of Religion in the Soviet Union.* Ed. Richard Marshall. Chicago: University of Chicago Press, 1971. Print. 257–284.
Wolf, Lucien. *The Myth of the Jewish Menace in World Affairs.* London: Macmillan, 1921. Print.

16

The Fantastic Four: A Mirror of Cold War America

Rafiel York

There is little disagreement among scholars or collectors that comics' Silver Age began with DCs reintroduction of The Flash in *Showcase #4*. This issue marks the return of the superhero, which would go on to become comics' dominant genre for over fifty years. The Flash's return was followed by the revivals of Green Lantern, Hawkman, and the Atom, all of whom inhabit the same world and occasionally appear in one another's books. Inspired by fans like Roy Thomas and Jerry Bails, who wrote letters requesting the return of the Justice Society of America, DC created an updated version of the team now called the Justice League of America (Jones and Jacobs 35–36). This team's roster featured Superman, Batman, Wonder Woman, Flash, Green Lantern, Aquaman and the Martian Manhunter, and it proved to be immensely popular. So much so, that Marvel Comics' publisher, Martin Goodman decided to cash in on the resurgence of the superhero team. In *Origins of the Marvel Comics*, Stan Lee recalls,

> Martin mentioned that he had noticed one of the titles published by National Comics seemed to be selling better than most. It was a book called Justice League of America and was composed of a team of superheroes. Well, we didn't need a house to fall on us. "If the *Justice League* is selling," spake he, "why don't we put out a comic book that features a team of superheroes? [16].

The team that Lee and Jack Kirby created for Goodman was The Fantastic Four, and they were unlike any superhero team, or any superheroes, that had previously appeared.

Of The Fantastic Four, Gerard Jones and Will Jacobs observe, "they had the powers of superheroes, but they didn't act like superheroes. They acted something like monsters — and something like real people" (51). The Fantastic Four did not wear costumes, until fans wrote in demanding that they do so. They made no effort to conceal their identities. Most of all, they fought amongst themselves. Johnny Storm and Ben Grimm bicker and fight like siblings. Ben harbored anger and jealousy for Reed Richards — anger because he blamed Richards for turning him into the monstrous Thing, and jealousy because Richards was admired and loved, while the Thing was feared. Susan Storm becomes infatuated with the Sub-Mariner, and hides her feelings from her fiancée, Reed Richards. Randy Duncan and Matthew J. Smith explain that *The Fantastic Four*, "was a marked departure from DC's heroes.... The appeal of Marvel was this more human approach to its heroes" (46).

While the characters' behaviors differed from those of the traditional (DC) superheroes, as the comic progressed through its first year of publication, its approach to Cold War themes also broke away from those that had been established in the comics and popular culture of the previous decade. Cold War concerns with communists, family, gender roles, experts, and juvenile delinquency all appear at throughout the first eight issues of *The Fantastic Four*. However, rather than simply re-doing what had already been done thematically, Stan Lee and Jack Kirby used the tried and true approaches as a springboard into new interpretations of Cold War themes.

The Origin of the Fantastic Four

The first issue of *The Fantastic Four* includes the team's origin. Dr. Reed Richards has created a space ship with the goal of the United States becoming the first nation to travel into outer space. Susan Storm, his fiancée, expresses the importance of beating the Soviet Union when Ben Grimm, the group's pilot, threatens to back out of the project because he fears that the "cosmic rays" could kill them. "Ben, we've got to take that chance," Susan explains, "unless we want the commies to beat us" (*The Fantastic Four* #1, 9). The foursome, which also includes Johnny Storm, Susan's teen-aged brother, sneaks into the "spaceport," not waiting for official clearance, and essentially steals the space ship, blasting off into a cosmic storm that gives each of them different, but amazing, powers. They decide "we've gotta use that power to help mankind, right," and The Fantastic Four is born (13).

The origin story presents many of the themes of Cold War popular culture, and even at this beginning stage in the development of *The Fantastic Four*, Lee and Kirby twist the themes. Susan's argument that they had to beat the "commies" into space fails to convince Ben to pilot the ship. In her book *Anti-Communism and Popular Culture in Mid-Century America*, Cyndy

Hendershot writes, "Anti-communist sentiment was widespread in American life from the late Forties through the mid–Sixties, and, as pervasive as the sentiment was, it is not surprising that a variety of people and causes found opportunity to use the sentiment for their own ideological reasons" (1–2). Susan attempts to use Ben's anti-communist sentiment to persuade him to join her cause, but her appeal falls on deaf ears. Susan recognizes Ben's indifference to the threat posed by communism and shifts tactics almost immediately to accusing him of cowardice. Willing to endure a threat to his way of life, but not to his manhood, Ben smashes his fist through a table and declares, "A coward!! Nobody calls me a coward! Get the ship! I'll fly her no matter what happens!!" (9) Ben's different reactions to Susan's different attempts at motivation reveal his values; he is willing to endure a threat to his nation, but not to his manhood.

Ben's response reflects Handershot's assertion that, "by the early Sixties, American attitudes toward the Soviet Union began to alter. Instead of the Soviets being represented consistently in the entertainment media as an inhuman threat ... a process of looking at the Soviets, both government and people, in a more favorable light emerged" (130). Furthermore, Susan reveals that she is not overly concerned with the "commies" a few panels later, as the team races to the space port, and Reed voices his concern for her and Johnny's safety, saying, "Susan, Ben and I know what we're doing — but you — and Johnny." Wanting to hear nothing more, Susan interrupts, declaring, "Don't say it Reed! I'm your fiancée! Where you go, I go!" (9) This move on her part speaks to the unclear role of women in American society of the late fifties and early sixties. Susan recognizes that her "duty" is to support her man in his professional life, but at the same time, she overrules his warning and insists upon traveling into space with the rest of the all-male crew. Jo Freeman explains, "In the early sixties feminism was still an unmentionable, but its ghost was slowly awakening from the dead." On place where the ghost is seen is in *The Fantastic Four* #1. Susan Storm's demand to be included in the mission anticipates the fight for equality in the workplace of second wave feminism.

Reed's concern for Johnny's safety as well as Susan's elicits the response of "and I'm taggin' along with sis!" from the hot-headed youth. The phrase "taggin' along" echoes the role teenagers had played in comics since the introduction of Robin in 1940, the sidekick. However, Johnny is no sidekick; he is a full member of the team. At the end of the origin story the foursome pledges to use their powers to help mankind, and Johnny claims the name "The Human Torch" for himself. The Human Torch was not an original name, nor was the character entirely original, as Stan Lee explained in a 1981 interview,

The one that was totally unoriginal, of course, was the Human Torch, because we'd had a character like the Torch many years ago. I thought we'd give Johnny Storm, the kid brother of Susan, the same power but we'd change him by making him a teenager. The original Torch was an android as I remember. And also, I attempted to give him a personality that would be unique to Johnny Storm [Pitts Jr. 94].

Despite the lack of originality of the Johnny's powers, Lee and Kirby's approach to writing the character was original. Johnny was a typical teenaged boy who was "more interested in fast cars and girls than saving the world" (Ro 72). By presenting a teenager as a full-fledged member of the team, Lee and Kirby argue that the juvenile delinquency scare of the previous decade is a non-issue, and that teenagers were as capable of acting for the good of humanity as adults were.

During the fifties, "faith in scientific wizardry permeated popular culture" (May 4). Dr. Reed Richards, the genius who created the space ship, is the personification of science and technology as an expression of America's greatness. His expertise falls short of success, however, as cosmic rays bombard the ship and penetrate its shielding. As the crew endures the effects of the "cosmic storm," one of the four astronauts, presumable Reed, though in a space suit and with his/her back turned it is impossible to tell, exclaims, "Ben was right!! We should have waited ... should have gotten heavier shielding!" (10) This admission of failure precedes the discovery of the group's new abilities, but even when the powers begin to appear they are not greeted with a sense of triumph. When Reed Richards and Ben Grimm's powers manifest, Johnny recoils, shouting, "You've turned into monsters ... both of you!!" (12) Johnny reacts to Reed and Ben's transformation with the fear that one might expect in that situation, but he also reflects the fear many people felt where scientists were concerned in the years following World War II, due to their roles in creating the atomic bomb (Badash 242). In the case of *The Fantastic Four,* it is not the mystery of nuclear power that creates trepidation, but the effects of cosmic rays on humans, but in a fundamental sense the source of the fear remains the same. It is the fear that scientists will be unable to control the forces with which they tamper.

It is common among scholars and fans alike to view The Fantastic Four as a family, even during the early years when the only members who were related were Susan and Johnny. This approach to writing a superhero team was a dramatic break from what had been done in the past. As Simcha Weinstein writes, "The family dynamic was unmistakable from the start. Prior to The Fantastic Four, the family unit had never been explored within the comic book genre" (74). During the origin story, Reed assumes the role of the "father" of the family that is The Fantastic Four. He is the recognized leader of the group, who expresses concern for the other family members as they prepare to steal the space ship, and who deals out discipline when Ben reacts violently to his transformation. As the creator of the space ship, Reed is placed in the position of bread-winner, as he clearly has a respectable, well-paying job. Susan falls into the role of "mother" almost by default in the origin story, because she is the only female character and because she is identified as Reed's fiancée. She does very little nurturing in the story, and there is no home for her to "make," thus she falls short of the traditional role assigned to a wife and mother. At this point, the attempt to shoehorn The Fantastic Four into the roles of the nuclear family falls apart. Johnny is clearly identified as Susan's brother, and refers to her as "Sis" throughout the origin story. If there were only the three members of the group, there would be a family dynamic in place (though, it would not be a nuclear family). However, the group is The Fantastic Four, and it is the fourth member who creates the biggest problem for reading this superhero team as a family.

Ben's relationship to the rest of the group is unclear. In later years Ben's history of being Reed's college roommate would be explained, but in the origin story, Ben is simply the pilot. In fact, in response to a letter published in *The Fantastic Four #7*, Stan Lee explains the relationships of the various members of the team, after explaining that Reed and Susan are "good friends," Lee writes, "The Thing (Ben) was the pilot they hired to fly them on their ill-fated space voyage." The way Ben Grimm interacts with the other members of the team does not come across as if he is a hired pilot. After the ship crash lands, Ben becomes infuriated and attacks Reed with a tree. Susan screams a warning and her concern for her fiancé, prompting Ben to reply, "I'll prove to you that you love the wrong man, Susan!" (12) Ben's jealousy reveals that he has been around the other members of the group long enough, and he has worked closely enough to develop feelings for Susan. Reed defends himself, and in the process, he discovers his ability to stretch his body. Entangling Ben in his arms, Reed proclaims, "You've had this coming to you for a long time, Ben!" (12) If Ben were just a hired pilot, they would not have established a relationship that has stood for "a long time." Ben's distemper and jealousy add to the family dynamic by creating opportunities for the members of the group to fight among themselves, and to put their differences aside when the family needs them to do so. The Fantastic Four is clearly not the saccharine family portrayed on TV and in comics of the time.

Body Snatching, Brainwashing, and Foreign Powers

In another throwback to the themes of the previous decade, *The Fantastic Four #2* introduces the Skrulls, a shape-shifting alien race that intends to conquer the Earth after doing away with The Fantastic Four. In order to get rid of the super-powered humans, the Skrulls take on the shapes of the members of the team and brazenly commit crimes like destroying an oil platform, stealing jewels, melting a statue during its dedication, and shutting off the power to the city. The government demands that The Fantastic Four, who have been on a camping trip, turn themselves in. Being heroes, they comply, but not before hatching a plan to infiltrate and stop the Skrulls. Of course, the team has to escape from prison in order to enact the plan, but that is a small concern since they are clearly innocent. Johnny poses as a Skrull posing as Johnny, and signals the rest of the team once he's found the aliens' lair. After defeating the Skrull scouts, the team again uses the ruse of posing as Skrulls posing as The Fantastic Four to infiltrate the mother ship. Reed convinces the Skrull commander that Earth's forces are too formidable for the Skrull army to conquer, and that he and the rest of his team should stay behind "to remove all evidence of our presence on Earth!" (8). Upon returning to Earth, The Fantastic Four tracks down the remaining Skrulls, and Reed informs the invaders that he will "hynotize [sic] you so you will forget your previous identities! You will remain what you become — for as long as you live!" The Skrulls agree to Reed's plan, admitting that they, "hate being Skrulls," and ask to find contentment in their new lives, which turns out to be as cows in a pasture (24).

The Skrulls' ability to change shape and imitate any person they choose is reminiscent of aliens in the 1956 film *Invasion of the Body Snatchers*. Of the film, Brian Vizzini writes, "Politically speaking, Invasion of the Body Snatchers is little more than a restating of what conservatives like McCarthy had been saying all along — i.e. that subversives had infiltrated all of our most cherished social and political institutions" (30). The Skrulls imitate Earth's only defense against their attack, and by doing so encourage the government to imprison The Fantastic Four, thus making Earth vulnerable to invasion. The fear of "imposters" was rampant in the United States in the early fifties, as Senator Joseph McCarthy spearheaded the movement to ferret out the communists who were hiding in our midst. Of course, Marvel released *The Fantastic Four* #2 in 1962, several years after Joseph McCarthy's witch-hunt had come to an end, but the anxiety over infiltration persisted into the 1960s. The film and the comic differ in their outcomes, however, and it is this difference that adds poignancy to the conclusion of The Fantastic Four story. *Invasion of the Body Snatchers* takes the stance that America is powerless to prevent communist infiltration. The film ends with the FBI being notified of the invasion, but all indications are that it is too late to stop it. *The Fantastic Four* #2 ends not only with the defeat of the imposters, but with them agreeing to be hypnotized into believing they are cattle. The Fantastic Four stops this invasion, and by hypnotizing them Richards gives them the contentment that they have been missing as members of the Skrull army. Through Reed Richards' expertise, America achieves victory over the Skrulls, just as American scientists would provide the means to defeat the Soviets.

It is also of note that Reed Richards uses hypnotism to imprison the Skrulls. In the years following the Korean War, a new fear manifested itself in the minds of many Americans, communist brainwashing. The fear was based on the belief them "Having cracked the brain's codes, Reds were now believed capable of remodelling [sic] humans at will" (Carruthers). Whereas the old fear had been that communists were masquerading as good Americans, the new fear was that good Americans could be transformed into communists against their will. The United States government attempted to influence North Korean and Chinese POWs to reject communism by introducing "'voluntary repatriation,' a novel interpretation of the Geneva Convention on the return of POWs which argued that individuals who chose to go elsewhere did not have to be repatriated" (Young). When they are left behind by the mothership, the Skrull scouts in this story become POWs, and by admitting they hate being Skrulls, they choose to accept the ways of Earth. They refuse repatriation, and choose to change their lives — going elsewhere.

Stan Lee and Jack Kirby would return to stories of hypnotism and mind-control three times in the first year of *The Fantastic Four*. Issue #3 tells the story of "The Miracle Man," a stage magician who performs feats so incredible that not even The Fantastic Four can duplicate them. Along with being a stage magician, The Miracle Man is also a jewel thief, and with his amazing powers he is able to avoid capture at the hand of The Fantastic Four. He then declares war on "the whole human race," and announces his intention to "conquer the earth" (8). Reed Richards soon deduces that The Miracle Man is actually powerless, and nothing more than a "clever hypnotist, a master of mass illusion," who had tricked The Fantastic Four into believing that their powers were ineffective against him.

The Fantastic Four #7 returns to the theme of brainwashing, as Kurrgo, the master of Planet X, uses his "hostility ray" to turn the rest of the world against The Fantastic Four. He then offers the team refuge on his planet, in exchange for a favor, saving Planet X from an impending collision with another planet. Reed is unable to devise a way to prevent the destruction of Planet X, but using a shrink ray he reduces the size of all five billion inhabitants of the planet, allowing them to evacuate to a new planet in one of Kurrgo's two functioning spaceships. The Fantastic Four take the other ship back to Earth, where the effects of Kurrgo's hostility ray have worn off the population.

The next issue, *The Fantastic Four* #8, introduces The Puppet Master, a villain who uses puppets constructed from radioactive clay to control peoples' minds. He kidnaps Susan Storm, takes control of The Thing, and sends him to kill the rest of The Fantastic Four. Then, The Puppet Master constructs a model of State Prison, and engineers a prison break. Reed and Johnny stop The Thing's attack by temporarily transforming him into his human form, then the threesome stop the prison break and free Susan. With his prison break halted, The Puppet Master prepares to launch his back-up plan, but his blind step-daughter, Alicia Masters, attempts to stop him. As they struggle, The Puppet Master trips over Alicia's arm and plunges out the window to his apparent death.

In each of these stories the villain uses a form of mind-control to combat The Fantastic Four. The Miracle Man attempts a fairly direct attack, Kurrgo turns the world against the super-heroes, and The Puppet Master uses one of their own against them. In the first two stories, the villain is defeated by Reed's cunning, showing once again that American scientists are capable of solving any problem and giving the nation the means to win any war. The Puppet Master is defeated, in part, because his step-daughter awakens to his evil, and turns on him. Having previously been an accomplice by imitating Susan Storm, the oppressed Alicia rises up against her tyrannical step-father and scores a victory for morality and goodness, just as the oppressed citizens of communist nations would need to rebel against their rulers (with the assistance of the United States).

The other stories that appeared in the first year of *The Fantastic Four's* publication centered on two of The Fantastic Four's greatest and most frequent adversaries: The Sub-Mariner and Dr. Doom. The Sub-Mariner makes his first Silver Age appearance in *The Fantastic Four* #4. The story sees Johnny quitting the team and running away. Seeking a place where his former teammates will not find him, Johnny spends the night at a "men's hotel" in the Bowery. While he's there, he finds a *Sub-Mariner* comic from the 1940s, which leads another man to point out a bum who's "as strong as that joker" (8). The bum becomes violent when the other men approach him, and Johnny diagnoses him as having amnesia, which he attempts to cure by cleaning up the bum. When Johnny uses his flame to give the bum a shave, he discovers that the bum is in fact The Sub-Mariner. Johnny returns the amnesiac to the ocean, where his memory returns, and he declares war on the surface world for having destroyed his undersea kingdom. Using a magical "trumpet-horn," The Sub-Mariner summons Giganto, "the largest living thing in all the world" and unleashes it on New York City. After several unsuccessful attempts to halt Giganto's progress, The Thing devises a plan to stop the monster. Strapping a nuclear bomb to his back, Ben Grimm walks into Giganto's mouth and into its stomach, where he drops off the bomb and runs out of the monster's mouth to safety. The bomb kills Giganto, and The Fantastic Four defeats The Sub-Mariner, and he returns to the ocean, swearing to get vengeance in the future.

Giganto, an enormous, armed whale hearkens back to the fifties, and the giant monsters that Jack Kirby drew in comics like *Journey into Mystery* and *Tales to Astonish*. These monster stories were obviously inspired by the giant monster movies like 1954's *Gojira* and its American version, 1956's *Godzilla, King of the Monsters!*, and like their inspirations, these stories "equate the monster with the atomic bomb" (Anisfield 53). When The Sub-Mariner unleashes his atomic bomb on New York, it is only fitting that The Fantastic Four should retaliate with its own nuclear bomb. The Thing only acquires the necessary ordnance after racing "from one military depot to another" (18), indicating that the United States government in not only aware of the intended use of the bomb, but that it is complicit in the bomb's detonation. The Thing's bomb proves to be more powerful than Giganto, and in this story, the U.S. emerges victorious in the arms race.

The Fantastic Four #5 introduces the team's arch-enemy, Dr. Doom, and while in later years Doom would become the monarch of the small country, Latveria, at this point he was a brilliant scientist in a suit of high-tech armor. In the story, Dr. Doom, a former classmate of Reed Richards who was disfigured when one of his experiments went awry, wraps The Fantastic Four's headquarters, The Tower, in an energy draining net. He demands Susan Storm as a hostage to "insure that you do what I demand of you" (5), and what he demands of the team is to travel back in time to acquire Blackbeard's treasure chest for him. The team has a few adventures as members of the crew of a pirate ship, and when they battle another pirate ship, The Thing, disguised as a black bearded pirate, gains the nickname "Blackbeard." The Fantastic Four's ship is destroyed, but when they wash ashore they find a treasure chest, which Ben loads with chains and brings to the present with him. Having thwarted Doom's plan through the clever use of semantics, bringing Blackbeard's treasure chest, but not the actual treasure, The Thing punches the villain, who is revealed to be a robot. The real Dr. Doom flips a switch that drains the oxygen from the room where Mr. Fantastic, The Human Torch, and The Thing are trapped. At this point, Doom's hostage, The Invisible Girl, short-circuits Doom's machine and frees her teammates from the trap.

Dr. Doom is a perfect foil to Reed Richards. Both men are brilliant scientists, but Doom is motivated by selfish reasons while Richards acts for the good of humanity. Of the perception of scientists in post-war America, Lawrence Badash writes, "Praise of science and scientists soon coincided with doubts, criticism, fear, and even hostility.... From being heroes who ended the war, scientists were almost immediately seen as evil geniuses that created unthinkable horrors: the atomic apocalypse" (242). With his amazing suit of armor, time machine, energy sapping net, and robot duplicates, Dr. Doom positions himself as a scientist to be feared. Furthermore, the first panel of the story shows him with books entitled *Demons* and *Science and Sorcery*, indicating that Doom is not only a scientist, but also a magician, dabbling with the unknown forces of black magic. Richards, on the other hand, is a heroic scientist, a man whose first invention is a space-ship which will be used to beat the "commies" into space (*The Fantastic Four* #1). By presenting these character foils, Lee and Kirby, also examine the potential of science to do good or evil, and conclude that it is not the science, but the scientist, that is good or evil.

The next issue of *The Fantastic Four*, issue #6, features a team-up between Dr. Doom and The Sub-Mariner. The story opens with The Human Torch unsuccessfully searching for Dr. Doom, who escaped in the previous issue. Meanwhile, Dr. Doom travels to The Sub-Mariner's undersea home to propose an alliance against The Fantastic Four. As the two villains discuss the plan, Doom notices a framed photograph of Susan Storm, which The Sub-Mariner warns "is no concern of yours" (7). Dr. Doom then reignites The Sub-Mariner's desire for revenge against the surface world, leading The Sub-Mariner to proclaim, "I ... I ... I cannot harm the girl! But I will aid you in defeating the others!" (8). As Doom and The Sub-Mariner launch the initial stage of their plan, the story cuts to The Fantastic Four's headquarters, which is now identified as the Baxter Building, where Susan catches Johnny snooping in her room. Johnny confronts Susan about a photograph of The Sub-Mariner that she had hidden in a bookcase. The brother and sister wrestle for the photo, and Johnny incinerates it as Reed and Ben enter the room to check on the commotion. When Johnny reveals the subject of the photo, Reed tells Susan, "I think you owe us an explanation, Sue!" (12).

Before Susan is able to explain her attraction to The Sub-Mariner, he enters the headquarters and The Thing and The Human Torch attack him. Susan steps in between the combatants while Reed restrains The Thing, but Susan's intervention does not cool The Human Torch's temper, and he and The Sub-Mariner fight. When Johnny exhausts his flame, The Sub-Mariner proposes a truce between himself and The Fantastic Four, and after checking out his story, Reed hesitantly accepts. Just then, Dr. Doom triggers his trap. Using his "grabber," Doom rips the Baxter Building from its foundation and launches it into space. As the team's headquarters loses oxygen, Mr. Fantastic searches for solutions to the problem, while The Sub-Mariner tends to Susan who "has nearly passed out from lack of air!" (17). After a pair of failed attempts to recues themselves, and a scuffle between The Thing and The Sub-Mariner, Namor leaps into space, chasing Doom's space-ship. When he catches his duplicitous partner, The Sub-Mariner forces Doom to abandon ship, and returns the Baxter Building to its foundation. Recognizing that their former enemy has saved their lives, Ben ponders, "How do you thank an enemy?" Susan responds, "Oh, he isn't our enemy! I just know it! He's so full of pain and bitterness that it blinds his better instincts! Submariner [sic] needs time ... time to heal!" (24).

Susan and Namor's mutual affection serves as both a threat to the family dynamic of the team, and as an expression of Susan's sexuality. While the team is not a nuclear family, Lee and Kirby did establish a definite sense of family in the first issue of *The Fantastic Four*. When Reed and Ben walk in on the Storm siblings fighting over the photograph of The Sub-Mariner, Ben opines, "Bah! I knew it! All a gal wants in a good-lookin' guy! It doesn't matter if he's the most dangerous creep on earth!" When Reed demands an explanation, Susan begins to say that Namor is "gentle and...," but she is interrupted when he arrives at the Baxter Building. Here The Sub-Mariner acts as a threat not only to the surface world, but also to the sanctity of the family that The Fantastic Four has become. He is the "other man," and he wants to steal the family's mother. Susan has announced her intention to form a family with Reed, and she and Johnny are siblings, thus she is a part of the two actual family relationships in the team. Of The Sub-Mariner, Stan Lee explains, "I also planned to have him fall in love with Sue, and have some interesting complications" (Jankiewicz 118). One such complication could have been the destruction of the team itself. Without Susan, Johnny and Reed have no connection, and it is conceivable that the team would crumble. Susan's desire for Namor, the "good-lookin' guy," reflects a trend that becomes prominent in the fifties. Elaine Tyler May writes, "Sexual attraction was an important component in the choice of a mate — too important, according to some observers at the time" (112). The sexual attraction between Susan and Namor threatens to destroy the family, and while this portrayal may seem abnormal for the era, as Warren Susman writes, "by the end of the decade [the fifties] ... the American Dream turns into a decaying marriage, and the family is assaulted, as it has never before been assaulted, as a total failure" (26).

The stories published during the first year of *The Fantastic Four* virtually overflowed with Cold War themes. The concerns of Americans in the late fifties and early sixties are examined through the lens of a superhero story, and exemplifying an idea that Stan Lee expressed in a 1970 interview, "you got to make your comic magazines ... relate to the real world because unless they do, you have meaningless cardboard characters, and that's not really what people are into today. They want stories that will tell them something about the world they are living in now" (interview with Van Gelder and Van Gelder 29).

Works Cited

Anisfield, Nancy. "Godzilla/Gojiro: Evolution of the Nuclear Metaphor." *Journal of Popular Culture* 29.3 (1995): 53–62. Print.
Badash, Lawrence. "From Security Blanket to Security Risk: Scientists in the Decade After Hiroshima." *History and Technology* 19.3 (2003): 241–256. Academic Search Premier. EBSCO. Web. 1 April 2011.
Carruthers, Susan L. "'The Manchurian Candidate' (1962) and the Cold War Brainwashing Scare." *Historical Journal of Film, Radio and Television* 18.1 (1998): 75. Academic Search Premier. EBSCO. Web. 5 April 2011
Duncan, Randy, and Matthew J. Smith. *The Power of Comics*. New York: Continuum, 2009. Print.
Freeman, Jo. "The Women's Liberation Movement: Its Origins, Structures and Ideas." jofreeman.com. n.p., 1971, Web. 27 April 2011.
Hendershot, Cyndy. *Anti-Communism and Popular Culture in Mid-Century America*. Jefferson, NC: MacFarland, 2003. Print.
Jankiewicz, Pat. "The Marvel Age of Comics: An Interview with Stan Lee." *Stan Lee Conversations*. Ed.
Jeff McLaughlin. Jackson: University Press of Mississippi, 2007. 107–120. Print.
Jones, Gerard, and Will Jacobs. *The Comics Book Heroes* 2d ed. Rocklin: Prima, 1997. Print.
Lee, Stan. Interview with Lawrence Van Gelder and Lindsey Van Gelder. *Stan Lee Conversations*. Ed. Jeff McLaughlin. Jackson: University Press of Mississippi, 2007. 20–29. Print.
Lee, Stan. *Origins of the Marvel Comics*. New York: Simon and Schuster, 1974. Print.
Lee, Stan. Reply to letter of Barbara Stock. *Fantastic Four* #7 (Sept. 1962): Marvel Comics. Print.
[Lee, Stan (w) and Jack Kirby (a)]. "Captives of the Deadly Duo!" *The Fantastic Four* #6 (Sept. 1962), Marvel Comics. Print.
_____. "The Coming of Sub-Mariner!" *The Fantastic Four* #4 (May 1962), Marvel Comics. Print.
_____ *The Fantastic Four* #1 (Nov. 1961), Marvel Comics. Print.
_____. "The Miracle Man." *The Fantastic Four* #3 (March 1962), Marvel Comics. Print.
_____. "Prisoners of Doctor Doom!" *The Fantastic Four* #5 (July 1962), Marvel Comics. Print.
_____. "Skrulls from Outer Space." *The Fantastic Four* #2 (Jan. 1962), Marvel Comics. Print.
May, Elaine Tyler. *Homeward Bound*. 20th Anniversary Ed. New York: Perseus, 2008. Print.
May, Lary. Introduction. *Recasting America: Culture and Politics in the Age of the Cold War*. Ed. Lary May. Chicago: University of Chicago Press, 1989. Print.
McLaughlin, Lary, Ed. *Stan Lee Conversations*. Jackson: University Press of Mississippi, 2007. Print.
Pitts Jr., Leonard. "An Interview with Stan Lee." *Stan Lee Conversations*. Ed. Jeff McLaughlin. Jackson: University Press of Mississippi, 2007. 85–100. Print.
Ro, Ronin. *Tales to Astonish: Jack Kirby, Stan Lee, and the American Comic Book Revolution*. New York: Bloomsbury, 2004. Print.
"The Soviet Union is First to the Moon." *History Today* 59.9 (2009): 10. Academic Search Premier. EBSCO. Web. 1 April 2011.
Susman, Warren. "Did Success Spoil the United States? Dual Representations in Postwar America." *Recasting America: Culture and Politics in the Age of the Cold War*. Ed. Lary May. Chicago: University of Chicago Press, 1989. Print.
Vizzini, Brian. "Cold War Fears, Cold War Passions: Conservatives and Liberals Square Off in 1950s Science Fiction." *Quarterly Review of Film and Video* 26 (2009): 28–39. Print.
Weinstein, Simcha. *Up, Up, and Oy Vey! How Jewish History, Culture, and Values Shaped the Comic Book Superhero*. Baltimore: Leviathan, 2006. Print.
Young, Charles S. "Missing Action: POW Films, Brainwashing and the Korean War, 1954–1968." *Historical Journal of Film, Radio and Television* 18.1 (1998): 49. Academic Search Premier. EBSCO. Web. 8 April 2011.

About the Contributors

Nathan **Atkinson** is an assistant professor of communications at Georgia State University. He is working on a book about how the Navy worked with newsreel companies to film the 1946 atomic blasts at Bikini Atoll.

John **Donovan** is an assistant professor of history at the Air Force Academy in Colorado Springs. He has extensively studied and taught world and American history, with an emphasis on the Cold War. He specializes in the analysis of media, politics, and popular culture (especially as it pertains to comics) from the 1940s to the present.

Jeanne **Gardner** is working towards a master's degree in history of the decorative arts, design history, and material culture at the Bard Graduate Center in New York City. She is writing a thesis on American romance comics from 1947 to 1954.

Christopher B. **Field** is a Ph.D. candidate in the Department of English at Southern Illinois University, Carbondale. His primary research interests are twentieth-century American literature and twentieth-century American culture. He has presented papers devoted to the study of comics at numerous conferences.

Diana **Green** teaches comic art history and graphic novel at Minneapolis College of Art and Design. An editor on the *Encyclopedia of Comic Books and Graphic Novels*, she is working on a book on the comic *Concrete*.

Christopher J. **Hayton** is a doctoral student in the College of Social Work at Florida State University, studying British social work education reform. He has spent many years studying, collecting and selling comics and, more recently, writing as a comic book scholar.

Sheila **Hayton** has been a mother, a homemaker, an auxiliary nurse, a shorthand typist, a medical receptionist, a teacher, an office worker, and a medical foster parent. An avid consumer and student of medical romantic fiction, she read British girls' comics in the 1950s and '60s, but her primary interest in comic books centers on the adaptations of traditional Indian literature in the Amar Chitra Katha series. Originally from Ely, Cardiff, she has traveled widely.

Peter **Lee** has a master's degree from California State University, Northridge, where he studied American cultural history and the European Middle Ages. He has contributed to *Americana: The Journal of American Popular Culture*.

Alexander **Maxwell** is a senior lecturer in history at Victoria University in Wellington, New Zealand. He has written *Choosing Slovakia: Slavic Hungary, the Czechoslovak Language and Accidental Nationalism*, edited *The East-West Discourse: Symbolic Geography and Its Consequences*, and translated into English Jan Kollar's *Wechselseitigkeit*. He has published short pieces on Hungary, Macedonia, and Slavic language codification.

Ruth **McClelland-Nugent** received her doctorate in history from Dalhousie University in Nova Scotia, Canada. She is an associate professor of history at Augusta State University in Georgia. Her previous research includes a study of the gendered portrayal of Nazism and gender in D.C. Comics and an examination of family dynamics in the *Wonder Woman* television series.

Phillip **Payne** is a professor of history at St. Bonaventure University, where he teaches a variety of courses on United States and public history. He is the author of *Dead Last: The Public Memory of Warren G. Harding's Scandalous Legacy* (2009) and numerous essays and articles.

Lawrence **Rodman** is a visual arts educator, writer and artist. He is a long-time contributing writer and illustrator for comics and graphics-oriented publications such as *The Comics Journal* and other Fantagraphics publications.

Paul J. **Spaeth** is the director of the library and special collections librarian at St. Bonaventure University. He regularly teaches courses in film, literature, history and theology. Among his publications he has been most active in writing about and editing the works of the poet Robert Lax.

Frederick A. **Wright** is an assistant professor of English at Ursuline College in Pepper Pike, Ohio. His writings have appeared in *The Journal of Electronic Publishing* and *Books and Beyond: The Greenwood Encyclopedia of New American Reading*.

Chris **York** teaches English and American studies at Pine Technical College. His writings range from pedagogy to poetry, and from baseball literature to comic books.

Rafiel **York**'s thesis, "Generic Transformation and the Superhero," was nominated for the distinguished thesis award at St. Cloud State University. He writes the comics blog *The Fanboy Scholar* and teaches English at Jackson County Central High School in Jackson, Minnesota.

Index

Numbers in **_bold italics_** indicate pages with illustrations.

Acheson, Dean 36
Action Comics 20, **_23_**, 24, **_25_**
All American Comics 58
All-American Girls Professional Baseball League 110
All-Flash 58
All Star Comics 58
All True Romance 141, **_142_**
Allen, Barry 57, 60, 64–65; *see also* The Flash
Allen, Woody 176
Alley Awards 58
American Comics Magazine Publishers (ACMP) 167–168
Andrews, Archie 103–114, **_108_**
Andru, Ross 117, 118, **_119_**, **_135_**
Aquaman 204
Archie Comics 95, 103, 110, **_111_**, 112
Archie's Joke Book **_108_**
Astonishing 32
Atlas Comics 46; *see also* Marvel Comics
The Atom 204
Atom-Age Combat 81, 83, 87
Avon Publications 81

Bails, Jerry 60, 204
Barton, Clara 131
Batgirl 123
Batman 8, 85, 103, 116, 123, 181, 204
Batman 123
Batwoman 123
The Baxter Building 213–214
Bean, Orsen 173
Bentley, Elizabeth 30
Berle, Milton 147, 174
Berlin Uprising 192, **_193_**
Bert the Turtle 27
Bikini Atoll (Bikini Islands) 11, 19, 24–26, 28
Biro, Charles 157, 159, 163, 164
Blackhawk 73
Blackhawks 192

Blandy, Admiral William H.P. 19–21
Bob and Ray 172–173, 175–176
Bond, James 64
Boy Meets Girl 137
Broken Arrow 180
Brooks, Mel 174, 176
Broome, John **_64_**
Bruce, Lenny 172, 177
Bumpo, Natty 183
Byrnes, James 104

Caesar, Sid 173–175; and ethnic stereotyping 176
Captain America 36, 38
Captain Cold 62
Cavell, Edith 131
Central City 11, 56
Central Intelligence Agency (CIA) 34, 62
Chabas, Paul 82
Challengers of the Unknown 68–77
Challengers of the Unknown 11, 68–70, 72–74, 77
Charlton Comics Publishing 132, 137
Chingatchgook 183
Classics Illustrated 88, 170
Clifford Report 30
Collins, Al "Jazzbo" 172–173, 175
Colombia Pictures Corporation 89
Comic Cavalcade 58
Comic Media 141
The Comics Code 5, 8, 11, 13–14, 41, 58, 60, 96, 101, 141, 143–144, 151, 157, 167, 170–171, 175, 186
Comics House Publications 157; *see also* Lev Gleason Publications
Comics Magazine Association of America (CMAA) 5, 167; and *Better Homes and Gardens* 170; *see also* The Comics Code
Commissioner Gordon 85
Committee on the Evaluation of Comic Books 158
Cooper, Betty 105, 107–110, **_109_**, 112–113

219

Cox, Wally 173, 177
Crandall, Reed 149, 192–193, *193*, *195*, 196–98
Crane, Nurse Betty 132
Crime and Punishment 163, 165–167, *166*
crime comics (genre) 58, 142, 157–158, 167, 169
Crime Does Not Pay 13, 142, 156–167, *162*, *165*
Crime SuspenStories 147
Crisis on Infinite Earths 65
The Crypt Keeper 167
Cuban Missile Crisis 190

Date with Danger 32
Daughters of Bilitis 152
Davis, Alan 148
Davis, Jack *51*, 172, 175
Davis, Rocky 69–70, 76
DC Publications 13, 41, 56, 82, 134–135, 204; see also National Periodical Publications
Dell Publishing 89, 130, 136, 170, 179, 183, 186
Detective Comics 123
Devil's Doorway 180
Disney, Walt 82
Ditko, Steve 36, 70
Dr. Doom 211–214
Doyly, Dilton 108–109
Drucker, Mort 173, 175–176
Dutch, Dana 97

Educational Comics (EC) 169; see also Entertaining Comics
Eisenhower, Dwight 34, 79; administration 26, 78, 80, 83, 89
Eisner, Will 152, 171
Elder, Will 172
Entertaining Comics (EC) 2, 13, 41, 45, 146, 132, 146, 150–152, 167, 169–173, 171, 177
espionage comics (genre) 11, 37
Esposito, Mike 117, 118, *119*, *135*

Fantastic Four 70, 75, 204, 205, 207–214
Fantastic Four 13–14, 70, 76–77, 205–214
Farmer, Philip Jose 147
Federal Civil Defense Administration (FCDA) 27
Feiffer, Jules 177
Feldstein, Al 13, 148, 149, 171–177
The Feminine Mystique 125–126
Fiction House 80, 130

film noir 148
First Love Illustrated 139
The Flash 11, 56–65, *60*, *63*, *64*, 69, 74, 204; see also Allen, Barry; Garrick, Jay
The Flash 64
Flash Comics 58
Flash Gordon 47
Four Color Comics 89, 179
Fox, Gardner 58, *85*
Friedan, Betty 126
Frontline Combat 45, *51*, 53
Fujitani, Bob *166*
Fury, Nick 42

Gaines, M.C. 58
Gaines, William 10, 41, 45–46, 170–173
Garrick, Jay 58; see also The Flash
Gates, Lewis 191
Gelbart, Larry 176
Geneva Convention 210
Giella, Joe *64*, *85*
Gilbert World-Wide Publications 88
Gilda 148–149
Gleason, Lev 158, 163
Godzilla, King of the Monsters! 212
Gojira 212
Goldwater, John 103, 106
Good Girl Art (GGA) 130, 138, 140
Goodman, Martin 204
Gorilla Grodd 62
Great Lover Romances 141
Green Lantern 204
Griffith, Andy 173
Grimm, Ben 205–208, 212–214; see also The Thing

Hart, Stan 172
Harvey Comics Hits 136, 139, 141
Harvey Hits 8, *9*
Harvey Publishing 131
Hawkman 204
Hedy DeVine 138
Hefner, Hugh 171, 172, 177
Hi-School Romance 92, *93*, 95, *99*, 100
Hiroshima 55, 81, 84
Hiss, Alger 31
Hoover, J. Edgar 191–192
horror comics (genre) 58, 167, 169
Hulk 42, 75
The Human Torch 206–207, 212–213; see also Storm, Johnny
Humbug 83
Hungarian Revolution, in *This Godless Communism* 195–196

Index

I Aim at the Stars 89
The Illustrated Story of Space 88
Infantino, Carmine 58, *60*, *63*, *64*, *85*
Invasion of the Body Snatchers 209
The Iron Curtain (film) 197
Iron Man 42
Is This Tomorrow: America Under Communism 191

Jefferson, Thomas 179
Joint Task Force One (JTF-1) 19–20, 22–23, 25–26, 28
Jones, Jughead 107, *109*, 112–113
Jorgenson, Christine 152
Journey into Mystery 212
Jungle Comics 6, *7*
jungle comics (genre) 6, 8
Justice Society of America 58, 204

Kanigher, Robert 58, *60*, *63*, 115, 117, 118, 124, 126, *135*
Kaye, Danny 172–173, 177
Kefauver, Sen. Estes 104
Kennan, George 104, 156
Kent Blake and the Secret Service 32
Khrushchev, Nikita 80, 191
Kid Flash 57, 65
King Kong 71
Kirby, Jack 11, 14, 68–77, *87*, 96, 132, 204–205, 207, 210, 212–214
Kogan, Artie 172
Korean War 11, 46, 53, 185, 210
Kovacs, Ernie 172–175; as Percy Dovetonsils 175
Krassner, Paul 177
Kubert, Joe *60*, *63*
Kurtzman, Harvey 11, 45–46, *51*, 52–53, 170–172, 177

Lampert, Harry 58
Landers, Anne 96–97
Lane, Lois 21, 120
Lang, Fritz 147
Laugh Comics *109*
Leatherstocking Tales 183
Lee, Stan 14, 70, 77, 138, *139*, 204–208, 210, 213–214
Lehrer, Tom 173
Lenin, Vladamir, in *This Godless Communism* 191–194, 197
Lev Gleason Publications 137, 142, 157, 163, 165
Linda Lark, Student Nurse 136
Lodge, Veronica 106–113, *108*

Lois Lane 120
The Lone Ranger 183
The Lone Ranger's Companion Tonto 183
The Long Telegram 156
The Lovers 147

MAD 13, 169–178
Mainline Comics 69, 75
Man in Space 82
The Manchurian Candidate 186
Mantle, Reggie 110, 112–113
Marston, William Moulton 12, 115–117, 126
Martian Manhunter 204
Martin, Jane, War Nurse 130
Marvel Boy 30–31, 32–33, *33*
Marvel Comics 42, 70, 75, 135, 138, 142, 204, 209
Marx, Karl, in *This Godless Communism* 191, 198, 200–201
Masters, Alicia 210–211
Matinée en Septembre ("September Morn") 82
Mattachine Society 152
Mayer, Sheldon 58
McCarthy, Sen. Joseph 37, 209; the McCarthy era 171
McKinley, William 185
MD 132
Men's Adventures 36
Mer-Boy 118–119
Metropolis 21, 24, 28
Midway 47–48
Military Comics 192
Millie the Model 138
Mirror Master 62
Miss Grundy 112
Mr. Crime 159–165, *162*, *165*, 167
Mr. Fantastic 212; *see also* Richards, Reed
Mr. Lodge 107, *108*
Mr. Weatherbee 112
Morgan, Ace 69
Morgan, Henry 173
Mortimer, Win *23*, *25*
Muggs, J. Fred 173
Myra North, Special Nurse 130
Mystery in Space 82, 84, *85*

Nagasaki 81
The National Office of Decent Literature 158, 191
National Periodical Publications 58, 84; *see also* DC Comics
Navy's Office of Public Relations 19
Nellie the Nurse 130, 131, 138, *139*, 143

Index

Neuman, Alfred E. 177
New Heroic Comics 132
Night Nurse 142
Nightingale, Florence 130, 131
Nixon, Richard 108
Nostradamus 72

Officer Common Sense 165–166; *166*
The Old Witch 167
Operation Crossroads 19–20, 22–24, 26, 28
Oppenheimer, J. Robert 37
The Organization Man 178
Our Army at War 134–135, *135*

Palais, Rudy 163
Pep Comics 103, 105–106
Peter, Harry G. 117, *118*
Pflaum, George 191–192, 194, 196–198
The Phantom 8, *9*
Planet Comics 80
Post, Howie 138, *139*, 143
Prince, Diana 117, *118*, *119*, 120; *see also* Wonder Woman
Professor Haley 69
Psychoanalysis 150–152
pulp magazines 140
The Puppet Master 210–211

Quality Comics 34, 41
Queen Hippolyte 116, 118, 123–4

Race for the Moon 86, *87*
Richards, Reed 76, 205–209, 211–214; *see also* Mr. Fantastic
Rio Grande 180
Riverdale 12, 109
Riverdale Gang 104–105, 113
Riverdale High School 108, 112
Robbins, June 69, 71–72, 76–77
Robin 8, 85, 123, 181, 184, 206
The Rogues 62
romance comics 2, 12, 58, 92, 94–96, 98, 100–101, 131–133, 136–137, 138, 140–142, 167, 169
Romance Picture Novelette 132
Romita, John 36
Rosenberg, Ethel 37
Rosenberg, Julius 37
Rosie the Riveter 116
Ryan, Red 69

St. John Publishing Company 83
Schwartz, Julius 58

Seduction of the Innocent 5–6, 8, 10, 152
Senate Subcommittee Hearing on Juvenile Delinquency 5, 10, 104
Sensation Comics **118**, 191
Sergeant Fury 135
Sergeant Rock 135
Severin, Marie *51*
Shepherd, Jean 172–173
S.H.I.E.L.D. 42
Showcase Comics 11, 56, 69, 204
Siegel, Jerry *23*, *25*
Siegel, Larry 172
Silver Streak Comics 159; *see also Crime Does Not Pay*
Simon, Joe 68–69, 96–98, 132
Simon, Neil 176
Sirk, Douglass 149
Skrulls 208–210
Space Cards 89
Speed Comics 131
Spider-Man 75
The Spirit 152
Sputnik 12, 79, 82–83, 85, 88–89
Spy and Counterspy 40
Spy Cases 32, 38
Spy Hunters 31, 33, *39*
Spy Thrillers 32
Stalin, Joseph 86, *87*; in *This Godless Communism* 191
Stevenson, Adlai 116–117
Storm, Johnny 205–209, 211, 213–214; *see also* The Human Torch
Storm, Susan (Sue) 76, 205–208, 211–214
Strange Worlds 81
Sturgeon, Theodore 147
Sub-Mariner 205, 211–214
Supergirl 41, 123
superhero comics (genre) 60, 126, 157
Superman 2, 11, 20–28, *22*, *25*, 41, 58–59, 75, 103, 120, 122, 123, 204
Superman 123
Sweetheart Diary 137

T-Man 30, 32, 33–34, *35*, 40, 41
Tales to Astonish 212
Teen Secret Diary 132
Teen Titans 124
Terry and the Pirates 47
Tessie the Typist 138
The Thing 208, 211–212; *see also* Grimm, Ben
This Godless Communism 13, 190–203
Thomas, Roy 204
Time (magazine) 83

Toby Press 141
Tonto 183
Top Secret 31, 38
Topps Company, Inc. 89
Toth, Alex 97, 133
Trask, Pete 30–36, *34*, 38–41
Treasure Chest of Fun and Fact 190–194; *193*, *195*, 196–198, *199*
Trevor, Steve 115, 117, 119–122, *121*
The Trickster 62
Trotsky, Leon 198–199, *200*
Truman Administration 19, 26; and the Truman Doctrine 34
Turok, Son of Stone 13, 179–188; *182*, *187*
Turtle Man 61
Tuska, George *162*, *165*
Twain, Mark 185
Two-Fisted Tales 45–46, 51–53

United Nations (UN) 26, 84, 89

The Vault Keeper 167
Venus Plus X 147, 150
von Braun, Werner 82, 89
Vonnegut, Kurt 175–176

Walt Disney's Man in Space: A Science Feature from Tomorrowland 82
War Comics 46–48, *50*, 51
war comics (genre) 58, 131–133, 169

Weather Wizard 62
Weisinger, Mort 170
Wellman, William 197
Wertham, Frederic 1, 5–6, 8–10, 13, 96, 152, 158, 162; and Batman 8, 123; and racism 6, 8; and Wonder Woman 115, 123
West, Iris 64
western comics (genre) 13, 58, 179–180, 183–184
Western Tales, Inc. (Harvey Comics) 86
While the City Sleeps 147
Whyte, William H. 178
Wings Comics 130
Wonder Girl 118, 123–4
Wonder Woman 12, 115–126, *118*, *119*, *121*, 191, 204
Wonder Woman 120, *121*, 123, 124, 125–6
Wonder Tot 123–4
Wood, Bob 163
Wood, Dave 69–70
Wood, Wally 172, 175–176, 177
The World Around Us 88
World War II 30, 47, 68, 100, 207

Yellow Claw 36
Yellow Claw 36
USS *Yorktown* 47
Young Catholic Messenger 191
Young Love 75
Young Romance 75, 96, 131–132, 134